MW00780975

BENCHMARKING MUSLIM WELL-BEING IN EUROPE

Reducing disparities and polarizations

Pamela Irving Jackson and Peter Doerschler

First published in Great Britain in 2012 by

The Policy Press
University of Bristol
Fourth Floor
Beacon House
Queen's Road
Bristol BS8 1QU
UK

Tel +44 (0)117 331 4054
Fax +44 (0)117 331 4093
e-mail tpp-info@bristol.ac.uk
www.policypress.co.uk

North American office:
The Policy Press
c/o The University of Chicago Press
1427 East 60th Street
Chicago, IL 60637, USA
t: +1 773 702 7700
f: +1 773-702-9756
e:sales@press.uchicago.edu
www.press.uchicago.edu

British Library Cataloguing in Publication Data
A catalogue record for this book is available from the British Library.

Library of Congress Cataloging-in-Publication Data
A catalog record for this book has been requested.

ISBN 978 1 84742 887 5 hardcover

Cover design by Robin Hawes
Front cover: image kindly supplied by istock
Printed and bound in Great Britain by MPG Book Group
The Policy Press uses environmentally responsible print partners

FSC
www.fsc.org
MIX
From responsible
sources
FSC® C018575

Contents

List of tables and figures

Tables

Figures

Acknowledgements

We are grateful for the support and encouragement of our families. Assistance from the Fulbright Scholar Program and its German Studies Seminars, Rhode Island College, Bloomsburg University, and the American Sociological Association as well as spirited exchanges with many scholars, political leaders, and others have improved this investigation. We take full responsibility for our findings, but are well aware of how much we owe to the colleagues and organizations with whom we have worked over the years. We also wish to thank GESIS, *Leibnitz-Institut für Sozialwissenschafiten*, for the use of ALLBUS data and the Norwegian Social Science Data Services (NSD) for the ESS.

Preface

The central questions of this book look to the future. We investigate what Muslims expect from Europe, how they evaluate the democratic institutions of the member state in which they live, and whether their well-being in Europe is comparable to that of their non-Muslim neighbours. In examining bias and intolerance directed at the religious minority, we take our lead from the warnings of European minority protection study agencies (including the European Agency for Fundamental Rights, and the European Commission against Racism and Intolerance) that Muslims are a vulnerable group in Europe. Our comparative measurements of well-being follow the definitions and strategies put forward by the Council of Europe and the European Parliament.

We identify four states as reflective of the direction of minority integration in Europe – France, Germany, the Netherlands and the United Kingdom – and recognize significant differences among Muslims within them. Considerable scholarship has demonstrated that members of the religious minority in each state differ in their origins and immigration history, as well as in the historical relationship between the country of family background and the European nation in which they are now at home. Previous research has also clarified relevant differences among European nations themselves: the states we examine vary in the nature and strength of the state's involvement in setting the criteria for minority integration, in the form of the church/state relationship, and in bureaucratic support for religious diversity. We utilize previous research and build on the understandings established by these bodies of scholarship.

In moving forward from the points established in existing examinations of where Muslims came from and of the institutional structural arrangements in the European states where they now live, we consider how Muslims feel about their present situation in Europe. Are they happy? Are they satisfied? Do they give high marks to the criminal justice system, the parliament, the political parties, the educational system, health care agencies and other institutions of the member state in which they live? As we explain, these questions are becoming a routine part of national efforts to measure well-being in ways other than the Gross Domestic Product per capita. Current conceptualizations of diversity buttressing data collection in most European states do not permit application of these measures to Muslims. The United Kingdom is an exception in this regard, gathering official data on Muslims and other religious groups, and its inclusion in our investigation provides a touchstone for evaluating the unofficial quantitative data available in other states.

What we learn about the attitudes and expectations of Muslims in these European states raises questions about assumptions that the religious minority has failed to integrate into Europe. Their support for agencies of the state sometimes rivals that of their non-Muslim neighbours. While Muslims experience more discrimination than do non-Muslims, and are more worried about the effect that fear of crime victimization has on their lives, they are about as happy and satisfied as others in Europe once their personal circumstances are taken into account. On some measures in some states, Muslims are more supportive of the way democracy is practised in Europe than are non-Muslims. Prevailing assumptions about young Muslims and the highly religious are also put to the test in our analyses. The results leave popular stereotypes wanting. Also unclear on the basis of these results is the value of state-imposed requirements designed to further the integration of Muslims or to clarify the extent to which their religious organizations do not fit into Europe – including host-nation language acquisition requirements for those from non-western nations, dress requirements in civic institutions, and church tax stipulations preventing the same financial support for social services delivered by mosques as by churches. We hope that our results open a new discussion about the ways in which the needs of Europe's largest religious minority can be accommodated in the democratic traditions of the member states and the doors that can be opened to provide for the full utilization of Muslims' talents.

ONE

Benchmarking the well-being of European Muslims

European agencies focused on stimulating research that draws attention to the situation of minorities have signalled that if Europe is to benefit fully from the intellectual and creative potential of its minorities, including its Muslims, the assumption that they fail to integrate must give way to efforts to reduce the 'disparities' and 'polarizations' between them and the non-minority population (European Parliament, 2007: 71). (See also ECRI (European Commission Against Racism and Intolerance), 2000; European Agency for Fundamental Rights, 2007, 2009; EUMC (European Monitoring Centre for Racism and Xenophobia), 2006.) Nonetheless, minority protection study agencies seeking to examine the circumstances of non-European cultural groups living in EU nations are hampered by the conflation of ethnicity, religion and citizenship in some states (cf. EUMC, 2006; Jackson, 2009). This blurring of ethnic, religious and national identities threatens to stymie the effort to benchmark minority integration in the European Union, initiated by the European Parliament (2007: 139) and intended to reduce disparities between Europe's minority populations of immigrant background and its 'natives' in the eight key areas of life specified by the Council of Europe (2003: 7): employment, housing, health care, nutrition, education, information, culture, and basic public functions (which include equality, anti-discrimination and self-organization).

We demonstrate the utility of measuring Muslim well-being following the definitions and guidelines put forward by the Council of Europe and the European Parliament. We start from the foundation provided by the European agencies that focus on scholarly examination and improved public awareness of the situation of minorities, especially as their research efforts relate to the practices, policies and concepts supporting the structural segmentation and reduced life chances of Muslim minorities in France, Germany, the Netherlands and the United Kingdom. The relative population size of Muslims in these four states (cf. EUMC, 2006) and the involvement of their governments in shaping the EU-wide debate (Jackson, 2009) render consideration of these cases important in understanding the ability of European Muslims to thrive. But to some extent, as we consider in the next chapter, the political salience of the presence of Muslims differs among these states because of their varying methods of coordinating ethnic and state identities (cf. Bleich, 2003; Brubaker, 1992; Buijs, 2006; Feldblum, 1999; Fetzer and Soper, 2005; Jackson, 2009), and their differing degrees of state primacy in stipulating the requirements of minority integration (cf. Haller, 2002; Jackson, 2009).

Below we discuss the sources of information that enable examination of both the structural and legal barriers to Muslims' achievement in European states, and the changes required for the cohesion sought by the framework of integration envisioned by the European Commission (2005). Some of these data are gathered by official European minority protection study agencies, often in collaboration with polling agencies such as Gallup-Europe. The information these agencies provide is not official, in that it is not necessarily gathered under the authority of the member state, but it does demonstrate the utility of such data. Some state agencies (especially in the UK) provide official data permitting the comparison of Muslims' well-being to that of others. Other state agencies (Statistics Netherlands, for example) no longer gather data on religion as part of the Census, though religion is included in some of its large-scale surveys, including the annual Permanent Survey on Living Conditions. Additional useful, but unofficial, data are the product of collaborations between research centres and universities. We discuss all of our data sources in detail below in this chapter. They include: the *European Union Agency for Fundamental Rights* (FRA); the *European Commission for Racism and Intolerance* (ECRI); the *European Social Survey* (ESS) (a joint project of the European Commission, the European Science Foundation and European Union member states); state level information resources, including the *UK Office for National Statistics* and the *UK Home Office*, the *Survey of Muslim Life in Germany*, the *German General Social Survey* (ALLBUS), and *Statistics Netherlands* (SN, CBS or the *Netherlands Central Bureau of Statistics*).

The importance of examining Muslim well-being in Europe

While history and context are important, key aspects of the future of European states are being determined now through the interaction of European policy and national preference. In this environment, though discussion of the source of the Muslim population in any specific European member state is important, it is, perhaps, less so than examination of the aspects of European and state institutional and bureaucratic policy that can facilitate Muslims' ability to fully utilize their talents in Europe and contribute effectively to both state and European projects. Several excellent books examine the situation of Muslims in European states, but none 'benchmark' Muslim integration in the eight key areas of life put forward by the Council of Europe (2003: 7) and the European Parliament (2007: 139).

We offer an extensive quantitative examination of the well-being of Muslims in Europe and the mechanisms through which their access to legitimate opportunities is blocked by bureaucratic regulations, public policy, discrimination and prejudice. Some texts and edited collections (for example Laurence and Vaisse, 2006; Modood, Triandafyllidou and Zapata-Barrero, 2006; Triandafyllidou, 2010) move in the latter direction, but we offer more attention to the European policy and data reporting environment in which individual European states operate. Utilizing the terms of discourse currently being established by the Community Statistics initiatives of the European Council and Parliament, we build upon and extend the work of previous researchers in our effort to demonstrate the utility of the benchmarking process in illuminating and removing the obstacles to Muslims' achievement of legitimate goals as members of European states.

Previous efforts to examine the well-being of European Muslims in more than one state have been offered in edited collections that provide contextual and historical detail, but little examination of the impact of either the Council of Europe's initiatives toward social cohesion indicators, or of the evaluation priority of the EU's Justice and Home Affairs Hague Programme (2004–2009) agenda (cf. Niessen and Huddleston, 2009: 20, for a description of the environment in which the benchmarking framework is developing). As Schmeets and te Riele (2010: 3) note, 'The Council of Europe aims to foster research on social cohesion. A Social Cohesion Development Division was set up in 1998 by the Council of Europe Committee of Ministers to undertake, in close cooperation with the member states, conceptual and methodological analysis.' The Council of Europe (COE) has a Social Cohesion website on which the COE definition of social cohesion is stated as follows: 'Social cohesion is the capacity of society to ensure the well-being of all its members, minimizing disparities and avoiding marginalization.' This definition is central to the *Report of the High Level Task Force on Social Cohesion in the 21st Century* (Council of Europe, 2008: 15).

Direct examination of the disparities and polarizations between Muslim and non-Muslim Europeans through the benchmarking process proposed to enhance social cohesion would also support the Europeanization of policies relating to Muslim well-being. It would thereby reduce conflict in a contentious area of domestic politics. The establishment of supranational norms central to the process of creating a united Europe has already been recognized with regard to integration policies for third-country nationals (TCNs). Kerstin Rosenow (2009: 133) demonstrates the importance of the European Parliament, the Council of Europe and the European Commission in 'promoting integration policies at the European level ... [and in strengthening] the status of integration policies by emphasising the linkage between successful integration policies and economic and social cohesion'. She describes as 'unexpected' the shift from national to supranational decision making in areas related to the rights of third-country nationals, 'a policy field that was once one of the last bastions of national sovereignty' (Rosenow, 2009: 134).

European involvement in the areas of citizenship and national identity has been influential in moulding state policies, even as it has been shaped by areas of agreement among the member states. Religion is a third area of contention – in addition to citizenship and national identity – that has triggered interaction between European and state-level policy makers. Matthias Koenig (2007b: 911) details both the emergence at the European level of a 'convergence of basic legal principles of religious governance as well as ... the persistence of divergent national patterns of incorporating religious minorities'. (For more discussion of 'Europeanization', see Graziano and Vink (2006) regarding development of connections between domestic and European policies in several areas; Ladrech (1994) for an examination of the Europeanization of domestic politics and institutions in France; and Lavenex (2001) for further consideration of the problems involved in the Europeanization of refugee policies.)

Besides place of birth, citizenship, religion and its expression in religiosity, two additional aspects of the personal identity of Muslims trigger discrimination and perceptions of minority threat in Europe: youth and gender. Young Muslim men are viewed as potential terrorists, susceptible to radicalization through religious instruction. The cultural organizations they join are suspected of being a source of radicalization. Muslim women who identify their religious orientation by wearing a headscarf are seen as subjugated, or as representing a threat to feminism, secularity and modernity. In examining Muslim well-being in Europe, we pay special attention to the impact of these five aspects of personal identity – age, religiosity, gender, citizenship and place of birth – on each of the eight dimensions of well-being proposed as part of the European benchmarking effort.

In the current context, contradictions between the aims of European and member-state agencies have created areas of tension that complicate efforts to understand and improve the well-being of Europe's Muslims. European agencies can be seen as leading in the direction of the development of immigrant integration data including religious orientation gathered at the national level, with appropriate anonymity protections despite resistance in some states to requesting religious and ethnic information from citizens (cf. EUMC, 2006: 25; European Parliament, 2007: 197; European Parliament and Council, 1995; Jackson, 2009). A key example can be found in the fourth report on France by the Council of Europe's European Commission Against Racism and Intolerance (ECRI France 2010: 45), where the ECRI:

> strongly encourages the French authorities to pursue their efforts aimed at establishing a comprehensive, consistent system for collecting data making it possible to assess the situation regarding the various minority groups in France ... In this connection it recommends that they envisage collecting data broken down according to categories such as ethnic or national origin, religion, language or nationality, so as to identify manifestations of discrimination, while ensuring that this collection is systematically carried out in accordance with the principles of confidentiality, informed consent and individuals' voluntary self-identification as members of a particular group ... The system should also take into consideration the potential existence of cases of double or multiple discrimination.

Some states, including France, insist that their 'national integration models' prevent examination, recognition or correction of disparities between Muslim minorities and non-Muslims. As we discuss in the next chapter, in these states, the 'politics of statistics' (cf. Geddes and Wunderlich, 2009: 196) ensures that data collection policies do not provide for examination of the extent to which Muslims' access to legitimate opportunities for success is blocked. Rather than seeking avenues through which they can develop programmes and policies to assist Muslims in finding a comfortable place in Europe, state authorities sometimes engage in 'venue-shopping' (Guiraudon, 2000) through which they shift back and forth between European and state-level regulations on immigration and immigrant integration to justify policies that in the long run support the *status quo*, even where they disadvantage Muslims within the state.

The fourth principle of the Council of Europe's November 2004 statement on immigrant integration policies, for example, has been used to justify the requirement for understanding the host nation language and culture that is now mandatory in the 'immigrant integration contracts' of the Netherlands, France and Germany (cf. Joppke, 2007). This fourth principle states that basic knowledge of the host society's language, history and culture is necessary for successful immigrant integration. But less emphasized as a key element of these policies is the first principle specified by the Council of Europe, requiring social, economic and political opportunities for immigrants because integration is a dynamic, two-way process (cf. Council of Europe, 2004: 19), necessitating change on both sides. Instead, immigrant integration contracts put forward by European states in the twenty-first century view the new migrant as 'responsible for his success in the host society' (Guiraudon, 2008: 1) and require those of immigrant background to find their way through the maze of relatively unyielding national customs and institutions protected by the 'national model of integration'. This policy approach leaves unexamined the structural and legal changes required for the cohesion sought by the framework of integration envisioned by the European Commission (2005). It also ignores a further principle of integration specified in the Council of Europe's (2004: 21) document: that equal access to institutions and goods and services, as well as equality of treatment (in comparison to natives) should be provided to those of immigrant background.

The presence of Muslims in European states has not been framed in terms of civil rights but, rather, in terms of immigration and security. Perceptions of long-standing problems of immigrant inclusion (say of Turks in Germany, North Africans in France or Pakistanis in the UK) have been distilled in the public discussion to questions about the integration of Muslims. In the wake of the tragic events of 9/11 and the subsequent attacks in Madrid, London and Amsterdam, policy makers and the public increasingly distinguished between the integration of Muslims and non-Muslims. In 2005, the Migration Policy Institute rated the integration of Muslims in Europe as the top migration issue of the year, heading its list of 10 (available at the following link: www.migrationinformation.org/Feature/display.cfm?id=350). Increasing attention has been devoted to the threat posed by Muslims to European (and western) security and culture. As a result, examination of structural barriers to minority achievement in the host society is often missing in these discussions, or is viewed only through the lens of securitization. Reducing institutional impediments to the full engagement of minorities in economic, political and civic arenas is often of secondary concern, though various structural and legal impediments prevent the full incorporation of Muslims as a permanent part of the European religious and political landscape. Instead, discussion of Muslim minority groups in Europe frequently refers to a 'Muslim diaspora' (cf. Leweling, 2005) whose members 'fail to integrate' (cf. *Spiegel* Online, 2009) and whose youth are tempted by the 'seductive fundamentalism' (cf. Heitmeyer, Müller and Schröder, 1998; Open Society Institute, 2005) of Islam. Such a conceptual framework presents Muslims as temporary residents of their 'host' nations, dissatisfied with 'western culture', opposed to modernity, and yearning for the traditions of the 'old country'. This interpretation provides a one-sided view of integration that places the entire burden on immigrants. It neglects to consider the obstacles hampering Muslims' contributions to Europe and its member states. It also prevents recognition of the extent to which Muslims think of themselves as European, feel satisfied with the institutions and policies of the host country and seek the possibilities for advancement available there for their children.

To understand the situation of Muslims in Europe, we have moved beyond studies based on single respondent accounts (for example, Baran, 2010) or direct questioning of small groups, even while we appreciate the perspectives they offer. We develop the picture provided by aggregate statistical data comparing Muslims and non-Muslims in their ability to move forward in the key areas of life central to well-being, and in the concerns and attitudes related to Muslims' ability to feel at ease in Europe and contribute effectively to their communities. Developing this picture of the situation of Muslims in Europe provides a basis for evaluating some politically charged policy areas, including: *civic integration contracts* with their emphasis on language acquisition and limits on family reunification for non-western applicants; policies relating to the *expression of religious orientation in schools* (regulating, for example, the wearing of headscarves); *church funding regulations* (for example, the German 'church tax') providing *public resources to religiously affiliated organizations for their social service activities*; the *securitization of immigration policy and resulting criminalization of Muslims.* We examine the impact of these and other policies on the life chances of Muslims in Europe, and the possibility that the perspective on which these policies are based does not permit recognition of the contributions Muslims can make to the European communities in which they live.

Key to this examination is our use of quantitative data to assess the *degree of trust expressed by Muslims in specific public institutions* (including the police, courts and other justice institutions; local government, political leaders, government officials, the education and health systems) in comparison to that of other religious groups. The claim that Muslims won't integrate into European states has at its core the assumption that Muslim Europeans distrust agencies of the European state in which they are living. Anecdotal evidence is often provided to support this claim – Turkish Germans carrying the Turkish flag during World Cup matches, Muslim parents' refusal to permit their children to engage in coeducational physical education activities in school, the preference of some Muslim women and girls for wearing head coverings to work and school, preferences for *halal* meat. But the meaning attached to these symbols has been imposed by non-Muslims, not Muslims themselves, who may think of their preferences as unrelated to their degree of satisfaction with the institutions of their European state. Rather than engaging in speculation about the extent to which European Muslims seek to live in a 'parallel society', we assess their degree of satisfaction with key areas of institutional life in the state in which they are living and compare their responses to those of non-Muslims in the same European state.

In **Chapter Two**, we prepare for our evaluation of data on Muslims' well-being in Germany, France, the Netherlands and the United Kingdom by examining the role of each state in facilitating or restricting opportunities for Muslims to find a comfortable place in the society. We offer detail on the extent to which each of the four states we use as examples in benchmarking Muslim well-being has a unique method of ethnic/state identity coordination and differing scope for the nation-state in minority integration. All four nation-states are bound by EU policy in this area, even as they shape it, but the contextual differences among them are likely to influence the process of reducing disparities and polarizations which is the goal of the benchmarking process.

The eight key areas of life delineated by the Council of Europe (2003:7) and European Parliament (2007: 139) as important in gathering community statistics for EU member states are examined in Chapters Three to Six using the data sources listed above and detailed below. Besides comparing Muslims and non-Muslims on well-being in each key area, we also examine how Muslims' circumstances vary by age, religiosity, gender, citizenship and place of birth (in the member state or not). We begin in **Chapters Three** and **Four** with the areas of greatest concern to both Muslims and non-Muslims alike: *worry about crime and confidence in the justice system*; and *trust in the political community and its institutions*. The implementation of integration contract policies in the Netherlands, Germany and France, and discussions of the need for such a policy in Britain, reflect a questioning of the extent to which immigrants from non-European cultures will fit into a democratic, secular Europe. Simultaneously, while integration contracts were being developed, European states cooperated in the securitization of immigration policies – that is, in the development of rules and procedures intended to allow police to 'ferret out networks of illegal migrant workers ... tackle abuse of political asylum' (Prime Minister's electronic *Portal du Gouvernement*, 2008) and closely monitor those who share their demographic or linguistic characteristics. Greater police scrutiny of those likely to be Muslim and increases in the proportion of Muslims in both prisons and immigrant detention facilities for non-violent, largely petty offences, including those involving their documentation, have criminalized the image of Muslims and contributed to their segmentation (Beckford, Joly and Khosrokhavar, 2005; Jackson, 2010). This environment can be expected to have made Muslims uneasy with their place in Europe, to have reduced their confidence in the police and other public institutions, and to have provided a fertile groundwork for discrimination against them and hostility toward them. We compare Muslims to non-Muslims in examining their experiences and attitudes relating to crime and justice, and their trust in public institutions as part of our consideration of the key area of life specified by the Council of Europe (2003: 7) and the European Parliament (2007: 139) in terms of *basic public functions*, defined as including *equality, anti-discrimination*, and *self-organization*. The key areas of *culture* and *information* are also considered here, through satisfaction with democracy, evaluation of democracy as an idea, and understanding of the agencies of government.

In **Chapter Five**, we provide data on the extent of discrimination against Muslims and its increase during the first decade of the twenty-first century. We also investigate the level of multiple discrimination against them, a topic of current examination by the European Agency for Fundamental Rights (2010). **Chapter Six** provides data on the general well-being of Muslims: their reported happiness and life satisfaction. Information benchmarking Muslim integration in the key areas of *education* and *employment* is also assessed. Statistical data benchmarking Muslim integration in the key areas of information acquisition, health, housing and satisfaction with economic, educational and health care institutions are also evaluated in **Chapter Six**.

Our summary **Chapter Seven** highlights the importance of data in evaluating the well-being of Muslims in Europe by comparing the findings of our analyses to assumptions about Muslims reflected in official government policy and in anti-Muslim extremist party rhetoric. We consider the policy implications of the findings. The central goals of the European benchmarking process, to reduce disparities and polarizations within Europe and its member states, are the guideposts that we use in evaluating the distance gained through our 'benchmarking' effort.

Sources of data on Muslim well-being in Europe

Research undertaken by Official European Minority Protection Study Agencies

The European Union Agency for Fundamental Rights (FRA)

FRA (http://fra.europa.eu/fraWebsite/home/home_en.htm) was created in 2007 as an umbrella organization linking EU research and study efforts focused on safeguarding minorities. FRA subsumed the European Monitoring Centre on Racism and Xenophobia (EUMC) and its subsidiaries in 2007. The EUMC was 'an independent body of the European Union created by Council Regulation (EC) No 1-35/97 of 2 June 1997' during the *European Year Against Racism* (FRA, 2007 website (origins): http://fra.europa.eu/fraWebsite/about_us/origins/origins_en.htm). FRA, the new umbrella organization, is 'a body of the European Union ... established through Council Regulation (EC) No 168/2007) ... based in Vienna' (http://fra.europea.eu). In addition to initiating research, data collection and analysis, FRA provides advice to EU institutions and member states and promotes awareness of fundamental rights in the civil society.

One of FRA's investigative spokes is RAXEN, established by EUMC, and shorthand for the Racism and Xenophobia Network, consisting of a National Focal Point (NFP) in each EU member state with responsibility for data gathering related to the situation of minorities and the preparation of regular related reports. Current RAXEN reports demonstrate the paucity of direct attention to the situation of Muslims in some EU member states. In Germany and France, for example, the NFPs do not gather data on religious orientation, and public support for an ideological or political form of secularism pays limited attention to the distinctions between ethnicity and religious orientation. Estimates of characteristics of the Muslim population are usually made on the basis of Turkish nationals (Turkish *Ausländer*) in Germany; in France those of North African nationality (North African *étrangers*) serve as the proxy for Muslims.

In those states where official data on religious orientation are not gathered, even minority protection study committees sometimes estimate the size of the Muslim population and its characteristics without attention to determining the best proxy group. In the Netherlands, for example, those of migrant descent (*allochtonen,* who are 18.4% of the Dutch population), are sometimes used as proxy for Muslims (cf. EUMC, 2006: 45). But even though national statistics in the Netherlands do not include data on religion, a better estimate of those likely to be Muslim could be obtained by limiting the consideration of *allochtonen* to the sub-group within them referred to as *ethnic minorities* (cf. RAXEN, 2005, Focal Point for the Netherlands). Those classified as *ethnic minorities* represent 9.4 % of the Dutch population and are deemed to be of 'non-Western background'. *Ethnic minorities* include those of Turkish, African, South American or Asian (but not Indonesian or Japanese) background, and also represent an inaccurate proxy for 'Muslims', but certainly less so than the wider *allochtonen* group. (See Guiraudon, Phalet and ter Wal (2005), and Prins and Sahaarso (2010) for discussion of minority policy in the Netherlands, and Jackson (2009), for examination of the problem of measuring Muslim integration in Europe.)

Like the RAXEN reports, the EUMC (2006) report, *Muslims in the European Union*, relies on information provided by each nation's National Focal Point. Even in this EUMC effort to examine Muslims directly, in Germany, for example, those classified as Turkish nationals serve as proxy. Many members of the German 'proxy' group (Turkish nationals) were born and lived their entire lives in Germany, but do not have citizenship (which was difficult for those of immigrant background to obtain until the citizenship law changes of 2000). Recent estimates suggest that not more than 63% of Germany's Muslims are of Turkish background (estimate from *Bundesamt für Migration und Flüchtlinge* (BAMF), 2009), and just under half of Muslims in Germany (49%) are classified as Turkish nationals (estimate from ALLBUS, the German General Social Survey, see Doerschler and Jackson, 2010b). Perceptions of Muslim religious identity in Germany are conflated with perceptions of Turkish ethnic identity.

The European Monitoring Centre on Racism and Xenophobia's 2006 report *Muslims in the European Union*, as noted above, was limited to data on nationality groups of immigrants likely to be Muslim for most EU states because of the lack of official data on religious groups. In the report, EUMC noted the lack of data as a problem. (Only the UK collects and publishes official social and economic data on religious groups, having begun this effort in 2001.) The National Focal Points (NFPs) for the Racism and Xenophobia Network (RAXEN) established by EUMC have regularly reported (to EUMC in the past, and now to FRA) on racism and bias in the member state in which they are located. Though they sometimes use the term 'Islamophobia', the NFPs do not gather information on victims by religion, except in the UK where those data have become available since 2001. In states other than the UK, the NFPs make assumptions on the basis of nationality groups most likely to be Muslim (for example, Turks in Germany and North Africans in France).

EU-MIDIS

FRA initiated the *European Union Minorities and Discrimination Survey* (EU-MIDIS) to 'measure minorities' integration into European societies, as well as the extent of discriminatory treatment and criminal victimization, including racially motivated crime, experienced by minorities [including] ethnic minorities, immigrants, national minorities and EU citizens as they move into and around the EU' (FRA, 2009 01: 4). EU-MIDIS was conducted in 2008 in all 27 EU member states and used a standardized 150-item questionnaire to conduct 20–60 minute interviews of 23,500 immigrants and members of ethnic minorities about their experiences related to discrimination and racial crime victimization, and their awareness of their rights. In 10 member states, an additional 5,000 majority group members living in proximity to the minorities were interviewed to permit comparisons on some topics. One of the 'Data in Focus' reports drawn from the survey provides summary information on respondents who self-identified as Muslim. The report is offered in the face of what FRA describes as the 'shortage of extensive, objective and comparable data on Muslims in the European Union ... [and provides] for the first time, comparable data on how Muslims across the EU experience discrimination and victimisation' (FRA, 2009 02: 2).

While the EU-MIDIS survey is important in its effort to spur member states to actively consider the impact of religious preference in bias and discrimination, it does not avoid the conflation of ethnic and religious identity in the selection of respondents. Minority groups were chosen for examination in delimited (urban) geographical areas within each EU member state. Where a majority of the minority group members self-identified as 'Muslims', the minority group was selected for examination in the special focus study of Muslims. In Germany, for example, the only minority group examined for the Muslim subset was Turkish; in addition, the German sample was taken from Berlin, Frankfurt and Munich. In these cities, those members of the Turkish sample who also self-identified as 'Muslim' formed the 'Muslim sample' in Germany. A similar process of selection was undertaken in each member state. In the Netherlands, for example, respondents classified as North Africans and those identified as Turkish formed the basis of the 'Muslim' subsample. Only members of these groups who also self-identified as Muslims were examined for the actual 'Muslim sample' in the Netherlands. The 'coverage area' for the Netherlands included Amsterdam, Rotterdam, The Hague and Utrecht. In France, North and Sub-Saharan Africans formed the basis of the 'Muslim sample' and the coverage area included the Paris metro area, Marseille and Lyon. In the United Kingdom, the coverage area was limited to London, and no majority Muslim ethnic group was identified. Central and Eastern Europeans were the minority group sampled for the study of discrimination in general, and the UK was not included in the sub-study of Muslims. Muslims are generally estimated to be between 3% and 4% of the UK population. Pakistanis, Bangladeshis and Indians comprise the major groups, and they were not part of the EU-MIDIS survey. (FRA EU-MIDIS Main Results 2009 03: 21, 23; FRA EU MIDIS Data in Focus Report: Muslims 2009 02: 4.). The omission of Muslims in the UK and the ethnic background limitations (as well as the within-state geographic coverage limitations) imposed in the data gathering for EU-MIDIS require care in interpretation of the data. They cannot be used in any official benchmarking (European Parliament, 2007) effort.

The EU-MIDIS study of Muslims provides a snapshot of the experiences of some Muslims from the ethnic groups examined in the geographical areas from which the samples were drawn; it does not allow for careful consideration of either Muslims in each EU member state, or of Muslim groups throughout the EU. This latter point is occasionally difficult to keep in mind when reading the FRA sponsored reports on EU-MIDIS. The *Data in Focus Report* on Muslims (FRA, 2009 02: 8), for example, sometimes combines groups across countries to provide comparative summaries of those who self-identify as Muslims by ethnic group and to extrapolate across the 14 EU member states in which Muslims were interviewed. This type of generalization is statistically problematic and such examples appear throughout the FRA documents on EU-MIDIS. Nonetheless, EU-MIDIS results provide preliminary evidence of the unfairness experienced by Muslims in Europe in some of the key areas of life examined by the benchmarking effort. The results presented in the EU-MIDIS sub-report on Muslims are more important for their focus on experiences of discrimination in general and instances of ethnic bias by justice officials than for the findings themselves. They represent quasi-official recognition of the need to examine both the marginalization of Muslim minorities in European societies and the crystallization of inequality between Europe's core non–Muslim groups and its Muslim minorities, deemed to be culturally peripheral. An additional EU–MIDIS report focuses on multiple discrimination, providing information on the extent to which respondents (Muslim women, for example) experienced discrimination based on more than one personal characteristic (such as their religion, gender and ethnicity) (FRA, 2010 05). Data from the *Special Eurobarometer 296* are utilized in conjunction with EU–MIDIS data in the report on Multiple Discrimination (FRA, 2010 05: 8) to compare perceptions of the minority and majority population on the prevalence of religious and other types of discrimination.

In later chapters we examine the EU–MIDIS results for both discrimination and multiple discrimination against Muslims, as well as evidence provided in other FRA/RAXEN-sponsored research studies. Data on the situation of minorities in Europe is offered in periodic FRA studies, most of which focus on specific topics, including education, housing, employment, discrimination, and racist violence and crime. While these reports sometimes make reference to the situation of Muslims, they most often are limited to following member-state policies in minority definition because they have shaped institutional data collection practices. As we noted above, both FRA and its predecessor EUMC have clearly stated that these limitations prevent an understanding of the situation of religious groups and that even the national integration models on which they are based would not be undermined by collection of data including religious orientation where the individual remained anonymous. EU–MIDIS represents an effort to go beyond state obstacles to examine the difficulties faced by Muslims in Europe. We use all the information that FRA and RAXEN have to offer, supplementing it with other sources of information on Muslims' well-being.

ECRI

Operating distinctly from FRA (which is located in Vienna), the **European Commission against Racism and Intolerance** (ECRI) is an agency of the Council of Europe and is based in Strasbourg. It is 'an organ of the Council of Europe', which has '47 member countries', and 'has no coercive powers to oblige states to make changes' (Hollo, 2009: 10). But, as explained in its mandate, ECRI is 'entrusted with the task of combating racism, racial discrimination, xenophobia, anti-Semitism and intolerance in greater Europe from the perspective of the protection of human rights, in the light of the European Convention

on Human Rights' (ECRI website: www.coe.int/t/dgh/monitoring/
ecri/activities/mandate_en.asp).

In her analysis of the history and impact of ECRI during its first 15
years, Lanna Hollo (2009: 11) describes ECRI as having 'considerable
weight and authority vis-à-vis European states' because they have
established and reinforced it, and committed themselves to its aims.
Yet, she points out, the primary influence of ECRI lies in its top-
down pressure on states in the fight against racism, discrimination and
intolerance; and the pressure that ECRI can exert from above is most
effective when joined by that of other supranational agencies, and with
organizations (often internal to states) that provide bottom-up pressure
towards the same goal.

General Policy Recommendation Number 5, *On Combating
Intolerance and Discrimination Against Muslims,* was adopted by ECRI
and published with the Council of Europe in Strasbourg on 16 March
2000, before extremist attacks in New York City, Amsterdam, Madrid
and London fuelled the problematization of Muslims within the
European population. In light of the stigmatization of Muslims during
the first decade of the twenty-first century, the significance of the
points made in ECRI recommendation number 5 is indisputable. In
it ECRI (2000: 3) 'recalled' the first summit (in 1993) of the 'Heads of
State and Government of the member States of the Council of Europe'
in which they established a 'Plan of Action on combating racism,
xenophobia, anti-Semitism and intolerance'; the Final Declaration and
Action Plan adopted in 1997 affirming the goal of member states to
'build a freer, more tolerant and just European society and ... [calling
for] the intensification of the fight against racism, xenophobia, anti-
Semitism and intolerance'; and the 1991 Recommendation numbered
1162 'on the contribution of the Islamic civilization to European
culture adopted by the Parliamentary Assembly'. Five years before the
Migration Policy Institute's annual list of 'Top 10 Migration Issues'
placed the challenge of integrating Muslims in Europe as number
one (www.migrationinformation.org/Feature/display.cfm?id=350),
ECRI warned of 'signs that religious intolerance toward Islam and
Muslim communities is increasing in countries where this religion is
not observed by the majority of the population ...[and that] Islam is
sometimes portrayed inaccurately on the basis of hostile stereotyping
the effect of which is to make this religion seem a threat' (ECRI, 2000:
3; available at: www.coe.int/t/dghl/monitoring/ecri/activities/gpr/
en/recommendation_n5/Rec5%20en21.pdf).

In addition to its effort to provide top-down pressure toward greater
inclusion and equality in member states, the foresight evidenced in

ECRI publications regarding potential challenges to states in ensuring 'that in practice individuals may fully realize their right to be free from discrimination and enjoy full equality' (Hollo, 2009: 13) makes these publications extremely valuable in examining member states' specific problems in providing for the well-being of their Muslim members.

ECRI publishes a report on each EU member state at four-year intervals. (For example, four have been published on Germany (1998, 2000, 2004, 2009), four for France (1998, 2000, 2005, 2010), three for the Netherlands (1998, 2001, 2008), and four for the UK (1999, 2001, 2005, 2010). The most recent ECRI report on each state explicitly details examples of anti-Muslim bias and recommends direct action to improve the religious minority's integration into the civil society through efforts to create greater tolerance on the part of non-Muslims. For example, ECRI criticizes public discourse in the Netherlands for having:

> portrayed Muslims as invading the country in waves, thereby posing a major threat to the country's security and identity. Policies have accordingly been advocated to close the borders to them. Islam has been repeatedly qualified as a 'subculture' and Muslims have been presented as the carriers of backward values, generally incompatible with democracy and the values of Western societies. Islam has also been portrayed as a violent religion in itself, many of whose aspects Muslims need to abandon to adapt to life in the Netherlands. (ECRI Netherlands, 2008: 37)

In his 'Welcome' on the Commission's website, ECRI Chair Nils Muiznieks marks 15 years of work by ECRI, and alludes to the increasing bias against Muslims as an outgrowth of anti-immigration sentiment and anti-terrorist security strategies. In his words:

> Persistent and recurring forms of intolerance, such as anti-Gypsyism, anti-Semitism, and prejudice against other 'traditional minorities' have in recent years been compounded by Islamophobia and increasingly negative attitudes, discrimination and violence against immigrants, asylum seekers and refugees. In the years ahead, the challenge of integrating recent arrivals to European societies will become all the more complicated, as attitudes and legislation have hardened, xenophobic political and media discourse become mainstream in many European countries,

and security concerns have often been invoked to justify discriminatory practices. (ECRI website: www.coe.int/t/dghl/monitoring/ecri/welcome_en.asp).

The third cycle of ECRI country-by-country reports, which began in January 2003, included recommendations on measures intended to ameliorate 'specific forms of racism', including Islamophobia (cf. Hollo, 2009: 61). These recommendations have been described as reflecting 'the broad ranging changes that it believes European countries need to make to their laws, policies, practices and attitudes in order to effectively counter racism and discrimination ... a sort of road map for action' (Hollo, 2009: 61). We will examine the evidence of anti-Muslim bias provided in ECRI reports and the agency's recommended road map toward minority inclusion.

Data gathered by European Agency and Member State Collaboration

The European Social Survey

A relatively new effort toward comparative, longitudinal data related to well-being, funded through the European Commission's Framework Programmes, the European Science Foundation, and national funding bodies in each country, is the European Social Survey (ESS) (www.europeansocialsurvey.org). Conducted on a biennial basis since 2002, the European Social Survey (ESS) is a joint project of the European Commission, the European Science Foundation and funding agencies from the approximately 30 participating countries, which include the UK, Germany, France and the Netherlands (for a full list of participating countries see http://europeansocialsurvey.org/index.php?option=com_content&view=article&id=41&Itemid=73). The main substantive focus of the ESS is the 'mapping of long-term attitudinal, social, political and moral climate' among European publics (Centre for Comparative Social Surveys 2010: 1). Each survey contains a Core Module of questions covering diverse issues such as political trust and participation, cultural attitudes, socio–political orientations, education and occupation, social capital, demographics and socio-economics, ethnic and religious allegiances, social exclusion and overall health and well-being (see http://ess.nsd.uib.no) and Centre for Comparative Social Surveys, 2010: 4). Because these questions appear consistently across all participating countries, the Core Module is particularly appropriate for repeated cross-sectional analysis. The ESS contains a randomly drawn sample with comparable estimates of each country's eligible residential population age 15 and older. A minimum effective sample of 1,500 respondents is targeted for each country. (For a more detailed description of sampling procedures used in the ESS, see www.europeansocialsurvey.org/index.php?option=com_content &view=article&id=80&Itemid=365.)

State-sponsored data gathering

Office for National Statistics and the Home Office of the United Kingdom

In the 2001 census for the United Kingdom, a voluntary question on religious identification was asked, including 'Muslim' as a category to be checked in England and Wales. (It was not on the census for Northern Ireland.) These data have been mined for several official and unofficial reports comparing the situation of those who self-identify as Muslim with members of other religious groups (cf. Office for National Statistics (ONS), 2006; 2004; Open Society Institute, 2005). Until the 2011 UK census is ready for use, the 2001 data are the only official census information. In the meantime, where it is possible and instructive, we compare them to the more recent data on Muslims in the UK from the European Social Survey, which were gathered in 2008, and note any discrepancies or changes in the relative well-being of Muslims in comparison to members of other religious groups. We also use both sets of data to compare the impact of religion and ethnicity on the benchmarking indicators. The 2004 ONS report titled *Focus on Religion* examines the situation of Muslims in several of the Council of Europe's key areas of life, updating 2001 census data with data from a national labour statistics survey in 2003–2004; and the 2006 ONS report, *Focus on Ethnicity and Religion*, provides further analyses using 2001 census data.

Data from the *British Crime Survey* (BCS) 2006/7 and 2005/6 contain information by race, ethnicity and religious orientation on individual attitudes, perceptions and risks of crime (cf. Jansson et al., 2007). A nationally representative victimization survey, the BCS is based on interviews with 47,000 adults in private households in England and Wales. Home Office researchers calculated logistic regressions to assess the relationship between respondents' religious orientation and their experiences with crime and attitudes toward the justice system, and to assess whether any existing differences between religious groups for these outcomes were due to their socio-economic profiles or their attitudes (cf. Jansson et al., 2007: Appendix 2). We examine these results and compare them to those from the European Social Survey.

From 2001 to 2011, the Home Office also collected a biennial social survey focused on community cohesion, race, faith and related topics (www.communities.gov.uk/communities/research/citizenshipsurvey). In 2007, the title of the survey was changed to the *Citizenship Survey* (simplified from the Home Office Citizenship Survey), though the acronym *HOCS* was retained. For reasons of fiscal austerity, HOCS was terminated in 2011 (www.communities.gov.uk/communities/resarch/citizenshipsurvey/surveycancellation). We utilize the data for preceding years to compare Muslims and non-Muslims on several indicators related to commitment to community and the state in Britain.

Survey of Muslim Life in Germany

The German Ministry of the Interior conducted a survey in 2008 in preparation for the 2009 German Islam Conference. This study can be seen as moving toward recognition that European Muslims have more in common with Europeans of other religious persuasions, possibly even in their degree of secularity, than with Muslims living in societies without European cultural traditions (cf. *Spiegel ONLINE*, 2009). The target population was 'persons ... 16 and over in private households in Germany in which at least one person lives with a migrant background from a predominantly Muslim country ... The gross sample was taken from the telephone directory' (BAMF, 2009: 37) selecting likely names for the (largely Muslim) countries of focus. These respondents were asked about their religion and denominational preference (Sunni, Shiite, Alevis and so on). The 200-page report, *Muslimisches Leben in Deutschland* (www.integration-in-deutschland.de/nn_286290/SharedDocs/Anlagen/EN/Migration/Publikationen/Forschung/Forschungsberichte/fb6-muslimisches-leben.html), based on these data suggested the need for the upward revision (to just over 5% of the German population) in official estimates of the size of the Muslim population and provided some details on the daily life of respondents who identified as Muslim, including how many wear headscarves, the religiosity of those who wear headscarves, the likelihood of missing a school outing because it was of mixed gender. Questions on these seemingly insignificant personal habits and preferences may have been asked to provide for evaluation of the accuracy of stereotypes about Muslims' dress and impressions of their 'self-imposed isolation'. But these questions seem irrelevant in light of a notable omission in the survey: there are no questions on Muslims' experiences of discrimination or perceptions of institutional or bureaucratic barriers to legitimate avenues of achievement.

Nonetheless, areas in which the state could better support Muslim integration in German institutions were apparent in the results. For example, three-quarters of respondents indicated the desire for Islamic religious instruction in schools. (German children can receive religious instruction in public schools.) But comparisons between religious groups in the report are limited to those between 'Muslims' and other members of their migrant group who do not identify as 'Muslim'. Examination of differences between Muslims and other religious groups in the general, non-migrant background German population is not provided, though it would be necessary for efforts toward the reduction of disparities between minority groups and the majority in Germany to begin in earnest.

Statistics Netherlands

Dutch population and household statistics are gathered by Statistics Netherlands (CBS, Central Bureau of Statistics in the Netherlands) from municipal population registers that have been fully automated since 1994. As Guiraudon et al. (2005: 80) note, 'It should be underlined that there is no question on religion in the registers'. In its 2004 report on the Census of 2001, *Statistics Netherlands* explains:

> Except the variable 'religion' the Census of 2001 contains the general demographic items. Since 1994 religion is no longer part of the population registers. From that year on, data on religion have been collected and stored in the database SILA of the Dutch churches. The variable religion is also part of some inquiries carried out by Statistics Netherlands [as we noted earlier in this chapter]... the Census of 2001 contains more detailed information on nationality and ethnicity than previous census.

Currently, the Statistics Netherlands website (available at www.cbs. nl/en-GB/menu/methoden/toelichtingen/alfabet/r/religion-or-ideology.htm) indicates that, 'To determine how many people in the Dutch population say they belong to a certain religion or ideology, every year 10 thousand people are asked ... The sample is drawn from the Dutch population, excluding the institutionalised population.' But the website also indicates that the figures for 2003, though also on the website, were gathered on the basis of an estimate determined by 'the number of foreigners in the Netherlands per country of origin, and the percentage of Muslims in the populations in these countries of origin'. In any case, we will not be able to benchmark Muslim well-being with census data for the Netherlands, but will be able to gauge some aspects of trust in institutions and involvement in community for Muslims in comparison to other religious groups in the Netherlands through the large-scale surveys conducted by Statistics Netherlands, the *Permanent Survey on Living Conditions.*

Research institute–university collaboration

The German General Social Survey (ALLBUS) (GESIS 2009) (www.gesis.org/en/allbus) provides survey data relevant for measuring Muslim well-being in Germany. The ALLBUS is conducted on a biannual basis and consists of face-to-face interviews drawn using clustered, random sampling from the population of noninstitutionalized adults (age 18 and older) residing in the Federal Republic. Starting in 2004 and including 2006 and 2008, the ALLBUS gives respondents the opportunity to state whether they belong to Islam. The ALLBUS also contains a number of questions relevant for assessing well-being, specifically respondents' trust in various political institutions.

Data gathered by survey organizations and NGOs

Private researchers, non-profit organizations and think tanks increasingly undertake unofficial studies and surveys examining some aspects of the situation of Muslims in Europe (for example the **Pew Global Attitudes Initiative**, the **Eurobarometer**, the Open Society Institute's **Muslims at Home in Europe** project). These unofficial data are useful, but not sufficient. We utilize these sources and point out their importance in underscoring specific obstacles to equality for Muslims in the European states in which they are members. But the results of unofficial studies may be ignored (as the Open Society Institute's (2007) analysis suggests) or dismissed as inaccurate by those who do not support the goals of the organization and do not want to devote resources to Muslim well-being. In addition, the detailed, focused, longitudinal and comparative European data sought by the European Parliament's (2007) benchmarking effort are not provided by unofficial studies (cf. Jackson, 2009).

Open Society Institute

At Home in Europe

The Open Society Institute's (OSI) focus on monitoring the situation of minorities 'in a changing Europe' has led to several excellent research reports on Muslims in Europe. *Muslims in Europe* reports on eleven cities, indicating at the outset that 'there are very little data available on Europe's Muslim and minority populations. What does exist is extrapolated from ethnic and country-of-origin data, which provides a limited picture of the lives, experiences and needs of Muslims in Europe' (OSI, 2010: 22). OSI (2010: 32) focused on 'countries with significant Muslim populations, whose history dates back to relatively recent waves of migration – in most cases the last 60 years'. The four states central to our investigation were included in the study (France, Germany, the Netherlands and the United Kingdom), in addition to three others (Belgium, Denmark and Sweden). OSI (2010: 33) explains that 'emphasis was placed on the older Member States of the EU, in particular the northern European states, as the issues faced by these states are largely similar'. Eleven cities were chosen from these states (*Amsterdam,* Antwerp, *Berlin*, Copenhagen, *Hamburg, Leicester, Marseille, Paris,* Rotterdam, Stockholm and *London*), seven of which (italicized) are located in the states on which we focus. Two hundred residents were selected from each city, 100 Muslim and 100 non-Muslim, and interviewed in face-to-face in-depth sessions with a researcher in the first language of the respondent. In addition, OSI (2010: 33) researchers conducted focus groups with Muslim residents, and interviews with 'local officials, practitioners such as teachers and health workers, community representatives, non-governmental organizations and experts engaged on anti-discrimination and integration issues.'

OSI (2010: 35) acknowledges several limitations to the research, and these largely evolve from contextual differences faced by Muslims in member states and the difficulty of ascertaining the trigger for discrimination as racial or religious. National and political differences may influence 'the challenges surrounding the categories of Muslim and non-Muslim', OSI (2010: 35) explains, and, in addition, the sampling method used for the study is not representative of the population as a whole. The use of national statistics to extrapolate the necessary characteristics of the sample was limited by the omission of ethnic and religious affiliation from national statistics. OSI (2010: 35) describes its respondents as a 'non-random cross-section of individuals chosen from the subgroups of the population within the selected neighbourhood of the city'. While the limitations of OSI data underscore the importance of continuous national data collection processes that include religion in examining disparities of well-being among segments of the population, the OSI reports nonetheless offer careful examination of the key areas of life specified by the Council of Europe. OSI findings, for example, highlight disparities between Muslims and non-Muslims in employment, housing, health care, nutrition, education, information and culture, civic and political participation and related knowledge (OSI, 2010: 187–210), media (OSI, 2010: 210–217), and basic public functions (equality, anti-discrimination, trust) (OSI, 2010: 197–202); policing and security, cohesion, belonging, discrimination and interactions (OSI 2010: 59–91). On-the-ground access problems in these areas are described by respondents interviewed by OSI researchers. OSI investigators looking into complaints by Muslim patients in hospitals regarding lack of access to *halal* meals found that in Marseille, for example,

> hospital staff's ignorance of dietary restrictions that may be relevant to Muslim patients is only part of the explanation. Stakeholder interviews implied that some officials see the provision of *halal* food as compromising on state secularism and so resist it on that basis. While the hospitals provide kosher meals for Jewish patients, providing *halal* food is perceived by these officials as giving into the demands of 'Muslim fundamentalists' (OSI, 2010: 158–159).

Open Society Institute Justice Initiative

The 2009 OSI publication, *Ethnic Profiling in the European Union: Pervasive, Ineffective and Discriminatory*, summarizes available research on the extent of ethnic profiling in ordinary policing and in counterterrorism (the latter since 2001), and makes related recommendations to European authorities, national elected authorities and policymaking bodies, law enforcement managers and to the civil society. For all four of the states on which we focus (as well as Italy) OSI details the use of ethnic profiling described in both official reports and those of non-governmental organizations (NGOs). Only the UK routinely collects information on religious orientation as part of its data on criminal victimization and stop and search activities. For France, Germany and the Netherlands, the Open Society Justice Initiative often cites data presented in reports of the European Commission against Racism and Intolerance (discussed above). Nonetheless, OSI (2009: 4) provides an invaluable compilation of available information in sections titled: *ethnic profiling in mass controls and stop and search practices; data mining, raids on Muslim institutions and harassment of Muslim businesses; arrest and imprisonment, identifying individuals in the process of radicalizing; monitoring mosques, Muslim organizations, and their members.* Their examination is useful in assessing the well-being of Muslims with regard to equality and discrimination (subsumed under basic public functions, which reflects equality of access and protection by institutions and justice systems). Also worthy of attention is its compilation of data sources evaluating the effectiveness of profiling practices (in terms of the number of cases of security threats they uncovered).

Primary aim of this investigation

Our goal is to examine disparities between Muslims and others in Europe to provide a basis for reducing the polarizations that prevent full utilization of the talents of members of the religious minority. We seek to demonstrate the utility of the benchmarking process in promoting member states' capacity for integration as defined by the European Parliament (2007: 73) in its benchmarking report: 'a society's ability to integrate all its members into new arrangements of active citizenship that ensure the long-term well-being of all in a diverse society'. Besides comparing Muslims to non-Muslims on well-being, we examine differences by age, religiosity, gender, citizenship and place of birth.

It is not our goal to detail the specific historical situation of European Muslims in each member state: several previous publications examine the transitions that drew Muslim population groups to Europe after the Second World War, and the specific political and social problems they face in the European states that are their home. We review this previous work in the next chapter. Our goal is to move beyond analyses of state-level context to demonstrate the utility of the benchmarking process in examining disparities between Muslims and others in Europe and providing a basis for equalizing life chances, thereby enabling Muslims to fully commit their abilities to Europe and its member states.

In key areas where the benchmarking indicators distinguish Muslim well-being negatively in comparison to non-Muslims or 'natives', we review structural and policy-imposed conditions to assess their impact. We consider institutional responsiveness to the cultural requirements of inclusion in several areas, including school, employment, policing, justice and other agencies of government. Anti-immigrant policy initiatives that attach suspicion to the demographic and linguistic characteristics of those most likely to be Muslim are examined along with the extent to which securitization contributes to the stereotypical image of the 'Muslim threat' and to the perception that Muslims prefer to live in a parallel society. Where the data suggest mechanisms of mitigating obstacles to the reduction of disparities between Muslims and non-Muslims in an institutional area, state-specific recommendations are made. We illustrate the ways in which the European Benchmarking process can provide the official information necessary to erode biases against Muslims and undermine inaccurate assumptions about them. This information would provide a firm platform from which state policy makers could develop effective approaches to reduction of the disparities in life chances that promote polarization between Muslims and non-Muslims in Europe.

TWO

State involvement in Muslim well-being

Despite their collaboration as key players in a united Europe, the nations examined differ in the degree of state involvement in immigrant integration. As a result, we can expect variation in both strength and form in their efforts to productively use benchmarking information on disparities between Muslims and non-Muslims. This chapter clarifies differences in the national role on key questions of the relationship between the individual and the civil society, and between religion and the state. At the end of the chapter, we provide information on each state's Muslim population.

European state involvement in minority integration policy does not refer solely, or even primarily, to the removal of barriers to a group's participation in educational, political, social, civic and other institutions (cf. Doerschler and Jackson, 2010a; Jackson and Parkes, 2007). Rather than simply legislating equal access to opportunities for success (for example, in education, employment or access to public facilities), European nations open state and social structures to minorities and immigrants only after they have met certain cultural gateways, or in order to ensure specific equality goals set by the state.

Some scholars of Europe have described relatively fixed and historically grounded national models of state/citizen relations guiding minority integration policy (cf. Bleich, 2003; Brubaker, 1992; Castles, 1995), and offered data on the continuing relevance of 'national citizenship regimes for incorporating migrants' (Koopmans and Statham, 1999: 659). But recent examination documents continuing change in these paradigms, in the requirements for cultural gateways to access membership privileges in European nations, and in the nature of the equality goals to be met by the state (cf. Faas, 2010a; Grillo, 2010; Joppke, 2007; Prins and Saharso, 2010; Modood and Meer, 2010; Schönwälder, 2010; Sunier, 2010a, 2010b). Change in states' conceptualization of the national model of integration is reflected in the shifting mechanisms of their accommodations to the requirements of Muslim well-being.

Mechanisms of state accommodation to Muslim well-being

Britain

Geddes (2003: 44) describes UK minority and immigrant integration policies as situated on a framework of multiculturalism described by former Home Secretary Roy Jenkins 'as "not a flattening process of assimilation", but "equal opportunity accompanied by cultural diversity".' Geddes notes that Adrian Favell (1998a) termed the result, '"multiculturalism on one island" with immigrant and ethnic minorities "nationalised" in relation to British social and political institutions and in a way that is distinct in both practice and conceptual terms from responses in many other European countries' (Geddes, 2003: 44). Tight controls between immigration and immigrant policies provided a foundation for policy in the UK and were seen to lead to better race relations (Geddes, 2003: 45). In discussing the first two Race Relations Acts of 1965 and 1968, Geddes (2003: 45) comments:

> The institutional architecture of race relations was also interesting. Responsibility was devolved to local institutions. The Community Relations Commission set up in 1968 sponsored local Community Relations Councils whose task was the promotion of good race relations. These committees were often composed of the local 'great and good', rather than by immigrants themselves. The good intentions of such organisations may have been overshadowed by their objectification of the immigrant presence: immigrants were a 'problem' to be solved rather than actors with some capacity to shape their own chances for social and political inclusion (Crowley, 1993). (Geddes, 2003: 45)

Geddes (2003: 46–51) describes continued evolution of British integration policy, focused largely on race relations and influenced gradually by European integration.

As Modood and Meer (2010: 78) explain, 'analysis of political and institutional responses to Muslim "difference" in Britain details a pattern of engagement that has evolved over time'. Muslims entering Britain as post-war migrants and the British-born generations that followed were first recognized as ethnic and racial (but not religious) 'minorities requiring state support and differential treatment to overcome distinctive barriers in their exercise of citizenship' (Modood and Meer, 2010: 79). Grillo (2010: 50) makes a similar point: 'despite misgivings about the growing diversity of British society, and often open hostility toward multiculturalism, government policy has, in a complex dialectical relationship with the reality of everyday lives, emphasized religion as a mode of recognizing and working with minorities. Thus, the construction of difference and diversity in Britain has moved from "race" ... to "ethnicity", to "culture", and thence "faith".' According to Modood and Meer (2010: 79), implementation of the third of the Race Relations Acts (1976) eventually 'cemented a state sponsorship of race equality', led to the imposition of a 'statutory public duty to promote good "race relations"' and the creation of the Commission for Racial Equality to 'assist individual complainants and monitor the implementation of the Act'. The goals of multiculturalism in Britain were eventually apparent in the work of local councils and municipal authorities (cf. Singh, 2005, and Swann, 1985, both cited in Modood and Meer, 2010: 80; see also Geddes, 2003, and Schain, 2008). Recognition of the barriers faced by Muslims to full inclusion in British society evolved through the creation of opportunities for minorities to voice their concerns, for example, through the Muslim Council of Britain.

Modood and Meer (2010: 81) cite several successes resulting from Muslims' greater voice in 'the corridors of power', including the addition of a question on religion to the national Census, state funding for some Muslim schools, and the development of policies to improve the socio-economic situation of deprived Muslim groups. Muslims, like other religious groups in Britain, have been able to establish themselves as deserving of the same provisions for education extended to members of the Anglican Church. (See Modood and Meer (2010: 86–88) for examples of accommodations to Muslims' other faith-related needs, including state-level legal changes assuring the supply of *halal* meat, and city council and local authority provisions enabling observance of faith-based burial requirements to be met.) Recognition of British Muslim organizations as part of the conventional establishment can also be seen in state efforts to involve them in counter-terrorism initiatives implemented at the state and local levels. (For examples, see Modood and Meer, 2010: 91–92.)

The changes wrought by the long-term presence of distinct cultural groups within Britain are unlikely to be undone by crises or by policies shoring up the importance of 'traditional' British culture. Though intended to incite the British public against ethnic minorities, Enoch Powell's famous 1968 'Rivers of Blood' speech and other attempts from the far right have been largely rejected by the mainstream. In the following quote, Grillo (2010: 62) describes the evolutionary process of cultural blending over time:

> [t]he picture [in Britain] is confusing. Multiculturalism is under pressure across the political spectrum, in a climate dominated by the events of 2001 and much tension around the Islamic presence. But faith communities are promoted, and in sites where hybridity is produced (schools, playgrounds, mixed marriages, the arts, music) there is a multiplicity of voices, languages, dialects, registers, joking, playing, crossing, engaging in dialogues through which new identities and relationships emerge.

Grillo's comments point out that creativity and new perspectives have emerged in Britain during the process of multicultural transition, even under the stressful conditions inherent to the twenty-first century securitization of policies related to minorities and immigrants. Maleiha Malik (2010) concurs, and underscores the importance of policies through which both minorities and majorities become involved in the project of creating a new national identity. In Malik's (2010: 59) words:

> Debates about the appropriate place of cultural minorities in Britain, therefore, are best understood as part of an ongoing process whereby not only minorities but also majorities are integrated into national life. Debates about 'multiculturalism' are at the heart of more profound national questions about what it means to be 'British'.

Malik's discussion suggests that acceptance of the idea that 'traditional' society provides a morally cohesive bulwark against terrorism obscures recognition of the societal decay that follows from long-term exclusion of a minority population.

Netherlands

Changing cultural gateway criteria utilized by the state in opening institutional structures to minorities and immigrants in the Netherlands are also evident. While the Netherlands has moved beyond the 'pillar' system, which was largely based on individuals' orientation to religion (Calvinism, Catholicism, Socialism and Liberalism), this history legitimized a form of multiculturalism without guarantee of equal access to integrated institutions. In making this point, Sunier

(2010a: 125) indicates that, 'an ongoing debate is taking place ... about the question of whether these typical Dutch political arrangements offer Muslims the opportunities to integrate into Dutch society on a more collective basis and whether an "Islamic pillar", reminiscent of the "traditional" pillars, can be considered as a viable option'. On the surface, this observation may seem at odds with recent developments in immigrant integration policy in The Netherlands. The Dutch 'Immigrant Integration Contract' was revized in 2006 to require Dutch language acquisition and understanding of Dutch culture as gateways to immigrant entry (cf. Joppke, 2007), and this requirement would appear to work against structures supporting maintenance of a collective identity on the part of Muslims. But, Sunier (2010a: 126) points out the importance of constitutional revisions in 1983, which severed all financial relations between church and state, in placing all religions on an equal footing. Along with the Dutch history of pillarization, this change supported acceptance of 'the idea that all religious denominations should have an equal share and should be treated equally' (Sunier, 2010a: 126); and this understanding has fuelled Muslim demands to open religious (confessional) schools, where the state is responsible for the curriculum but religious lessons are based on Islamic religious convictions. (There are 40 Islamic schools today, the first of which opened in 1998 (cf. Sunier, 2010a: 124)).

As Geddes (2003: 113) describes it, in the last two decades of the twentieth century, multicultural policies were blamed 'for maintaining social distance between immigrants and the Dutch, for contributing to social exclusion, and for not pushing Dutch institutions to become more accommodating of newcomers'. Despite decline in the social relevance of the pillars beginning in the 1960s, Geddes (2003: 114) points out that the assumptions of equality with respect for difference remained in place as they dissolved, providing the foundation for a minorities policy that embraced the importance of ethnic differences as key to social identity.

Since 1985 immigrants with five years or more of legal residence have been able to vote in municipal elections in The Netherlands, a process which, no doubt, has encouraged minorities' 'active use of the constitutional rights of consociational society' (Prins and Saharso, 2010: 74), even while 'by the end of the 1980s, the Dutch government already started to discard the perspective of collective rights and care, and to put more emphasis on individual responsibilities and obligations (Fermin, 1997)' (Prins and Saharso, 2010: 75). Recognition of the permanent residence of guest-workers at the beginning of the 1980s had led to a new discourse in which they were referred to as ethnic or cultural minorities and, later, as *allochthonous*. As Sunier (2010a: 131) puts it, 'since structural integration was the central aim of the new policies, culture became the single most important criterion by which integration came to be measured.' Islamic organizations were seen as part of the migrant network, 'and their activities were judged by their effects on the integration process' (Sunier, 2010a: 131). Redefined as foreign through

> the conflation of 'Muslim' with 'migrant' ... Muslims are formally able to make use of the legal opportunities in order to build their own religious infrastructure, [but] they have to seek commonalities, rather than emphasize religious boundaries ... [I]n order to be accepted as Muslims, they have to make themselves invisible as Muslims to the outside world. (Sunier, 2010a: 134)

As the quote below indicates, Prins and Saharso (2010a: 88–89) describe acceptance of the specific cultural demands of Muslims (and of multiculturalism) in the Netherlands as mixed, rather than closed.

> If we take account of the developments at the level of policies, the backlash against multiculturalism does not seem to have hit as hard as the tough public rhetoric suggests. Regarding, for instance, asylum seekers and immigration, the policy lines have surely become harsher. But at some points, the much praised pragmatic Dutch approach seems to have survived. We already mentioned how at the grass roots level problems of domestic violence are combated with culture sensitive measures wrapped up in culture blind terms. Another example is the issue of the Islamic headscarf. Despite much talk about entirely banning the all-covering burka, women in public offices, like teachers in state schools, are allowed to wear the headscarf without much further ado. (Prins and Saharso, 2010: 88–89)

Nonetheless, as Sunier (2010b: 233) explains, even with the more temperate approach of the new government of 2007, the prevailing view is that cultural and religious differences in the Netherlands will eventually be eroded by social and political integration. Geddes (2003: 117) asserts that the Netherlands has moved away from its early embrace of ethnic minority politics to 'a form of civic nationalism ... Lurking beneath the surface are also fears about immigrant loyalty, or disloyalty'.

While the ostensible shift to civic nationalism has not erased the Dutch history of policies protecting minority difference, a tug-of-war between the two policy directions is being played out in response to Muslims' requests for inclusion.

France

In two separate chapters in recent edited collections, Valerie Amiraux details the extent to which the politics of difference in France reflect 'hesitation, inconsistency, and faithfulness to historical ghosts and abstract principles' (Amiraux, 2010b: 93). Amiraux (2010a: 149) asserts that:

> Islam's place in France is still not stable. Its fate is decided on the basis of a number of issues (historical, political, legal, social) which all converge on an apparent loss of trust in the lay republican system. … The thoroughly modern, anti-Muslim racism that characterizes European public opinion relies in the French context on republican universalism, 'the new incarnation of post-colonial imperialism, which makes Islam into the "other" who cannot be assimilated' (Laborde, 2001: 721, as cited in Amiraux, 2010a: 149).

Amiraux (2010a: 145) traces the 'continuity between pre-and post-colonial imagination, discourse and practice in handling Muslim otherness in France'. She translates Guenif (2006) from the French in explaining that images of trouble and danger associated with young Muslim men derive from historical stereotypes of savage Muslim warriors, and reflect the belief that:

> the 'integration gap' for these post-colonial French people does not result from their social inadequacy, nor from their failure to adapt to the employment market. It lies within their own bodies, in their inability to submit to the rules of self-control required by the civilizing process in France (Guenif, 2006: 120, as cited in Amiraux, 2010a: 146).

While French republicanism was established in large part to ensure equal treatment of all citizens in the public arena by recognizing a private cultural and religious sphere, violation of this private sphere by the state has been turned into a

> normal state of affairs ... *laicite*, more honoured by some
> in the breach than in the observance, remains a founding
> concept of the republican spirit, a shared conviction,
> despite its many possible interpretations ... breaching *laicite*
> is therefore now punished. Is this enough to maintain the
> primary meaning of the post-revolutionary secular plan for
> peace-making and reconciliation? (Amiraux, 2010a: 150)

Amiraux (2010a: 145) argues that 'the story of the relationship between the French state (colonial and post-colonial) and the Muslim religion is *in fine* one of interference rather than neutral indifference'.

Amiraux (2010a: 143) describes 'French Muslim policy' as a 'product of the twentieth century', with the aim of developing 'systems of control for protecting the republican project and the colonial Empire from the threat of "Islam" in every area of society'. This approach provided the basis for what Amiraux (2010a: 143–144) refers to as 'the obsessive control and organization of the Muslim religion in accordance with republican principles' which became apparent in the 1980–90s period, and was followed by a period of relative 'laissez-faire' pragmatism and diplomacy resulting in the 'institutionalization of representation for Islam' in the CFCM, the Council of the Muslim Faith in France, in 2003. Expressions of Muslims' religious needs in France are viewed, Amiraux (2010a: 144) explains, as illegitimate and tinged with 'the suspicion of disloyalty'. As examples, she cites the public controversies over both the wearing of the Islamic headscarf and demands for official statistics (including the census) acknowledging racial, ethnic and religious differences within the French population. Simon and Sala Pala (2010: 101–105) similarly cite the controversy over these two issues as reflecting the potential challenge they raise to traditional conceptions of France, rather than to the Republic's political and legal framework (Bowen, 2007: 249, cited in Simon and Sala Pala, 2010: 103), its colonial history, and its management of immigration. Even with the creation of the ministry of immigration, integration, national identity and co-development, the integration model of France, Simon and Sala Pala (2010: 106) argue, 'has not prepared the country to provide any answers, nor any frames to figure out' problems of ethno-racial stratification and discrimination. Rather, they explain (Simon and Sala Pala, 2010: 106), 'by obfuscating ethnic and racial divisions', the model has reinforced systems of racial and ethnic inequality by denying their existence.

In the following quote, Geddes (2003: 66–67) provides background for this situation:

French 'national integration' rests on the idea that as immigrants become 'integrated' then they disappear as a distinct component of French society as they are emancipated from the 'status quo of minorities as collectivities or communities' (Gallisot, 1989: 27, see also Weil and Crowley, 1994; Favell, 1998b). An effect of this is that the concept of minority is absent from French law with policy-makers finding it very difficult to think about the notion of minority groups (Lochak, 1989) ... Despite the formal disavowal of ethnicity and ethnic minorities, Hargreaves (1995: 36) argues that there has actually been an 'ethnicisation' of French politics with 'political behaviour conditioned to a significant degree by consciousness of ethnic differences'. Lochak (1989) argues that the French authorities' position moved since the 1970s from a toleration of difference to the institutionalization and management of difference.

Geddes (2003: 67–71) suggests several examples of change in the French position toward what Schain has called 'the recognition of ethnicity in practice if not in theory' (Geddes, 2003: 67).

France currently offers universal access to social institutions to those who present themselves culturally as *Laic* Republican citizens. The question of Muslim integration in France has focused on group members' unwillingness to integrate themselves, rather than on the removal of barriers to the group's participation in major societal institutions. In other words: 'the question of opening access to public institutions and civil service opportunities to those with headscarves has had much less political salience among native populations in western European nations than has the question of how to persuade Muslim women to go without headscarves to avail themselves of these opportunities' (Jackson and Parkes, 2007–8: 11).

Despite passage of the 2004 law banning headscarves in public schools in France, Françoise Lorcerie (2010: 60) points out that 'the normative model of the "Republican school" ... is not against the expression of social or religious memberships: rather it ignores them'. The current ideological conceptualization of French institutions and of Republican public space, Lorcerie (2010: 60) explains, 'could well be not as naturally French and as old as it is currently supposed to be, despite the seduction it exerts upon certain foreign scholars – who helped legitimise it whether they chose to or not (Brubaker, 1992). The most probable hypothesis is that it has been contextually built and maintained in conflicting settings (Hobsbawm and Ranger, 1992)' (Lorcerie, 2010: 60). In their response to the headscarf ban, Muslim girls and their families made manifest their priorities and goals, even while the ban fuelled the sense of exclusion on the part of Muslims in French society. As Lorcerie (2010: 67) explains '[h]aving to choose between a religious command and school attendance, Muslim girls and families in France chose school. This illuminates the prominent logic of Muslim immigrant families and children in France. School achievement and social mobility are goods one must not reasonably put aside.' The significance of this logic may have gone unnoticed in the public clamour about implementation of the law, clamour which focused largely on perceptions of a threat to French ideals posed by Muslim religious identity.

Germany

In Germany, until recently, the state avoided responsibility for immigrant integration with the publicly expressed assumption that immigrants would return 'home' and that Germany was 'not a land of immigration'. Geddes (2003: 90–91) describes the post–World War Two situation this way:

> Germany's guestworker migrants were 'denizens'. They possessed legal, social, but not political rights ... The FRG's identity as a welfare state had important implications for non-national migrants. Foreign workers and their families were given access to social rights on a par with Germans ... Private welfare organisations 'represented' the immigrants. The Catholic organisation Caritas looked after Catholics from Italy, Portugal and Spain ... The result was the creation of cultures based on religious identities that many of the immigrants had not chosen for themselves.

Geddes (2003: 92) quotes Esser and Korte (1985: 201) in noting that Turks became more visible with their increased numbers, leading to efforts to 'demarcate an ethnic boundary', one aspect of which was with regard to religious identity. As Geddes (2003: 92) explains:

> In 1982, the Turkish Islamic Union (DITIB) was founded as the German branch of the Turkish government's Directorate of Religious Affairs (Diyanet). By 1987, more than 50 per cent of the 1.7 million Muslims in Germany were practicing

this form of Islam that conformed with the ideology of the Kemalist state (Amiraux, 2000). In Germany, as in France, adherence to Islam has been construed as reactionary or as evidence of an unwillingness to integrate ... On these grounds, it is wrong to see a permanent antithetical relationship between 'hosts' and 'immigrants' as though either of these constructs is static and unchanging. (Geddes, 2003: 92)

Geddes (2003: 92) provides several examples of change in the German model of minority integration in its definition of migrant workers in terms of their national cultural origin (whether or not the workers identified with it) and in its conceptualization of *Aussiedler* – though immigrants – as eligible for ethnic and welfare membership in the state because of their German ethnic identity. He argues that assuming a static perception of the national model of integration 'homogenises the host society and imputes to it a coherence that usually makes little sense' (Geddes, 2003: 92).

Since 2000, the German state has placed emphasis on language acquisition and citizenship as mechanisms of integration (cf. Doerschler and Jackson, 2010a). In his 'overview of the policy responses to the Muslim presence' in Germany, Daniel Faas (2010a: 61) highlights 'the shift from notions of "foreigner politics" between the 1960s and 1990s to a politics of integration under the latest two German governments'. While he describes integration as the new 'buzzword', Faas (2010a: 60) points out that 'German rather than Muslim attitudes were arguably the main factor precluding effective integration. The uncertainty of many Turkish Muslims about whether they would eventually return to their country of origin and a society-wide tendency towards social and linguistic segregation were reinforced for two generations.' Between 1974 and the early 1980s, the integration of 'those who have the right to live in Germany' (Faas, 2010: 62) was one of three principles that developed under the SPD leadership of Chancellor Helmut Schmidt. The other two were a continuation of the 1973 recruitment ban, and financial incentives offered to migrants for return to their country of origin fostered by the 1983 law for 'Promotion of Readiness to Return'(Faas, 2010a: 63).

Karen Schönwälder (2010: 153) similarly describes in Germany a process of 'policy reorientations ... incremental, slow policy change spanning three different governments ... to put an end to attempts to revise immigration processes resulting from past labour recruitment and instead to accept past immigration as a fact'. She highlights the

Citizenship Act (in effect in 2000) and 2005 Immigration Act as reflective of this change. Citing Interior Minister Schauble's comment in 2006 that 'immigration is no longer our problem ... our problem is integration', Schönwälder (2010: 154) argues that there is now a political consensus on this point. In explaining the 'paradigm change from migration to integration policy', Schönwälder (2010: 154) describes a lack of clarity regarding the meaning of 'integration': 'integration and equal opportunities are not promised to everyone ... there is an emphasis on cultural and identificational assimilation, and themes like sanctions, pressure and selection are constantly reiterated'. She further explains that '[i]n Germany, wide-ranging official policies linked to an explicit programme of recognizing and promoting ethnic plurality do not exist' (Schönwälder, 2010: 158). The paradigm shift called for in the 2001 so-called Süssmuth Report, from a focus on regulating 'foreigners' to a points system for selecting migrant workers to fit the needs of the economy and greater focus on programmes and services for immigrant integration, never fully materialized, though the more restrictive 2005 immigration law was influenced by the discussion that ensued (Lanz, 2010: 127).

Faas (2010a: 65) explains that amendments to the 2000 citizenship law that came into effect in 2007 and 2008 reinforced the importance of knowledge of the German language (2007) and 'knowledge of cultural, political and historical aspects of Germany' (2008), and enabled the federal states to place additional requirements on the citizenship process, including mandatory integration courses on themes related to democracy and gender equality. Some of the so-called 'Muslim tests' that were introduced by states even earlier (in 2006) and 'arguably played on stereotypes of Islam and Muslim beliefs', forcing demonstration of ideological conformity, were challenged (Faas, 2010a: 64–65). In describing the situation of Muslims in Germany today, Faas (2010a: 71) notes that literature and cinema reflect an 'openness to German society' on the part of the large Turkish community, even with a commitment to Turkish culture. But despite some electoral successes, there is a 'general imbalance between political representation and population. Less than 1% of parliamentarians are Muslims compared with over 4% of the general population. The same holds true for teachers, of whom less than 1% have a Muslim or migrant background' (Faas, 2010a: 72).

Stephen Lanz (2010: 105) describes multiculturalism in Germany as involving 'racism with a distance'. He describes related political discourse as framing Muslims in radical, culturally fundamentalist terms, 'increasingly excluded from an imagined community of the "self"' (Lanz, 2010: 141). Even among left-leaning politicians (from the

Green party), Lanz (2010: 136) explains, 'the antagonistic construction of the West as secular and democratic and of Islam as backward and undemocratic seems to be successfully separating the majority from Muslim immigrants'. At the same time, he argues, in some cities and especially Berlin, minorities (but Lanz does not specify Muslims here) are 'valued as a relevant social resource for the future' (Lanz, 2010: 141).

Policies of state involvement are not static

The processes of accommodating the needs of Muslim well-being in these four EU member states reflect considerable change in the models guiding state-led efforts related to the well-being of Muslims as a religious minority: Britain moved from a race-based to a faith-based policy; the Netherlands from a consociational rights-based policy, to a policy based on individual responsibilities; France from a *laïcité* policy ignoring individuals' religion, to one penalizing displays of religious identity in public institutions; and Germany from a policy based on the assumption that non-German difference has no place in German society, to a policy establishing a minimum threshold of commonality between those 'foreigners' who will remain and German citizens (placing on Muslims the burden to conform to the majority). In the context of efforts to measure well-being in Europe, accurate information about Muslims could demonstrate the importance of religion. The possibility exists of implementing a common set of standards of well-being in which religion is recognized as an aspect of personal identity that hinders success in the face of bias and discrimination.

Efforts to prevent examination of the extent to which life chances are limited through institutional discrimination and prejudice are sanitized by reference to the immutability of 'national models of integration'. This tactical procedural stumbling block has been branded as 'political discourse in disguise ... an argument in the normative conflict over the integration of migrants and minorities ... useless for the very simple reason that these models ... never existed in the way we usually picture them' (Bertossi, 2010: 1–2). In the case of France, the integration model blocks examination of discrimination and diversity in its reference to 'an imagined normative republic' (Bertossi, 2010: 4). Integration models may serve states poorly in 'the struggle to locate their racial, ethnic, cultural, or religious diversity at the heart of their program of equality' (Bertossi, 2010: 12). Careful historical examination of French republicanism and the multiculturalism of the Netherlands and Britain demonstrates their elusiveness rather than rigidity as definitions of national identity (cf. Amiraux and Simon, 2006; Bertossi,

2010: 9; Duyvendak and Scholten, 2010; Vertovec and Wessendorf, 2010). Bertossi (2010: 6) argues that debates about republicanism or multiculturalism can be seen as screens hiding 'widely varied and contradictory "problematizations" ... of integration and citizenship in [France, the Netherlands, and Britain]'. The fact that these 'models' are taken seriously in the political realm can be seen in discussion of the extent to which they are currently in 'crisis' (cf. Schain, 2008; Scheffer, 2000). The 2005 riots in France and the terrorist attack in London in the same year, as well as the 2004 killing of Theo van Gogh in Amsterdam by a Dutch Moroccan (and related warning to Hirsi Ali) (cf. Prins and Saharso, 2010: 81) have been framed as reflective of Islam's challenge to secularity, modernity and state integration models despite the fact that the incidents were executed by a few extremists who used religious ideology to justify their attacks and were condemned by European Muslim leaders.

Bertossi (2010: 10) argues that conceptualizing national integration models as 'social practices that guide interactions among actors in varying contexts ... as ... social construct(s) ... dependent variable(s)' (rather than as independent variables) illuminates the ways in which the models evolve. Duyvendak and Scholton (2010) make a similar point. National models of integration are reflective of demands for inclusion and efforts to retain dominance by competing interest groups. In seeking to utilize their talents and contribute to the societies in which they have grown up and been educated, the children of guest-workers and of former colonies are making legitimate demands for inclusion. These demands do not come in the form of terrorist attacks or violence; rather they are expressed in the form of applications for university entrance, for professional positions, for better housing, and for the same use of taxpayer funds for the social services provided by their religious organizations that is given to other religious groups in the European member state in which they live. Without the blinders imposed by notions of immutable national integration models, the extent to which Muslim Europeans want to be like other Europeans might be recognized, as would the structures that inhibit this possibility in some key areas of life. It is our goal to demonstrate the mechanisms through which the benchmarking process has the capacity to open this discussion, once data collection processes include religion as an aspect of individuality that influences well-being and creates disparities and polarizations within Europe.

Civic integration requirements and the securitization of policies relating to the well-being of Muslims

Both the life chances available to minorities and their image in the public arena are influenced by the degree of state involvement in stipulating the criteria through which those who are not deemed to be 'native' to the society can access state provided goods and services (such as education, employment in state-run agencies, social welfare assistance, unemployment compensation, or support for the social service and educational activities sponsored by religious organizations). Efforts to regulate manifestations of cultural identity, including host language acquisition, as well as clothing and other elements of religious observance, have increasingly been described as necessary for the security of the state: diversity in these areas in the public arena has been branded as threatening to the integrity of the state culturally, economically, and existentially. As Sara Goodman (2010: 768) explains:

> despite inherent institutional and experiential differences between conditional and prohibitive citizenship countries, the use of civic integration requirements to confront issues of immigration and integration predictions is an interesting new policy pattern across states ... it is important to consider the role that violence has played in infusing civic integration with a new sense of urgency. In Britain, the 'duty to integrate' by requiring applicants for settlement to pass the 'Life in the UK' test directly followed the London bombings of 7 July 2005, and Dutch integration requirements have grown increasingly prohibitive since their earliest incarnation in 1998, fuelled by a seemingly endless stream of events, including the murder of Theo Van Gogh.

Civic integration contracts, Goodman (2010: 767) points out, 'vet and exclude applicants', rather than facilitating integration or limiting it numerically. But even in light of converging pressures – such as open borders, economic needs, Europeanization, colonial precedents, and domestic political pressure toward restrictiveness – some differences remain in the nature and degree of integration requirements put in place by states. While Goodman (2010: 767) argues that institutional differences between states 'merely refract and mediate similar strategic pressures on policy-making in liberal citizenship regimes', nonetheless, significant differences remain. Again, in Goodman's (2010: 767–768) words:

> The politicisation of immigration by the far right in France prioritises integration policies in a way that an insulated civil service in Great Britain could never achieve ....The degrees of deterrence that integration requirements have achieved are far more pronounced in the Netherlands and France than they are in the UK; Human Rights Watch (2008) has condemned the Dutch for using civic integration tests as an unjustified device of discrimination. Where this approach is more covert, Nicholas Sarkozy's desire for France's ratio of *immigration subie* (endured; family unification) and *immigration choisie* (proactive; skilled migrants) is no secret (Bennhold 2006: 3). And evidence suggests that British requirements also play a small 'gatekeeper' role, with 16 per cent of refused applications for British citizenship in 2007 attributed to 'insufficient knowledge of English and/or knowledge of life in the United Kingdom (Home Office, 2008b: 7)' (Goodman, 2010: 767–68).

While Goodman explains that in all of these states integration requirements help to screen out certain types of immigrants, her examples consistently demonstrate that historical background, stance toward and degree of diversity, and institutional composition (such as Britain's insulated civil service) all influence the strength and nature of the policies through which the state can impose immigrant and minority group conformity toward the dominant culture. Nonetheless, requirements for integration have been strengthened in all four of the states we examine.

In the following quote Jef Huysmans explains the political utility of regulating the nature and degree of diversity that is tolerable through 'securitization' policies in the creation of a united Europe.

> The creation of the European Union as a European polity depends on whether a European cultural identity can be created and on sorting out how national political identities can be integrated into this European cultural identity. Immigrants and refugees emerge in this context as a complicating factor that further diversifies the question of cultural identity. Securitization is then a strategy of cultural discrimination that firmly places culturally different immigrants outside or in the margins of national communities and the European Union. (Huysmans, 2006: 118)

Huysmans (2006) describes the emergence of security policies from existing political arrangements in European states. The fact that cultural securitization has been applied to Muslims born in European nations can be seen as a case in point. Charges that those who wear headscarves are a threat to both the state and the position of women, continued confusion over the legitimacy of mosques and their social services in the national religious landscape, the inability of avowedly secular states to support requests for *halal* food in hospitals, schools and prisons all can be seen as examples of the marginalization of Muslims by the state, as a relegation of their demands for religious expression to their previous immigrant status (or that of their parents), rather than as legitimate demands made by European citizens. Expressions of frustration with the state in communities populated by Muslim youth, such as the 2005 riots in French *banlieue* outside of Paris, are attributed to 'immigrants' in news accounts and in quotes by public officials presenting the 'threat' posed by these implicit demands for change as unwarranted and coming from 'outsiders', not Europeans.

The states we are examining can be arranged on a continuum of state primacy in individual well-being and integration (cf. Jackson and Parkes, 2007; Jackson, Zervakis and Parkes, 2005) to facilitate our comparison of official responses to minority and immigrant groups. By state primacy, we refer to 'both the structural evidence of state intervention in society and the economy (anti-discrimination policy, social welfare, state education, regulation of the economy), and the legitimacy held by the state in promoting its values through these structures and by other means' (Jackson and Parkes, 2007: 16–17). France and Germany, examples of prime states, evidence both state intervention in society and the active promotion of cultural values. Britain and the Netherlands are less clear cut. Despite structural evidence of state intervention in society, both of the latter states have promoted themselves as 'multicultural', an ideology that suggests a limited state role in promoting official cultural behaviour. (See Penninx (2006) for a discussion complementing that of Goodman (2010) above regarding the importance of the murder of van Gogh in efforts to redefine state multicultural policy in the Netherlands.) While these states may be seen to promote some type of 'official behaviour' and, in the case of the Netherlands even an integration contract requiring an understanding of both the Dutch language and culture,

> entrenched liberal understandings ... have limited the state's scope to promote the exclusive values of the majority ... even though cultural engineering is accepted as in prime

states, the scope for the state to promote the exclusive values of the majority is narrower as in a limited state. (Jackson and Parkes, 2007: 17)

State primacy has implications for the securitization of immigrant policy: limited states regulate fewer societal, social and economic structures and have less legitimacy in the imposition of cultural gateways of access to them. Limited states are weaker in their ability to promote an exclusive 'national culture' than are prime states, and are, therefore, less effective in portraying minorities as threatening to the cultural and political stability of the state (cf. Jackson and Parkes, 2007–8: 18).

State primacy and benchmarking

The need for data comparing Muslim Europeans to members of other religious groups in the key areas of life specified by the Council of Europe (2003) and examined in the benchmarking effort initiated by the European Parliament (2007) is most pressing in prime states, which have the greatest influence on minority integration policies and provide the greatest social welfare cushion for their residents. Where the state plays a primary role in the well-being of residents, disparities between groups spark the greatest conflict with all sides blaming the state for the polarizations that develop. (See Jackson, 2009: 240–241.) Some residents of prime states resent what they see as evidence of the ineffectiveness of state policies in assimilating the minority population (where, for example, women wear headscarves, or families celebrate non-Christian holidays and speak the language of the country of origin in public). Others who live in prime states charge that state efforts are doomed to failure because they ignore important structural elements that keep the minority segmented (like the ambiguous place of mosques in the state's institutional network, and the lack of state financial support for mosques' social service activities). (See Schiffauer (2006) and Schuerkens (2007) for discussions of France and Germany, respectively, illustrating several aspects of conflict resulting from public perceptions of state involvement in minority integration.)

The same complaints are made in limited states (like the UK), but belief in the legitimacy of state action to correct the problem is less entrenched, reducing the impetus for the actual implementation of policies to change the situation. Examples include the failed effort to require that the identity card be carried by all British citizens (BBC, 2009) and the controversy over wearing the niquab in Britain – but lack of a ban on it (*New York Times*, 2007).

Even in light of the 2004 French ban on headscarves and conspicuous religious symbols for students in public schools, not all European member states have gone in that direction. There is even variation within individual member states. Some German federal states (see van der Noll, 2010: 194) have passed explicit regulations prohibiting religious symbols and clothing for teachers and other civil servants, though other German federal states have not. (Since Germany is less centralized than France, it is important to examine policies at the level of the *Bundesland* as well as at the federal level.) Faas (2010b: 49) reports that in several German states related legislation 'privileges the Christian cross over other religious symbols in schools'. While the headscarf is banned for teachers in public schools and civil servants in these states, van der Noll (2010: 194) notes that 'Christian crucifixes, nuns' habits and the Jewish Kippah are allowed'. Headscarves can generally be worn by school and university students in Germany (see Faas, 2010a, cited in van der Noll, 2010: 194).

But the situation is different in the United Kingdom and the Netherlands, even though their multicultural histories are believed by many to be insufficient to stem the tides of change toward nativism. As Jolanda van der Noll (2010: 194) explains,

> the United Kingdom has a very liberal approach to the wearing of religious symbols. In most teaching institutions the Islamic headscarf is accepted and if conflicts arise, they are generally resolved within the institution. There is no general legislation that prohibits women from wearing headscarves ... in the Netherlands there is a broad ability to live according to particular group identities and traditions, including in the public sphere. The Dutch Equal Treatment Commission generally rules in favour of women who want to wear the headscarf, ruling that it is an expression of their religious identity, and as such protected by the right of freedom to religion. Distinctions ... are made between institutional contexts; for reasons of neutrality, religious symbols (including the headscarf) are prohibited in courtrooms and the police force, but teachers and pupils are allowed to wear headscarves in schools (Saharso and Lettinga, 2008) (van der Noll, 2010: 194).

See also Dutch News.nl (2011) for discussion of a February 2011 decision supporting Muslim girls' headscarves in a Catholic school in the Netherlands. This decision of the Dutch Equal Opportunity

Commission was appealed to a local district court and overturned on 4 April 2011. It is currently on appeal again. See the Law Library of Congress (2011) for a discussion of the case in English. Despite extremist party rhetoric demanding a ban on headscarves in schools in the Netherlands, the restrictions being debated in Dutch courts refer only to Catholic schools and rest on the question of whether the schools' mission is damaged by the wearing of religious symbols relating to Muslim (rather than Catholic) traditions.

The importance of data in supporting state policy

Without data showing that disparities between Muslim minority groups and the non-Muslim majority are diminishing, states cannot defend their policies effectively. The persistent success of anti-foreigner and anti-Islam platforms by political parties in these states lead elected officials to avoid policies that would examine and improve the well-being of Muslims, even if these initiatives only focus on data gathering (EUMC, 2005a, 2006). The history of official misuse of personal data including religion during the Second World War is often brought up to legitimize the fact that Muslims are not officially counted in census enumerations in Germany, the Netherlands and France (Negrin, 2003). But while the political and historical context in continental European states supports the information gap on Muslims, European agencies responsible for stimulating research on minority populations have determined that states cannot afford to ignore the need for data. Some states, like the United Kingdom, have moved in the direction of gathering valid and reliable information on Muslims' situation by augmenting the census to include religious identification; other states, like Germany, have taken a preliminary step with an initial survey of a sample of Muslims (BAMF, 2009).

In the states with the greatest degree of involvement in assuring individual well-being and in controlling immigrant policies relating to integration, political conceptualizations of the place of an individual's religion in the establishment of their civic identity and access to rights are most likely to fan the flames of discord, creating both disparities and polarizations. In France, for example, even creation of the French Council of Muslims in 2003 failed to clarify the place of the mosque and the political representation of Islam in French society (cf. *Economist* 2007: 65). This confusion fuelled the 2005 riots in the *banlieue* surrounding Paris, sparked by the sense of illegitimacy associated with the routine identification checks by police of youth 'of colour' and perceived to be Muslim (cf. Mucchielli, 2009: 748).

To some degree, this lack of clarity regarding the place of mosques in the existing system of church/state relationships characterizes all four states we examine and fuels debates about issues symbolically related to minority inclusiveness in European states. These include, for example, state support for educational and social service activities of Muslim religious organizations, integration contracts for non-western immigrants, headscarves for students and public employees, the educational performance of Muslim minorities, the relationship between Muslim youth and the police, the impact on Muslim minorities of policies regulating illegal immigration and asylum, and the unacknowledged 'Islamization' of prisons (cf. Beckford, Joly, and Khosrokhavar, 2005). With regard to these and other specific issues of inclusion, a key aspect in examining the role of the state in Muslim well-being is the impact of the new immigration security environment that became explicit in the twenty-first century. Though its roots were in the previous century, the image of danger associated with those of immigrant background became explicit after several highly publicized terrorist attacks, including those in New York City (2001) and London (2005), and the killing in 2004 of film maker Theo van Gogh by a man of Dutch and Moroccan nationality (after van Gogh produced the film *Submission*, portraying violence against women in Islamic societies). States with the greatest influence in promulgating the image of the ideal insider had the greatest perceived legitimacy in defining the characteristics of outsiders.

Benchmarking indicators

The problems faced by third country nationals, including refugees and asylum seekers have been the focus of previous discussion of the indicators of individual well-being needed to assist European states in a two-way process of minority integration by reducing disparities and polarizations (cf. Ager and Strang, 2004a, 2004b; European Parliament, 2007; Niessen and Huddleston, 2009). While the earlier literature related to the topic is conceptual (Ager and Strang, 2004a; European Parliament, 2007) with the goal of establishing the dimensions of life that are important in the integration process, later efforts use the conceptual definitions to examine integration policies for third-country nationals, and public opinion outcomes associated with varying degrees of inclusiveness in states' integration policies. Benchmarking processes toward well-being have not been directly applied to the situation of Muslims in European states other than the UK, to some extent because the 'politics of statistics' has successfully thwarted such examination, contributing to the fact that benchmarking projects are focused on refugees and other third-country nationals. With the European Commission's (2005) Community Statistics Proposal and the European Parliament's (2007) benchmarking report diffusing new international understandings on reducing disparities and polarizations between groups, measuring and improving Muslim well-being in Europe could be one way (to use Geddes and Wunderlich's (2009: 196) terminology) 'in which the EU can "hit home" in domestic politics'.

There is little divergence in the definitions of 'integration' put forward by those who have been examining it conceptually. Ager and Strang (2004a,b; 2008: 167), for example, began with consideration of close to 200 integration indicators from the Council of Europe's (1997) report, *Measurements and Indicators of Integration* and other sources (cf. Ager and Eyber, 2002). With a focus on refugees, Ager and Strang conducted both fieldwork involving qualitative research and secondary analysis of cross-sectional survey data to support the salience of their conceptual framework. Ultimately, Ager and Strang (2008: 169–170) put forward four 'key issues' as 'discrete domains' providing both markers and means of integration: Employment, Housing, Education and Health. These constitute the top layer of their conceptual framework, which rests on three tiers below it. The foundation layer consists of *citizenship and rights*. These are balanced, Ager and Strang assert, on the 'nation's sense of identity,' which evolves over time (as we discussed earlier in this chapter, and they also consider). Above the foundation layer rest what Ager and Strang (2008: 182) refer to as the facilitators necessary for effective integration in the wider community. Facilitators include *knowledge of the host nation language and culture*, and the *safety and stability* that comes from an absence of conflict and tolerance of diversity, requiring the responsiveness of the host society. Above the facilitators in the conceptual model is what Ager and Strang (2008: 177) refer to as 'connective tissue ... driving the process of integration at the local level'. Connective tissue includes *social bonds* (connections with members of their ethnic group), *social bridges* (connections with members outside of their ethnic group), and *social links* (connections to state structures and services) (Ager and Strong, 2008: 177–182). What results from this layered framework are ten interdependent domains central to the conceptual understanding of integration, intended to stimulate discussion and inform 'policymakers, researchers, service providers and/or refugees themselves' (Ager and Strong, 2008: 185). These domains of integration do not differ significantly from those offered to operationalize the benchmark definition of integration provided in the report initiated by the European Parliament's Committee on Civil

Liberties, Justice and Home Affairs (European Parliament, 2007: 71): 'a society's ability to integrate all its members into new arrangements of active citizenship that ensure the long-term well-being of all in a diverse society,' where the key aspects of integration are those specified by the Council of Europe (2003; cf. European Parliament, 2007: 139): employment, housing, health care, nutrition, education, information, culture and an aspect referred to as integration of basic public functions and reflecting equality, anti-discrimination and self-organization.

The creation of a Migration Integration Policy Index (MIPEX) was begun in 2004 and more fully developed in 2007 'to establish a reliable biannual standard-setting and monitoring tool for governmental integration policies' (Niessen, 2009: 1). Rather than measure the degree of integration of third country nationals, the MIPEX project examines the national policies likely to have the greatest impact on the integration of minorities. For 28 countries, including EU member states, the MIPEX project compares legislation 'on the basis of a set of 142 legal and policy indicators' (Niessen and Huddleston, 2009: ix). By 2007, the index (MIPEX) had evolved to include these policy areas: 'labour market access, family reunion, long-term residence, political participation, access to nationality, and anti-discrimination law' (Niessen, 2009: 1). While education policies targeted toward migrants were not included in this list, Niessen notes their importance and suggests that they and other additional elements of integration could be considered for later editions of the index.

The utility of the index is explained in the first chapter of the MIPEX volume: 'a country's policies can be compared against the highest European integration standards, to other countries and the EU average, and over time' (Niessen, 2009: 1). MIPEX was developed

> as a tool to assess to what extent equality principles are applied to integration policies ... The MIPEX authors took as source proposals for Community law made by the European Commission and by non-governmental actors, European Council Conclusions and adopted Community law. In areas where the EU lacks legislative competence, MIPEX used two European Conventions, namely the European Convention on Nationality and European Convention on the participation of foreigners in public life at the local level. (Niessen, 2009: 3)

Designed as an effort to turn 'policies into numbers', and 'numbers into scores, comparisons and rankings' (Niessen, 2009: 7), MIPEX member-state rankings are based on a score key ranging from '0, Critically unfavourable for promoting immigrant integration' to '100, Best practice' (Niessen, 2009: 8).

Data from the *European Social Survey* (ESS) and from the *Eurobarometer* were linked to MIPEX in this examination (cf. Jacobs and Herman, 2009). Benchmarking standards have also been applied to anti-discrimination law and policy (Bell, 2009), and to nationality law (Toth, 2009). Geddes and Wunderlich (2009: 195) examine the impact of immigrant integration policies 'on the ground' in terms of employment and unemployment levels of third-country nationals in the EU. The MIPEX effort will provide an imperfect and incomplete picture of the effectiveness of integration policies in fostering inclusiveness in European member states because 'the politics of statistics on immigrant populations' has led to the exclusion in many European states of minorities who have become citizens (Geddes and Wunderlich, 2009: 196). While Geddes and Wunderlich indicate that the situation of ethnic minorities of immigrant origin will be outside of the scope of examination due to data politics, we extend their concern to the situation of Muslims, who face barriers to inclusion in Europe that are separate from their ethnic identity.

The MIPEX project is useful in examining integration policy as it is related to the inclusion of third-country nationals, and in evaluating the relationship between policy and public opinion toward immigrant minority groups. It does not, however, directly evaluate the progress of states in reducing disparities and polarizations among those who reside within the state, and, especially, between 'natives' and minorities of immigrant background who were born within the state, and may even be citizens of the European state. It can help us evaluate the legal framework, but not the degree of difference among residents. In addition, MIPEX does not evaluate policies related to the religious needs of migrants.

National Quality of Life benchmarking initiatives

The role of government in promoting the well-being of citizens has received increasing attention in the rich world. In the United Kingdom, for example, David Cameron (citing Robert Kennedy's assessment of the limitations of the Gross Domestic Product (GDP) as a measure of national well-being) committed the Office of National Statistics to measure quality of life and individual happiness beginning April 2011 (cf. Mulholland and Watt, 2010; Davies, 2010). Since January 2008 news reports have described Nicolas Sarkozy's plans to include happiness and well-being in measures of economic progress in France, under the guidance of two Nobel prize winning economists (Joseph Stiglitz and Amartya Sen) (*Economist*, 2008). (See also Mulholland and Watt, 2010 and Mail Online, 2009.) The so-called Stiglitz Commission (cf. Stiglitz, Sen and Fitoussi, 2009) examined measures of political voice, social connections and insecurity as predictors of life satisfaction (cf. Gjoksi, 2010: 11). Subjective well-being (SWB) has increasingly become a focus of Statistics Netherlands (which conducts the national census), and scholars date the beginnings of this interest to the 1974 Life Situation Survey (LSS) conducted by Statistics Netherlands for the Netherlands Institute for Social Research (NISR) (de Jonge, 2009). In Germany a National Welfare Index (NWI) has been developed and is under examination as complementary to Gross Domestic Product as a measure of national well-being (cf. Gjoksi, 2010: 13–15). Twenty-one variables comprise the NWI, including the green economics aspects of what is generally called the Genuine Progress Indicator (GPI) movement, as well as six indicators of social factors and two economic indicators. The latter two sets of factors include spending on education, health and prevention of criminality, but 'research on the NWI indicator is more strongly connected to the ecological economics framework and less to the well-being discussions on happiness or life satisfaction' (Gjoksi, 2010: 13).

It is fair to say that all four states examined here have moved beyond GDP as a measure of national welfare, with plans to devote some greater degree of attention to social well-being and to aspects of personal satisfaction. But while disparities in equality, political voice and social connectedness are cited as stumbling blocks hampering efforts toward greater well-being on the part of citizens, problems associated with assuring the well-being of Muslims in particular are not directly considered despite the relative inequality, lack of political voice and social isolation of the religious group in each of these states. In the pages below, we seek to demonstrate both a constructive approach toward inclusion of the problems of well-being specific to Muslims in the European and national efforts to benchmark and improve citizen satisfaction and reduce disparities, and the utility of expanding these national and supra-national well-being projects to provide for the greater well-being of Muslim Europeans.

Demographic characteristics of European Muslim populations

Relative youth

Demographic data demonstrate the relative youth of the Muslim populations in Europe. The European Social Survey estimates shown in Table 2.1 for the cumulative 2002–2008 sample indicate that Muslims were at least twice as likely to be under 30 than non-Muslims in the UK (48% of Muslims vs. 20% of non-Muslims), Germany (39% of Muslims in contrast to 18% of non-Muslims), France (39% of Muslims vs. 19% of non-Muslims), and in the Netherlands (where 36% of Muslims were under 30 years old in contrast to 17% of non-Muslims). (Comparison of the 2002 ESS age distribution data for the United Kingdom with the latest data collected by the British Office for National Statistics (2001) indicates considerable agreement about the relative youth of Muslims in comparison to non-Muslims. (See *Focus on Religion*, Office for National Statistics, October 2004: 3.) The UK is the only state for which census data can be used in comparison to ESS findings.)

Table 2.1: Summary profile of Muslims and non-Muslims (ESS 2008-2)

	France		Germany		Netherlands		United Kingdom	
Age (%)	Muslims	Other	Muslims	Other	Muslims	Other	Muslims	Other
15-29	39.2	19.3	38.7	17.7	36.1	17.3	48.1	20.4
30-44	37.8	26.6	39.8	26.7	42.8	27.5	30.3	27.7
45-59	18.0	27.4	14.1	27.4	14.4	31.0	15.9	25.4
60 and older	5.0	26.7	7.4	28.2	6.7	24.2	5.8	26.4
Average age	35.1 (221)	47.2 (6,821)	34.7 (256)	47.9 (10,988)	34.7 (180)	47.0 (7,720)	33.7 (208)	46.7 (7,147)
Female (%)	47.1 (221)	53.2 (6,821)	44.8 (268)	50.7 (11,136)	43.9 (180)	54.2 (7,721)	45.8 (212)	52.1 (7,187)
Non-citizen (%)	31.2 (221)	2.6 (6,821)	67.7 (269)	3.0 (11,133)	19.4 (180)	2.1 (7,721)	12.3 (212)	3.7 (7,195)
Foreign born (%)	53.8 (221)	7.4 (6,821)	72.0 (268)	7.7 (11,130)	66.7 (180)	6.7 (7,721)	64.6 (212)	9.3 (7,196)
Member ethnic minority (%)	31.9 (207)	2.9 (6,757)	57.1 (261)	3.4 (11,102)	85.6 (180)	3.8 (7,713)	74.4 (203)	5.4 (7,177)
Lives in big city[1] (%)	39.8 (221)	18.4 (6,819)	37.1 (267)	18.5 (11,118)	46.7 (180)	17.1 (7,699)	26.2 (206)	7.4 (7,173)
Average religiosity	6.6 (221)	3.6 (6,798)	6.7 (268)	4.2 (11,063)	7.4 (180)	4.9 (7,700)	6.9 (212)	4.1 (7,178)
N Muslim (% total)	221 (3.1%)		268 (2.4%)		180 (2.3%)		212 (2.9%)	

Note: Number of respondents for each question contained in parentheses.
Data: ESS 2008, 2006, 2004, 2002
[1] Other categories include suburb, town or small city, country village, farm or home in countryside.
Exact population sizes of each category were not provided to respondents in the questionnaire.

Their relative youth ensures that the impact of Muslims on European states will be significant, despite their small proportion in the population.

Table 2.1a: Specific characteristics of Muslims (ESS 2008-2)

	France	Germany	Netherlands	UK
Origin of non-citizenship (%)				
Middle East/North Africa[1]	84.5	78.5	74.2	41.9
Africa (excluding Maghreb)[2]	13.1	1.4	6.5	32.6
Europe[3]	2.4	11.9	6.4	0
Southern Asia + Indonesia[4]	0	8.2	12.9	25.5
	(221)	(269)	(180)	(212)
Primary language spoken at home (%)				
Residence (French, German, Dutch, English)	65.2	40.1	61.1	47.7
Arabic	23.1	3.7	8.9	4.2
Turkish	4.5	44.2	21.1	---
Other	4.0	9.7	8.9	45.8
Refusal/don't know/no answer	3.2	2.2	---	2.3
Secondary language spoken at home (%)				
No second language	59.3	9.0	37.4	62.4
Residence (French, German, Dutch, English)	9.0	54.1	18.1	5.6
Arabic	20.4	3.4	13.7	2.8
Turkish	---	26.1	18.7	---
Other	9.9	6.0	12.1	29.2
Refusal/don't know/no answer	1.4	1.3	---	---

Note: Number of respondents for each question contained in parentheses. Data: ESS 2008, 2006, 2004, 2002
[1] Includes Algeria, Azerbaijan, Brunei, Egypt, Iraq, Lebanon, Libya, Morocco, Syria, Tunisia, Turkey, Yemen
[2] Includes Democratic Republic of Congo, Guinea, Ivory Coast, Kenya, Mali, Nigeria, Senegal, Sierra Leone, Somalia, Togo
[3] Includes Albania, Belgium, Bosnia and Herzegovina, France, Greece, Macedonia, Portugal, Serbia and Montenegro, UK, Yugoslavia
[4] Includes Afghanistan, Bangladesh, India, Indonesia, Iran, Pakistan

By 2100, one estimate concludes that Muslims will constitute 25% of Europe's population (Jenkins, 2006). Problems in schools and in employment for young adults, as well as lack of inclusion in the political system will impact Muslims most heavily because of their age distribution. But Muslim youth who can fully develop their talents will be poised to contribute productively to their European states and to the European project. Recognition of this possibility should spur efforts to ensure that the schools attended by Muslim youth provide them with the technological experiences, linguistic training, and the educational and career development guidance that will ensure maximum utilization of their abilities even in the face of their minority backgrounds.

Estimates of size

According to most estimates, Muslims are 3% of the population in Great Britain (Jansson et al., 2007), 5% in Germany (BAMF, 2009), 6% in France (Laurence and Vaisse, 2006) and close to 6% in the Netherlands (U.S. Department of State, 2010). (A slightly lower figure of 5% is given on the website of Statistics Netherlands from its 2005–6 unofficial survey estimate.) Table 2.2 provides the estimates of percentage of Muslims obtained from the European Social Survey on the basis of its random sampling of the population of France, Germany, the Netherlands and the United Kingdom in 2002, 2008 and for the cumulative 2002–8 data. ESS respondents were asked which religion or denomination they consider themselves as belonging to.

ESS obtained the following figures for those identifying with Islam: 7.6% for France; 3.8% for Germany; 5.2% for the Netherlands; and 5.8% for the UK. But these figures are reduced when the population specifying 'no religion' is added to the population base. The largest category of response for religious identification in each of the four states we examine is 'no religion'. For the cumulative ESS sample (2002–8) that we have used, the figures of those selecting 'no religion' follow: Germany, 39%; France 52%; UK 52%; and Netherlands 57%. We included those not identifying with any religion in the total population base; their inclusion reduces the ESS estimates of the proportion that is Muslim. Since our goal is to compare the situation of Muslims to that of other members of their European state, not only to those who have a religious identification, we start by assessing Muslims' relative demographic size in the overall population.

Table 2.2: Estimates for percentage Muslim in ESS

	France	Germany	Netherlands	United Kingdom
2008	3.2	2.0	2.9	3.4
2002	3.5	2.4	2.2	2.1
2002-2008	3.1	2.4	2.3	2.9
Excluding respondents with 'no religion'	7.6	3.8	5.2	5.8
Percent 'no religion'	51.5	38.4	56.5	51.9

Data: ESS 2008, 2006, 2004, 2002.

Language skills may have prevented some Muslims from participating in the ESS survey. ESS provides translations to those groups representing at least 5% of the population; none were offered in the four countries on which we focus. Table 2.1a provides information on language skills, the importance of which we discuss later, in Chapter Seven. Some Muslims might have been hesitant to participate in the European Social Survey, though it is unlikely that this survey would have been of more concern than others, including the UK Census. Throughout the book, we compare the results of our ESS analysis to those obtained utilizing alternative data sources whenever they are available. These comparisons consistently support the ESS findings, and, as a result, thereby support the representativeness of the ESS sample of Muslims.

Citizenship, foreign birth, ethnic minority identification

The citizenship of ESS respondents for the cumulative 2002–08 sample is summarized in Table 2.1. In the UK, 12% of Muslim respondents are non-citizens, in contrast to just under 4% of non-Muslims. In Germany, the policy of limiting access to citizenship to German descendants is reflected in the citizenship figures, with 68% of Muslim respondents indicating they are not German citizens, in contrast to 3% of non-Muslims. The French citizenship policy of permitting citizenship to those born in France (with increasing provisions requiring children to request it by a certain age) is reflected in a lower rate of non-citizens among Muslims (31%), while for non-Muslims it is under 3%. In the Netherlands, 19% of Muslims are not Dutch citizens, in contrast to 2% of non-Muslims.

Table 2.1 indicates that in all four states, over half of the Muslim respondents in the ESS 2002–2008 cumulative sample were foreign born. (A comparison of the 2002 ESS respondents' foreign born figure (not shown in a table) for the UK (70%) with the 2001 UK Census (Office for National Statistics, 2004: 6) (54%) indicates that both estimates place the figure at over half.) To the extent that they are like migrants before them, Muslims who relocated to Europe were in search of a better life for their families. But like other religious minorities, Muslims may require specific accommodations to support their religious identity even while they contribute to and participate in European institutions.

Table 2.3 illustrates the pitfalls inherent in the prevailing strategies of estimating the size of the Muslim population and their well-being on the basis of characteristics of immigrant or non-citizen population groups. In France, for example, while 54% of Muslims were born abroad, only 19% of those born abroad are Muslim. A similar problem of comparison exists for the other three states in our analysis. Since the UK asks respondents to identify their religion in its Census, more accurate representations of the Muslim population can be obtained without relying on estimates gleaned from the immigrant population. Table 2.3 suggests that use of 'non-citizens' as the referent group for Muslims is also problematic as to overlap: in Germany, for example, the European Social Survey estimates that 68% of Muslims are non-citizens, while 35% of non-citizens are Muslims. The assumption that information about 'ethnic minorities' applies to Muslims is also risky: Table 2.3 indicates that in the Netherlands, for example, while 86% of Muslims identify themselves as a member of an ethnic minority (Appendix 1, Controls: Belong to an ethnic minority in country), only 35% of those who define themselves as 'ethnic minorities' are Muslim.

Table 2.3: Diversity of Muslim population

	% Muslim who fit each category	% of each category that are Muslim
France		
Born abroad	53.8	19.2
Non-citizen	31.2	27.9
Member of ethnic minority	31.9	25.4
Germany		
Born abroad	72.0	18.4
Non-citizen	67.7	34.9
Member of ethnic minority	57.1	28.6
Netherlands		
Born abroad	66.7	18.9
Non-citizen	19.4	17.9
Member of ethnic minority	85.6	34.5
United Kingdom		
Born abroad	64.6	17.0
Non-citizen	12.3	8.9
Member of ethnic minority	74.4	28.0

Data: ESS 2008, 2006, 2004, 2002.

Failure to distinguish Muslims as a group from the categories of 'immigrant', 'non-citizen' and 'ethnic minority' may obscure their similarities with other Europeans. Even the size of the Muslim population is not well understood in many states. Amiraux (2010a: 152) for example, discusses the '*querelle du chiffres*' (quarrel over the figures) regarding estimates of the number of Muslims in France: estimates are typically based on the size of ethnic groups with origins from largely Muslim countries, or on the number participating in the collective rituals of the religion, including prayer, fasting, consuming *halal* food (Amiraux, 2010a: 140). The criteria for identifying Muslims vary from study to study without firm agreement. Thus, estimates of the percentage of the French population that is Muslim do not rest on a firm foundation. The same is true for both Germany and the Netherlands. Faas (2010a: 60) describes the lack of statistical clarity in Germany as follows:

> The internal diversity of Germany's Muslims is still relatively unclear as is the exact number of Muslims living in the country. Since most federal statistics do not employ religion as a category, it is unclear precisely to what degree Muslims as a group are marginalized in housing and employment. Although the first representative study into 'Muslim Life in Germany' (Haug *et al.* 2009) throws some light on the socio-demographic and structural features of Germany's Muslim population, it does not yet move beyond a mainly descriptive account of religious orientations, the wearing of the headscarf and participation in educational opportunities at school. But it marks a clear departure from most previous research which focused only on Turkish Muslims. (Faas, 2010a: 60)

Estimates of the well-being of the Muslim population in the Netherlands are similarly fraught with inaccuracy. As Sunier (2010a: 122) describes:

> Official statistics on labour market position, educational performance and the socioeconomic status of the population indicate that there are two fundamental categories: *autochthonous*, denoting people of Dutch origin, and *allochthonous*, denoting people of non-Dutch origin (see also Geschiere, 2009). The latter category is divided into Western and non-Western *allochthonous*. Although this is an extremely vague statistical category without clear delineations, let alone any explanatory power, it serves as the basis of official policy reports. In the public eye, Muslims and non-western *allochtonous* are practically similar categories

(see CBS 2008). (Sunier, 2010a: 122) [Italics ours to denote language other than English.]

We make an effort to avoid the pitfalls of this failure to recognize the situation of European Muslims as distinct from that of immigrants, non-citizens and groups seen as 'ethnic minorities'. As we go along, we will point out several areas in which our investigation is more precise than is possible in analyses that conflate Muslims with groups that are seen to be foreign to Europe. We compare the situation and attitudes of Muslims in Europe to that of non-Muslims in their member state.

Religiosity

Much has been made of the possibility that Muslims are different from other migrants because of their religiosity. In fact, the visibility of Muslims in these states (and in Europe as a whole) may be explained not so much by the religious minority's proportion in the population (a percentage which is quite small regardless of the choice of estimating technique), but rather by the fact that between 39%–57% of the member state's population does not identify with any religion at all (as the ESS data in Table 2.2 suggests). ESS allows us to consider religious orientation not only in terms of respondents' self-identification as Muslim or not, but also in terms of three different measures of religiosity: self-assessment of religiosity, frequency of prayer outside of religious services, and attendance at religious services apart from special occasions. With regard to individuals' self-assessment of religiosity, Table 2.1 indicates that on the eleven-point scale utilized by ESS (from '0', least, to '10', most religious), Muslims on average rate their own degree of religiosity two or three points further along the scale than do non-Muslims in the same European state. The ESS results in Table 2.4 indicate that Muslims are also considerably more likely than their European neighbours to pray daily apart from religious services (46% more likely in the UK, 28% more likely in Germany, 36% more likely in France and 23% more likely in the Netherlands). Muslims are also more likely to attend religious services apart from special ceremonies once a week or more (38% more likely in the UK, 24% more likely in Germany, 9% more likely in France, and 15% more likely in the Netherlands). Throughout the analyses, we will examine the impact of religiosity on Muslims' commitment to democratic institutions in the European state in which they reside.

Appendix 1 (ESS Variables) provides a list of the variables used in our quantitative analyses benchmarking Muslim integration in these four states with the European Social Survey. ESS data allow us to examine differences between self-identified Muslims and non-Muslims in terms of the individual's estimate of their overall well-being; the nature and level of their education; their economic satisfaction, occupation, and pattern of employment and unemployment; respondent's estimation of their general health and of the health care system; respondent's facility with and attention to information concerning politics, news and current events, and respondent's use of the internet; cultural orientation in terms of dimensions related to lifestyle, acceptance of diversity, importance of democracy and of communitarianism, value of affluence, and importance of attention to nature and the environment; and several variables that come under the key area of basic public functions including equality, anti-discrimination and self-organization. These include: feelings of safety and security; trust in government, the legal system and the police; interest in politics and satisfaction with democracy. We also look at several individual characteristics of ESS respondents to better understand any differences that we find between Muslims and non-Muslims in these European states. Among these differences are their citizenship and country of birth, first language, age and gender, income and education. We begin to consider these aspects of Muslims' identity in contrast to their non-Muslim European neighbours in the next chapter, which focuses on Muslims' confidence in the justice system.

Table 2.4: Comparing religiosity between Muslims and non-Muslims

	France		Germany		Netherlands		United Kingdom	
	Muslims	Other	Muslims	Other	Muslims	Other	Muslims	Other
Pray apart from religious service (%)								
Every day	45.0	9.3	42.1	13.9	47.5	24.3	63.0	17.1
More than once a week	5.5	5.4	12.3	8.6	10.6	5.5	9.0	7.3
Once a week	2.7	4.5	8.4	6.3	3.9	3.6	7.1	5.2
At least once a month	3.2	7.5	7.3	5.8	2.2	4.4	6.6	5.8
Only on special holy days	6.4	2.8	7.3	4.4	5.6	1.8	3.8	1.9
Less often	13.2	14.9	12.3	23.0	15.6	12.3	4.7	16.7
Never	24.1 (220)	55.5 (6,782)	10.3 (261)	38.0 (10,943)	14.5 (179)	48.1 (7,696)	5.7 (211)	46.0 (7,155)
Attend religious services apart from special occasions (%)								
Every day	5.0	0.2	3.0	0.3	6.1	0.1	16.0	0.7
More than once a week	0.9	0.9	9.7	1.4	11.6	4.1	4.7	3.3
Once a week	9.5	5.2	21.0	7.3	9.9	8.6	29.2	8.1
At least once a month	6.8	6.4	15.7	10.7	8.8	8.5	6.6	6.0
Only on special holy days	33.6	18.9	20.2	20.4	13.8	12.9	10.4	12.8
Less often	21.8	16.2	13.5	22.1	19.3	14.7	15.1	18.6
Never	22.3 (220)	52.2 (6,811)	16.9 (267)	37.8 (11,085)	30.4 (181)	51.0 (7,717)	17.9 (212)	50.5 (7,189)

Data: ESS 2008, 2006, 2004, 2002.

European Muslims' confidence in the justice system

Agencies of criminal justice (particularly police and the courts) have a key but underappreciated role to play in creating a comfortable and productive environment for European Muslims. The effectiveness and fairness of police, courts, prosecutors and other elements of the legal and justice system are important in promoting a sense of safety, order and reliability within the community and, in the extreme, in preventing violent outbursts of frustration. Examination of the catalysts for riots involving racial and ethnic minorities – for example, in Toxteth in 1981 and Brixton in 1980 (both in England), and outside of Paris in 2005 – consistently underscores the fact that the violence began with a police-citizen encounter.

The April 1981 riot in Brixton was sparked by an arrest after a day of unrest fuelled by unsubstantiated rumours of police brutality. As explained by BBC News (2006):

> Many young black men believed officers discriminated against them, particularly by use of the Sus law under which anybody could be stopped and searched if officers merely suspected they might be planning to carry out a crime. In early April, Operation Swamp – an attempt to cut street crime in Brixton which used the Sus law to stop more than 1,000 people in six days – heightened tensions ... The mixture of high unemployment, deprivation, racial tensions and poor relations with police were not unique to Brixton. By the time Lord Scarman's report on the events in Brixton was published in November 1981, similar disturbances had taken place in a raft of other English cities, most notably Liverpool and Manchester.

Laurent Mucchielli (2009) paints a similar picture of the sources of urban riots in France. In his words (Mucchielli, 2009: 734–735):

> The scenario has been more or less the same since the first 'urban riots' in 1990 and 1991 ... The riots were triggered

by the death ... of local youths connected (in various ways) with police intervention. What happened this time, in the little town of Clichy-sous-Bois on Thursday 27 October 2005? It was late afternoon, the schools were on vacation, and three teenagers ... who lived in Clichy, all three of North African descent, climbed over the fence around a power transformer. Two of them were fatally electrocuted ... Why did they go into that particularly dangerous place? ... Youths from the neighbourhood were convinced that the boys had been forced to run to escape the police who were pursuing them for no good reason.

Mucchielli (2009: 740–741) indicates that in his investigation of the rioters' 'voice', discussion of the Clichy-sous-Bois tragedy largely focused on their conclusion that:

the police *was* involved and that the Minister of the Interior had tried to hide that fact ... Revenge against the police may ... be viewed as the main motivation of the rioters, especially when the police were not simply exposed to the violence of these youths, but ... they sometimes went there to provoke it (for example by deploying police forces massively around the neighbourhood and multiplying identity checks in areas where there had not yet been any rioting).

Mucchielli (2009: 748) notes that 'several local riots have already taken place in France since November 2005, always prompted by the same type of incident – death of a young person(s) in relation to police intervention.' While both Mucchielli's analysis, and the BBC report noted above clearly indicate that the sources of riots are to be found in the long-term marginality of the minority, including their economic and political exclusion, police behaviour is cited as triggering the expression of hostility. Minority youth perceived police as representative of 'the system' and, because of that, instances of apparent police unfairness are magnified in significance.

This understanding has broader implications for support for the wider political system. As Hurwitz and Peffley (2005: 764) explain, 'the justice system is as close as many come to the government; thus, low levels of confidence in the CJS can clearly undermine support for the broader system.' Citing Tyler and Folger (1980), Hurwitz and Peffley highlight the importance of the fairness of procedures, rather than the outcomes of police and other legal encounters as important in shaping citizens' perceptions of fairness in the criminal justice system. (They note that this is in contrast to the greater importance of outcomes over process in determining citizens' evaluations of the economic system.) Work by Lind and Tyler (1988) is put forward as demonstrating that 'people who believe the justice system to be unfair tend to evaluate the entire political system as less legitimate' (Hurwitz and Peffley, 2005: 764). Tyler's (1990) research is also cited indicating that 'citizens are more likely to comply with the law when they believe legal authorities to be fair' (Hurwitz and Peffley, 2005: 764).

Given their implications for the degree of legitimacy with which the state and its institutions are viewed, and for trust in 'the system', we focus in this chapter on Muslim Europeans' perceptions of police and justice system fairness. We also look at Muslims' degree of concern about criminal victimization and the level of crime in their neighbourhoods. We limit our focus here to the sense of safety and security expressed by Muslims and the extent of their trust in justice agencies. In the next chapter, we discuss trust in the political system.

British Crime Survey (BCS)

Analysis of the *British Crime Survey* provided in a Home Office Report (Jansson et al., 2007: 31) indicates that 'for the key crime types, religion was not independently associated with the *risk of victimization*' in England and Wales. For violent crimes, age and marital status were significant predictors of victimization risk, not religion. While Muslims appeared to have a higher risk of household crime victimization than Christians (22% vs. 18% respectively), it is likely that this difference is a reflection of the fact that Muslims are less likely to live in detached houses and more likely to be young than Christians (Jansson et al., 2007: 31). BCS examined religiously motivated crime, but less than one tenth of one percent (0.1%) of the population reported having been a victim of one, resulting in a number too small to provide useful estimates or further analysis (Jansson et al., 2007: 32).

Regarding *perceptions and experiences of the police and the criminal justice system*, the results suggest that Muslims' views are more optimistic than those of Christian respondents. Table 3.1 below summarizes some of the BCS findings. Fifty-eight percent of Muslims rated the police in their local area as doing a good or excellent job, in contrast to 51% of Christians; similarly, 58% of Muslims rated police in general as doing a good to excellent job in contrast to 52% of Christians. Muslims and Christians were about equally likely to have contacted the police during the last year (25% and 26% respectively). But Muslims were more likely to have experienced police-initiated contact in this time period (30% vs. 21% for Christians). The BCS Home Office report (Jansson et al., 2007: 33) suggests that this difference reflects the relative youth of the Muslim group. 'Being stopped while in a vehicle, being asked information about crimes, dealing with ringing alarms or having missing property returned' are listed as the most common reason for being contacted by the police (Table 3.7, Jansson et al., 2007, and page 33). Furthermore, in five areas of criminal justice system performance, Muslims (and Hindus) had higher levels of confidence than Christians (and Buddhists). These include: 'effectiveness in bringing people to justice, effectiveness in reducing crime, dealing with cases promptly and efficiently, meeting the needs of victims and effectiveness in dealing with young people being accused of crime' (Janssen et al., 2007: 34). Muslims were also more likely than Christians to rate as good or excellent specific agencies of the criminal justice system, including the Crown Prosecution Service (48% vs. 27%), judges (54% vs. 26%), magistrates (51% vs. 28%), prisons (31% vs. 22%), probation service (35% vs. 19%), and juvenile courts (37% vs. 13%). (See Table 3.11, and page 36, Jansson et al., 2007.) These BCS results cannot be seen as performance measures for police forces or other agencies of justice (cf. Feilzer, 2009). But they do reflect among Muslims a base of support for police and other criminal justice agency efforts in England and Wales.

Muslims are more worried about antisocial behaviour and crime than Christians. The BCS indicates that more than twice as many Muslims (33%) as Christians (16%) indicated that antisocial behaviour in their local area is a very or fairly big problem. BCS asked about seven specific areas of antisocial behaviour and, of all the religious groups measured, Muslims displayed the greatest concern about each area of antisocial behaviour. (We present only the differences between Muslims (the largest religious group after Christians) and Christians but, for every religious comparison, Muslims displayed the greatest degree of concern about antisocial behaviour of all religious groups.) Forty-eight percent of Muslims (in contrast to 27% of Christians) thought that *people using or dealing drugs* was a very or fairly big problem in their local area, and 48% of Muslims (vs. 32% of Christians) were similarly concerned about *teenagers hanging around on the streets.* Muslims (41%) were more likely than Christians (30%) to describe *rubbish or litter lying around* as a very or fairly big problem. Differences are also notable for those estimating the following as a big or fairly big problem: *people being drunk or rowdy in public places (3 7%* of Muslims vs. 24% of Christians); *vandalism, graffiti and other deliberate damage to property* (37% of Muslims vs. 28% of Christians); *noisy neighbours or loud parties* (17% of Muslims, 10% of Christians); and

Table 3.1: British Crime Survey 2006/7

Muslims' confidence in justice agencies and concerns about anti-social behavior and crime (% of total)		
Justice agency contact and ratings	**Muslims**	**Christians**
Respondent had a police initiated contact	30	21
Respondent contacted police	25	26
Effectiveness of criminal justice system	62	40
Local police doing good/excellent job	58	51
Police in general doing good/excellent job	58	52
Crown services doing good/excellent job	48	27
Judges doing good/excellent job	54	26
Magistrates doing good/excellent job	51	28
Prisons doing good/excellent job	31	22
Probation services doing good/excellent job	35	19
Juvenile courts doing good/excellent job	37	13
Concern about anti-social behavior		
% indicating the behavior is a very big or fairly big problem		
High level of perceived anti-social behavior	33	16
People using or dealing drugs	48	27
Teens hanging around on streets	48	32
Rubbish or litter lying around	41	30
People being drunk or rowdy in public places	37	24
Vandalism, graffiti, other deliberate damage to property	37	28
Noisy neighbors, loud parties	17	10
Abandoned or burnt-out cars	17	8
Concern about crime		
% with high level of worry about		
Violent crime	36	16
Burglary	28	12
Car crime	27	13

Note: For a related discussion and additional data see: Jansson, Budd, Lovbakke, Moley and Thorpe (2007) *Attitudes, perceptions and risks of crime: Supplementary volume 1 to Crime in England and Wales 2006/7* (2nd edn) Home Office (accessed 10 December, 2010).

abandoned or burnt-out cars (17% of Muslims, 8% of Christians). To some extent, but not completely, these findings were influenced by the fact that Muslims were more likely to be young and to live in areas in the ACORN (A Classification of Residential Neighbourhoods) category of 'Hard pressed' or 'Moderate means' (Janssen et al., 2007: 37). Concern about antisocial behaviour in their neighbourhood may provide an outlook leading Muslims to positive evaluations of the *effectiveness of the criminal justice system in bringing people who commit crimes to justice.*

Multivariate examination of the *effectiveness of the criminal justice system in bringing people who commit crimes to justice* demonstrated that its bivariate link with religion (where 62% of Muslims and 40% of Christians rated the CJS as effective) was due to respondents' age, perceptions of the level of antisocial behaviour in their neighbourhood, and perception of the appropriateness of sentence severity (Jansson et al., 2007: 34–35, and Table 3.9).

Muslims were much more likely to be worried about crime than Christians. For violent crime, 36% of Muslims in contrast to 16% of Christians had high levels of worry about crime. For burglary, 28% of Muslims vs. 12% of Christians had high levels of worry about crime; and for car crimes, 27% of Muslims in contrast to 13% of Christians had high levels of concern. BCS reports that in the multivariate equations for worry about crime, besides religion additional significant predictors were: perceptions of high levels of antisocial behaviour in the local area, being from a black or minority ethnic group (BME), belief that there has been an increase in the national crime rate, and having no educational qualifications (Janssen et al, 2007: 38).

The fact that Muslims are worried about antisocial behaviour and crime in their neighbourhoods – more worried than Christians – even in multivariate equations conducted by BCS including background demographic characteristics and neighbourhood status, allows us to suggest that Muslims are not as comfortable in their neighbourhoods as Christians in England and Wales. Yet despite their relative unease in their neighbourhoods, and the fact that they were 9% more likely to be contacted by the police than Christians, Muslims were 6–7% more likely than Christians to rate the police (on the general and local level respectively) as doing a good or excellent job. This greater positive evaluation (than Christians) of agencies and institutions of justice extends to prosecution services, judges, magistrates, prisons, probation services and even juvenile courts. On the basis of their confidence in the criminal justice system, it is hard to say that Muslims are not integrated into British society. Christians seem to have the greater degree of scepticism in the fairness of justice professionals and their institutions. These results are in stark contrast to popular assumptions that Muslims are not fully invested in British life and that they are distrustful of British institutions.

German General Social Survey (ALLBUS)

ALLBUS does not contain questions asking respondents about concerns regarding antisocial behaviour or crime. But it does ask respondents about their degree of trust in the police and in the judiciary (7=highest trust; 0=lowest trust). (See Figure 3:1 below.) And, like Muslims in England and Wales, Muslims in Germany evidence greater trust in both the police and judiciary than do non-Muslims.

Figure 3.1: Differences in mean levels of trust in Germany's judiciary and police (2008)

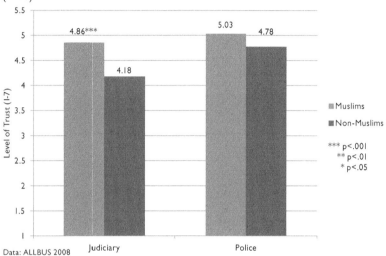

Data: ALLBUS 2008

In results not shown here, exposure to German society is positively and significantly related to Muslims' level of *trust in the police* even when several other background variables are controlled. In addition, also in results not shown here, even when several background variables are controlled, Muslims' level of religiosity is not related to their degree of political trust (in any of nine areas measured) or to their satisfaction with democracy. (For all of the results not shown here, see Doerschler and Jackson, 2010b, 2011). In addition, Figure 3.1 indicates that for trust in the judiciary, the difference between Muslims and non-Muslims is statistically significant, with Muslims having higher levels of trust in the bivariate relationship. As Table 3.2 (below) suggests, the results of our multivariate analysis (OLS) indicate that Muslims in Germany are like other Germans in terms of trust both in the police and the judiciary once we control for indicators of social capital, socioeconomic status, ideology and satisfaction with democracy. (These are standard indicators in sociopolitical research and are available in ALLBUS. We have controlled for them because it is likely that respondents' degree of trust in the judiciary is influenced by the stake in the system provided by their social capital and socioeconomic status, and by respondents' ideological perspective (as left or right) and degree of satisfaction with democracy.) Taken together, these results paint a picture of Muslims as no less supportive than others of the German state and its agencies of justice. The German results, like those for England and Wales, undermine the widespread assumption by non-Muslims that Muslims resent the agencies of European states.

Table 3.2: Effects of Muslim ID on trust in police, judiciary and legal system

	France		Germany		Netherlands		UK	
	Muslim	Full	Muslim	Full	Muslim	Full	Muslim	Full
Trust in Germany's police system[1]	–	–	.25 (3,326)	.21 (1,394)	–	–	–	–
Trust in Germany's judiciary[1]	–	–	.68*** (3,271)	.04 (1,381)	–	–		
Trust in police[2]	–.97*** (7,025)	–.74*** (4,467)	–.17 (11,360)	.06 (7,932)	–.09 (7,864)	.18 (6,231)	.46** (7,384)	.19 (5,378)
Trust in legal system[2]	.12 (7,019)	–.02 (4,463)	.17 (11,255)	.09 (7,910)	.15 (7,794)	.23 (6,214)	1.05*** (7,309)	.76*** (5,356)

***$p<.001$, **$p<.01$, *$p<.05$, figures represent unstandardized OLS coefficients.
Note: Number of respondents contained in parentheses.
[1] Data: 2008 ALLBUS. Full models control for R's level of social trust, religiosity, age, gender, income, citizenship, unemployment, education level, ideology, interest in politics, place of residence, amount of TV watching, and satisfaction with government.
[2] Data: 2008, 2006, 2004, 2002 ESS. Full models control for R's level of social trust, religiosity, age, gender, income, citizenship, unemployment, years of education, ideology, interest in politics, place of residence, amount of TV watching and satisfaction w/government.

European Social Survey (ESS)

Figure 3.2 allows us to compare Muslims and non-Muslims regarding trust in the legal system and police using data from the European Social Survey. Again, the data suggest that, for the most part, Muslims do not differ greatly from non-Muslims in their attitude toward the legal system, and that where they do differ significantly, Muslims have more trust than non-Muslims. There is more variation with regard to attitude toward the police, but, except for in France, Muslims do not differ significantly from non-Muslims in their level of trust in the police.

Figure 3.2: Cross-national comparison of Muslims' and non-Muslims' trust in the legal system and police

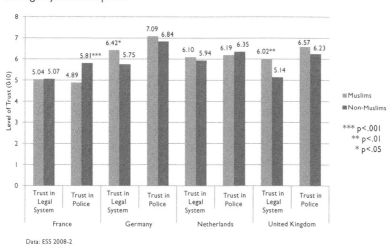

Data: ESS 2008-2

Further support for the British Crime Survey and German Social Survey findings above is provided by the multivariate results from the European Social Survey, shown in Table 3.2, in the previous section. In the United Kingdom, for example, Muslims have greater trust in the legal system than do non-Muslims, and these results are statistically significant even in the full model with controls. (The control variables selected are available in the European Social Survey and are background characteristics of individuals that are expected to influence their trust in both the police and the legal system.) In terms of trust in the police, the positive UK results are significant only at the bivariate level. For Germany, the ESS data in Table 3.2 suggest no statistically significant relationship between Muslim religious orientation and trust in either the legal system or the police. The fact that Muslims do *not* have significantly less trust in the legal system or the police than non-Muslims is surprising, in light of political rhetoric on the topic in Germany. The ESS results are positive (though insignificant) in the multivariate model, supporting the ALLBUS findings in their direction.

In both France and the Netherlands, as Figure 3.2 indicates, there is no statistically significant difference between Muslims and non-Muslims in terms of their reported trust in the legal system. The same is true for trust in the police in the Netherlands. But in France Muslims have significantly less trust in the police than do non-Muslims. These results for France are supported and explained by the EU-MIDIS findings regarding Muslims' perceptions of the police, discussed further on in Chapter Five. Since the early 1990s French police have been mandated to check the immigration status of minorities to facilitate the expulsion of those in France illegally. As we noted in Chapter One, the November 2008 website of then-French Prime Minister Hortefeux described an agenda of ferreting out networks of illegal immigrant workers and tackling abuse of political asylum (Jackson, 2010). Table 3.2 above indicates that this multi-decade policy approach has taken its toll on Muslims' confidence in the police, which remained significantly lower than that of non-Muslims, even in the face of controls for respondents' age, gender, income, citizenship, unemployment, education, ideology, interest in politics, amount of television watching and satisfaction with government.

Considerable additional support for this finding is available: a constitutional challenge to ethnic profiling by police in France is currently being reviewed by French courts. According the Open Society Institute:

> Under this new procedure introduced in 2010, the cases start in the ordinary courts, where legal proceedings have begun as a result of an ID stop. The judge concerned will be asked to refer the case for consideration of the constitutionality of the ID stop. Criminal cases will first be considered by the Cour de Cassation (Court of Cassation) and immigration cases will first be considered by the Conseil d'Etat (Council of State), which serve as filtering bodies for the referrals to the Conseil Constitutionnel ... The Justice Initiative is working in collaboration with a number of French nongovernmental organizations and lawyers to mount a legal challenge to ethnic profiling ... Ethnic profiling violates the rights of those stopped under both the French constitution and the European Convention of Human Rights ... Legal Certainty ... Personal Liberty ... Freedom of movement ... Discrimination ... [are all cited as aspects of personal freedom violated by ethnic profiling] (http://www.soros.org/initiatives/justice/litigation/qpc).

Furthermore, in its most recent report on France (ECRI, France, 2010) the European Commission on Racism and Intolerance also underscored the problem of racial profiling by French police, recommending that 'French authorities take measures to combat all forms of discriminatory conduct by law enforcement officials, including racial profiling ... by clearly defining and prohibiting racial profiling by law, carrying out research on racial profiling and monitoring police activities to identify

---

racial profiling practices ... ECRI recommends that French authorities guarantee the existence of a body ... independent of the police and prosecution authorities, to be entrusted with the investigation of alleged cases of racial discrimination and racially-motivated misconduct by the police (ECRI, France, 2010: 43).

This ECRI recommendation and the proposed constitutional challenge to ethnic profiling suggest a firm basis for French Muslims' negative attitude toward the police – a well-documented history of discriminatory treatment currently under investigation by European minority protection study agencies (ECRI), non-governmental organizations (OSI) and private and public attorneys, and the French courts. In light of this evidence, French Muslims do not appear to be pessimistic about the state, but rather realistic and accurate in their survey responses in assessing their negative treatment by the police.

The European Social Survey results, like those for the British Crime Survey, suggest some areas in which Muslims are more worried about crime than non-Muslims. Tables 3.3 and 3.4 provide ESS data for all four states. To simplify our discussion, we focus on differences (shown in Table 3.3) between Muslims and non-Muslims that are statistically significant in the full model with controls (shown in Table 3.4). In the Netherlands, for example, Muslims are significantly less likely to indicate that they 'feel safe or very safe walking alone in the local area after dark'. Table 3.3 indicates that Muslims are about 13% less likely than others to feel safe or very safe (69.6% of Muslims vs. 82.3% of others); and Table 3.4 indicates that the difference remains when we control for age, gender, citizenship, unemployment education and ideology. Muslims in the Netherlands are also significantly more likely in the multivariate model (Table 3.4) to indicate that 'worry about having their home burgled has an effect on their quality of life': Table 3.3 shows that Muslims are about 22% more likely to say that this concern has some or a serious effect on the quality of their life (46.4% of Muslims in contrast to 24.5% of others expressed this concern). The multivariate model in Table 3.4 suggesting that 'worry that being a victim of violent crime has an effect on the quality of life' also significantly distinguishes Muslims and others in the Netherlands. In Table 3.3 we see that Muslims are about 23% more likely than others to indicate this concern has some or a serious effect on the quality of their life (53% of Muslims vs. 29.5% of non-Muslims responded that concern about being the victim of violent crime has some or a serious effect on the quality of their life).

Table 3.3: Cross-national comparison of Muslims and Non-Muslims worried about crime

	France		Germany		Netherlands		UK	
	Muslims	Other	Muslims	Other	Muslims	Other	Muslims	Other
Feeling of safety walking alone in local area after dark...[1]								
very safe	47.0	35.0	14.0	23.3	11.6	17.0	26.1	19.8
safe	30.1	39.3	59.2	53.6	58.0	65.3	39.8	47.2
unsafe	12.3	16.7	22.3	18.5	28.2	15.2	26.5	24.1
very unsafe	10.5	9.0	4.5	4.6	2.2	2.5	7.6	9.0
	N=219	N=6,750	N=265	N=11,088	N=181	N=7,691	N=211	N=7,159
How often worry about your home being burgled...[2]								
all or most of the time	6.9	7.8	1.7	2.5	8.0	3.8	20.4	7.8
some of the time	34.5	36.1	27.7	18.4	19.0	23.1	22.1	25.8
just occasionally	26.9	28.1	24.4	33.0	29.0	28.5	26.5	36.6
never	31.7	28.0	46.2	46.1	44.0	44.5	31.0	29.7
	N=145	N=3,908	N=119	N=5,490	N=100	N=3,559	N=113	N=3,679
Worry that home burgled has effect on quality of life...[2]								
serious effect on quality of life	8.2	8.9	1.6	4.1	7.1	4.3	10.5	2.1
some effect	33.7	28.6	40.6	25.8	39.3	20.2	55.3	24.4
no real effect	58.2	62.5	57.8	70.1	53.6	75.5	34.2	73.6
	N=98	N=2,811	N=64	N=2,947	N=56	N=1,965	N=76	N=2,583
How often worry about becoming victim of violent crime...[2]								
all or most of the time	2.1	4.0	1.7	1.4	3.0	1.1	8.0	3.8
some of the time	22.1	27.2	22.5	13.2	17.2	13.7	28.3	18.0
just occasionally	32.4	33.6	29.2	33.5	29.3	28.1	32.7	37.3
never	43.4	35.2	46.7	51.9	50.5	57.2	31.0	40.9
	N=145	N=3,904	N=120	N=5,488	N=99	N=3,555	N=113	N=3,679
Worry that being victim of violent crime has effect on quality of life...[2]								
serious effect on quality of life	9.8	7.7	6.2	4.5	12.2	5.8	16.7	3.2
some effect	34.1	34.0	50.0	30.1	40.8	23.7	43.6	29.4
no real effect	56.1	58.2	43.8	65.4	46.9	70.5	39.7	67.5
	N=82	N=2,529	N=64	N=2,627	N=49	N=1,512	N=78	N=2,170

[1] ES 2008, 2006, 2004, 2002

Table 3.4: Effects of Muslim ID on feelings of crime and victimization

	France		Germany		Netherlands		UK	
	Muslim	Full	Muslim	Full	Muslim	Full	Muslim	Full
Feeling of safety walking alone in local area after dark[1]	.13* (6,970)	.10 (4,473)	−.13** (11,353)	−.07 (8,093)	−.18*** (7,870)	−.15** (6,315)	.07 (7,369)	.12 (5,400)
How often worried about home being burgled[2]	−.08 (4,052)	−.05 (3,328)	.09 (5,608)	.13 (4,017)	.06 (3,659)	.08 (2,983)	.19* (3,791)	.02 (2,745)
Worried about home burglary having effect on quality of life[2]	.04 (4,052)	.06 (2,401)	.11 (3,010)	.05 (2,203)	.25** (2,021)	.22* (1,698)	.48*** (2,659)	.45*** (1,945)
How often worried about being victim of violent crime[2]	−.16* (4,049)	.17 (3,327)	.15* (5,607)	.07 (4,014)	.15 (3,653)	.08 (2,979)	.30*** (3,790)	.07 (2,745)
Worried that being victim of violent crime has effect on quality of life[2]	.05 (2,611)	−.04 (2,148)	.22** (2,690)	.08 (1,968)	.31*** (1,560)	.27* (1,262)	.41*** (2,248)	.39*** (1,661)

***p<.001, **p<.01, *p<.05, figures represent unstandardized OLS coefficients.
Note: Number of respondents contained in parentheses.
[1] Data: ESS 2008-2002. Full models control for R's age, gender, income, citizenship, unemployment, education and ideology.
[2] Data: ESS 2008, 2006. Full models control for R's age, gender, income, citizenship, unemployment, education and ideology.

Table 3.3 indicates that Muslims in the UK are 39% more likely to indicate that 'worry about their home being burgled has an effect on the quality of their life' (65.8% of Muslims in contrast to 26.5% of others). This difference is statistically significant for the UK in the full model (Table 3.4), as it was in the Netherlands. Muslims in the UK, as in the Netherlands, are significantly more likely to indicate that 'worry that being the victim of violent crime has an effect on the quality of their life', demonstrated in the full multivariate model in Table 3.4. Specifically, Table 3.3 shows that Muslims are about 28% more likely to express this concern (60.3 % of Muslims indicate that this worry has some or a serious effect on the quality of life, in contrast to 32.6% of others).

The evidence in Tables 3.3 and 3.4 clearly suggests that regardless of their income, education, gender, employment, age and ideology, Muslims in the Netherlands and the UK worry more that the possibility of crime has some or a serious effect on the quality of their life; the results also suggest that in the Netherlands, Muslims are less likely to feel safe walking alone in their local area after dark. We do not have evidence as to why Muslims in the Netherlands and the UK are more concerned about crime than others, while we do not see this pattern in France or Germany. In the latter two states Table 3.4 indicates no statistically significant differences between Muslims and others on concerns about crime once controls have been imposed in the full model. We suggest, though, that greater social, and likely physical, separation between Muslims and non-Muslims in France and Germany than in the UK and Netherlands might be reflected in these data. The multicultural models characteristic of the UK and the Netherlands, despite recent controversy about their viability, provide more opportunities for social and geographic interaction between Muslims and non-Muslims and might, thereby, increase the concern of Muslims that they will be victimized, whether or not they actually experience crime victimization. The fact that Muslims can identify themselves in most public places with headscarves and other attire in the UK and the Netherlands might increase their sense of vulnerability at the possibility of encountering biased individuals in light of frequent new reports of hate crimes (for example, 'Paki-bashing') or less violent encounters (for example, passers-by responding to a women's headscarf by asking if she is a terrorist).

Implications of the results

In Chapter Two, we discussed the differences among Britain, Germany, France and the Netherlands in the nature of their minority integration models and in the degree of state primacy in stipulating integration criteria. It is not clear, though, that these structural aspects of state involvement in integration policy determine the degree of Muslim well-being in terms of their confidence in criminal justice agencies. In the multicultural, relatively limited state system within which England and Wales are contained, where minorities face comparatively few rigid demands for cultural conformity to 'Britishness', the findings above suggest that Muslims have significantly greater trust in state agencies of justice than others. But in the relatively closed state of Germany, characterized by its integration contract and active state involvement in stipulating specific cultural integration requirements, data from the German Social Survey (ALLBUS, 2008) indicated that Muslims' degree of trust in the German judiciary was not significantly different from that of non-Muslims in the full model with controls for individual background characteristics. Data from the European Social Survey provide similar findings for the difference between Muslims and non-

Muslims in Germany with regard to trust in the legal system, in that the difference is not statistically significant.

Muslims in France and the Netherlands displayed as much trust in the legal system as non-Muslims, despite prominent differences in these states regarding the demands for minorities' display of acceptance of the dominant state culture. In the Netherlands, minority policy has ostensibly moved from a foundation on group-based rights to one based on individual responsibilities, but with weak (limited) government legitimacy for requiring that minorities leave the cultural traits of their heritage behind. Yet the difference between Dutch non-Muslims and Muslims in terms of trust in the legal system mirrors the insignificant difference between the two groups in France, where an assertive state policy based on *laicite* is now used to legitimize penalties, including exclusion, for the display of religious identity in public institutions.

These findings are remarkable, both because of their failure to support popular assumptions about Muslims' lack of faith in the system, and because they reflect the views of Muslims in a decade of obvious justice system and cultural securitization, as described by Huysmans (2006) and others, during which those who display Muslim cultural traits have been viewed with suspicion. Like the recent analysis of ALLBUS data for Germany which focused on several areas of trust in government, democracy and individual institutions (where religiosity and exposure to German society were also controlled) (described above and detailed in Doerschler and Jackson, 2010b), the present study suggests that Muslims have at least as much, if not more confidence in the state than do members of the dominant religious group. France provides one glaring exception in the negative relationship between Muslim religious identity and trust in the police, and this view has the support of ECRI and the Open Society Institute.

Overall, the results indicate that Muslims are more integrated into their European homes than popularly recognized. In three of the four states, rather than distrusting the police and the legal system, Muslims are at least, if not more, willing than other Europeans to work with agencies of justice and rely on them for protection. In France, where state policy has mandated aggressive policing of those whose demographic characteristics are linked with undocumented immigrants, Muslims are significantly less likely to trust the police than are non-Muslims. But even while their distrust of the police appears to be based on facts documented by outside agencies, this distrust does not extend to the rest of the justice system: ESS data indicate that there is no significant difference between French Muslims and non-Muslims in trust in the legal system.

The British Crime Survey demonstrates the unease that Muslims in England and Wales feel at the crime and antisocial behaviour in their neighbourhoods, even after other background characteristics of their situation and neighbourhood type are held constant in multivariate equations. The BCS findings reflect the need for greater effort by police and other justice agencies to help in creating an environment in which Muslims feel comfortable in their European neighbourhoods. Data from EU-MIDIS presented later, in Chapter Five, will also support a picture of Muslims facing frequent discrimination in nine important societal areas (including employment, housing and health care), and targeted by profiling more often than are non-Muslims.

Data from the European Social Survey for the Netherlands and Britain and from the British Crime Survey similarly reflect Muslims' concern about crime, and indicate that they coexist with confidence in the justice system that sometimes surpasses that of non-Muslims. The well-being of European Muslims would be improved considerably by attention to their concerns about crime; and Muslims' positive attitudes toward the police, which are fairly widespread, and toward other justice agencies would provide a foundation for their involvement in the development of the networks of public, private and parochial relationships that foster neighbourhood collective efficacy and reduce crime.

It should not be ignored that these results provide clear evidence of the urgency of gathering official data examining the social and economic situation of Muslims in comparison to other Europeans in those European states in which these data are not currently collected. If they do not neglect Muslims, the benchmarking processes currently being initiated, focused on reducing disparities and polarizations between minorities and natives, are likely to have a significant positive effect in helping Muslims create a comfortable home in Europe from which they can contribute productively to the European project through full utilization of their talents in member states. Official data providing for comparisons between Muslims and others have the potential to dispel myths that currently limit the recognition of Muslims' integration in Europe and undermine the capacity of state agencies to work effectively with them.

The importance of these results cannot be underestimated: they challenge the core of the belief that 'Muslims don't integrate into European societies'. Those who put forward such beliefs are most convinced that Muslims do not accept agencies representative of the authority of European states. There is much less concern about the disparity between Muslims and others in regard to areas of well-being other than trust in the system. It is likely that unfounded and erroneous assumptions about their lack of confidence in the fairness of their European states constitute key roadblocks to Muslims' full engagement in Europe. It is also likely that the pervasiveness of bias and discrimination is sufficient to permeate the structures put in place to open institutions to religious minorities in multicultural states: Muslims' greater likelihood in the multicultural British and Dutch states of asserting that worry about crime affects the quality of their lives, even after we controlled for their personal circumstances, suggests that the quality of their interactions with non-Muslims needs further consideration (cf. Brüß, 2008). We will take up this examination in Chapter Five, focused on discrimination.

Trust in the justice system by Muslims deemed 'vulnerable' to dissatisfaction

The European Social Survey allows us to look within the Muslim population for differences in satisfaction with police and the legal system on the part of the 15–29-year-old population, the highly religious, males, foreign nationals and those born abroad. Table 3.5 below demonstrates that young Muslims, under 30, have lower average trust in the police in France, Germany and the Netherlands, and these differences are statistically significant in France and Germany (but not large, in that on average they are less than one rung on the eleven point trust scale which runs from 0–10). In the UK, young Muslims have significantly *more* trust in the police than those who are over 30. The British system of requiring each police force to 'answer to a Police Authority, an appointed body comprising councillors and others, which sets local priorities and a local policing levy' (*Economist*, 2011) might be partly responsible for creating an environment in which young Muslims report more trust in the police than others.

The level of religiosity that Muslims hold does not appear to influence their trust in the police in any significant way. While male Muslims in Germany have significantly less trust in the police than females do, the difference between the two groups on average is not much more than one point on the eleven point trust scale. Nonetheless, the reasons for male Muslims' lower level of trust in the police in Germany would be worth consideration by police departments in high Muslim areas, even if only because in the other three states there is no difference between males' and females' trust in the police.

Table 3.5: Average trust in the police among vulnerable groups of Muslims

	France	Germany	Netherlands	UK
Age groups				
15-29	4.35	6.18	5.70	7.03*
others	5.15*	6.82**	6.13	6.24
50 and older	5.52	6.87	5.80	5.55[1]
others	4.68	6.52	6.65	6.04
Religiosity				
high (7-10)	5.07	6.70	5.89	6.66
others	4.57	6.23	6.17	6.49
low (0-3)	4.58	5.89	5.86[2]	5.75[1]
others	4.85	6.65	5.95	6.64
Gender				
male	4.66	5.98	5.94	6.49
female	5.02	7.17**	6.01	6.72
Citizenship				
national	4.44	5.56	5.86	6.43
foreign	5.72**	6.48	6.46	7.81**
Place of birth				
national	4.14	6.04	5.60	6.44
foreign	5.44***	6.69	6.16	6.68

Data: ESS 2008-2002
***p<.001, **p<.01, *p<.05
[1]10<N<30; [2]N<10

Muslims with foreign citizenship in France and the UK appear to have even greater trust in the police than do those Muslims who hold the citizenship of the European state. These significant differences support a point made in the next chapter: The difficult circumstances from which Muslims have come to Europe may contribute to their greater satisfaction with policing as they see it practised there. This may be particularly true for those who have come to France (likely from Algeria, Morocco and Tunisia) and to the UK (often from Pakistan and Bangladesh).

Table 3.6 below allows us to examine variations in trust in the legal system comparing specific demographic groups of Muslims to each other. Young Muslims have slightly less trust in the legal system than other Muslims in France and this difference is statistically significant (but not large). This finding (and the lower level of trust in the police expressed by young Muslims in France) is not surprising in light of our discussion above, regarding the tough stance toward minority youth promoted by justice officials in France.

Table 3.6: Average trust in the legal system among vulnerable groups of Muslims

	France	Germany	Netherlands	UK
Age groups				
15-29	4.54	5.85	5.96	6.01
others	5.31*	5.89	5.66	6.27
50 and older	6.08**	5.90	5.80[1]	6.34[1]
others	4.77	5.87	5.76	6.12
Religiosity				
high (7-10)	5.02	5.93	5.89	6.11
others	4.94	5.75	5.56	6.14
low (0-3)	5.17	5.41	3.91[2]	5.86[1]
others	4.95	5.93	5.84*	6.15
Gender				
male	4.90	5.56	5.94	6.22
female	5.13	6.16	5.55	6.04
Citizenship				
national	4.61	5.92	5.74	5.89
foreign	5.92**	5.78	5.87	7.95***
Place of birth				
national	4.15	5.79	5.74	5.36
foreign	5.76***	5.89	5.78	6.58**

Data: ESS 2008-2002
***p<.001, **p<.01, *p<.05
[1] 10<N<30; [2] N<10

Highly religious Muslims are as trusting of the legal system as the less religious. In fact, the data for the Netherlands tentatively (given the low *n*) suggest a significantly lower level of trust in the legal system among Muslims with the lowest levels of religiosity. We consider the decline in trust in the political systems of Europe in the next chapter, and explore its relationship to the decline of religiosity.

There are no significant differences between the genders in terms of trust in the legal system among Muslims. Citizenship and place of birth, however, do make a difference, but not in the direction assumed in public discussions relating to minority integration. It appears, for example, that Muslims with foreign citizenship in France trust the legal system more than do those with French citizenship. In addition, trust among Muslim French citizens is low (4.6 on average on the 0–10 scale) in contrast to that of Muslims who are citizens in Germany, the Netherlands and the UK (where the figures are 5.9, 5.7 and 5.9 respectively). The low level of trust in the legal system on the part of those Muslims who have French citizenship calls into question the extent to which French courts are seen as upholding the basic rights of Muslim citizens. Muslims with foreign citizenship, on the other hand, have a greater appreciation of the French legal system rating it about as well (5.9) as the Muslims who are citizens in the other three states rate the justice system of their European state. The level of trust in the British legal system on the part of Muslims with foreign citizenship stands out as higher than for the other countries in our analysis. Muslims of foreign citizenship in the UK may feel more safeguarded in UK law and the court system than in other places.

The place of birth of Muslim respondents matters for their trust in the legal system in France and the UK. Muslims born abroad trust the legal system significantly *more* than those born in France or the UK. It is likely, as we noted above, that the courts and laws of European states appear to provide for greater safety than some groups of Muslim immigrants experienced in their country of origin. But the results also suggest that some attention should be devoted to consideration of the low level of trust in the legal system expressed by those Muslims born in France, especially in contrast to higher levels expressed by Muslims in other states and even by those Muslims born outside of France but living there now.

Exploring the question of why Muslims residing in the UK, but born abroad or with foreign citizenship, trust the legal system more than those born in the UK could also provide valuable information. Do foreign-born Muslims feel advantaged in the UK relative to their country of origin? Are there areas in which the UK legal system could better serve Muslims born in the UK or holding UK citizenship? We turn now in Chapter Four to consideration of Muslims' trust and involvement in the political system.

FOUR

Muslims in European politics: support for democracy and trust in the political system

A core facet of individual well-being concerns one's relationship to politics. Political attitudes such as support for democracy and trust in governmental institutions form the basis of legitimacy for democratic government while various forms of political participation illustrate citizens' capacity to affect policy outcomes. Critics of the presence of Muslims in Europe posit (often without providing evidence) that they threaten the stability of democratic systems (cf. Sarrazin, 2010: 267). Those with vested interests in Europe may also fear that despite the small size of the religious minority, Muslims may dramatically affect European politics in the future. Recent figures estimate the number of Muslim voters in France, for example, the country with the largest Muslim population, at approximately 1.5 million or only 3.75% of all French voters (Ajala, 2010: 84 and see Vaïsse, 2007). However, an aging native European population combined with relatively high birth rates among Muslim populations in the member states indicates the potential for these percentages to dramatically increase and with them Muslims' influence on European political systems.

Critics fear Muslims' relationship to politics, and question both their attitudes toward democracy and the form that their participation in government will take. In an effort to ascertain Muslims' relationship to politics in France, Germany, the Netherlands and the United Kingdom in this chapter, we examine existing scholarly literature and present data from several sources, including the European Social Survey, the Home Office Citizenship Survey, the German General Social Survey, and Statistics Netherlands. Our focus here is on Muslims' political well-being in Europe, a concept with several dimensions, including: their support for democracy, their trust in the political systems of Europe and its member states, and the backlash against them by others intent on using politics to prevent accommodation to Muslims' demands for recognition of their religious identity in Europe. Though some recent literature on these topics has looked specifically at European Muslims, much of the older literature has focused more generally on immigrant populations and ethnic minorities. While we caution against conflating these categories, we also discuss this literature.

Muslims' political participation and representation

Examination of core indicators of political integration such as voter turnout and representation in elected office reveals that though some progress has been made, most ethnic minorities, including Muslims, are less well incorporated politically than native citizens (Messina, 2006, 2007). As Pfaff and Gill (2006: 805) note, 'for the most part, Muslims have yet to become an organized force in European politics'. Interestingly, these deficiencies are at odds with the number of salient social and political issues affecting the Muslim community that would serve as the impetus for greater participation including large-scale collective action. Unfortunately a number of formidable obstacles stand in the way of greater political mobilization.

One factor inhibiting Muslims' greater political incorporation are state structures including administrative practices, social and political rights, integration policies and citizenship laws (Ireland, 1994; Warner and Wenner, 2006). In states with a more restrictive or closed institutional structure, members of ethnic, racial or religious minorities will typically base their political actions on their position as foreigners; in states with greater assimilationist policies, members will typically mobilize around issues of race, ethnicity or culture (Ireland, 1994). In France, an opening of the country's political opportunity structure precipitated by Mitterand's election to the presidency in 1981 significantly expanded immigrants' political rights and increased the power of ethnic organizations. In response to continued discrimination, immigrants were then better able to effectively channel their concerns through more responsive organizations and various forms of electoral and non-electoral participation (Ireland, 1994). On the basis of two case studies in Denmark, Togeby (1999) hypothesizes that immigrant voter turnout in local elections is higher in Denmark than in other European countries because of an open-list electoral system allowing preferential voting that increases incentives to participate.

Because they define political membership, citizenship laws together with criteria for naturalization are particularly important in determining the types and degree of political participation and representation available to Muslims (Brubaker, 1992). Until more liberal reforms were instituted in 2000, Germany's restrictive citizenship laws based squarely on principles of *jus sanguinus* denied citizenship to the children of immigrants born in Germany. While all children born in Germany now receive citizenship provided at least one parent has been a legal resident for no fewer than eight years, past practices have kept the number of citizens within the immigrant community relatively small, thereby reducing their collective power as a voting bloc. For example, Hunger (2001: 2) notes that the German party system has not responded much to immigrants because many immigrants do not have citizenship. In contrast, the UK and France instituted more liberal citizenship laws that use Commonwealth membership and *jus soli* as forms of inclusion. As a result of these laws, a significantly higher percentage of Muslims in the UK and France are citizens than in Germany. With greater ability to affect the political process through the vote, Muslims and other ethnic minorities in these states have a greater incentive to express concerns about and mobilize around ethnic issues. Several states, including the Netherlands, have compensated for low levels of participation and representation among their ethnic minorities by granting local voting rights to non-citizens.

As recent immigrants to Germany, many European Muslims, especially from the first generation, have enduring ties to the country of origin. One way in which these ties are manifested is in attachments to homeland politics. The strength of these attachments is dependent in part on differences in national citizenship policies (see Koopmans and Statham, 1999, 2000). More restrictive citizenship regimes effectively push individuals toward the homeland while liberal, more inclusive policies create incentives for greater investment of political capital in the country of residence. Homeland orientations may also persist where Muslims view themselves as persecuted minorities or where emotional attachments remain to friends and family. In many cases, the homeland has been known to encourage and nurture these ties since expatriates represent a potentially significant source of political and financial support. Such relationships seem particularly strong between Turkey and Algeria and their émigré populations in Europe (Castles and Miller, 2009: 279; Ögelman, 2003). There is ample evidence that Muslims, too, are drawn to homeland politics and sometimes even prefer to operate politically within a transitional diaspora network (Argun, 2003; Soysal, 1997; Warner and Wenner, 2006: 470). For example, conflict in Algeria between the military government and religious groups has spilled over into France (Warner and Wenner, 2006: 470).

Deep social divisions among European Muslims along ethnic, national and religious lines have produced a fragmented institutional structure that inhibits their ability to collectively mobilize behind a central, unifying organization, party or candidate (Ajala, 2010: 82; Pfaff and Gill, 2006: 807–810; Warner and Wenner, 2006: 457). Among these social cleavages, religious identity appears to take a back seat since 'only a minority of Europe's Muslims are intensely devout, and thus most are uninterested in organizing around a broad Islamic political identity' (Warner and Wenner, 2006: 459). In fact, '[i]n no Western European country has a dominant Islamic organization emerged that speaks with authority for the Muslim community, nor is there any successful pan-European Islamic organization' (Warner and Wenner, 2006: 458). In many cases, Muslims have even competed against each other on central issues such as the ban on headscarves in France or the teaching of Islam in public schools (Pfaff and Gill, 2006: 819). While past research has shown that non-citizens participate in a wide range of extra-electoral political activities (for example Ireland, 1994; Koopmans and Statham, 2000; Miller, 1981), much of this activity appears to be organized along class or nationality lines in response to socio-economic issues, events in a homeland or issues affecting the wider immigrant community such as the French riots in 2005 and union activities that occur periodically throughout Europe (see Castles and Miller, 2009: 281; Klausen, 2008). In response to specific economic grievances, Muslims may also be channelled into unions or workers' groups that have little to do with religious identity. The decentralized nature of European Muslim communities also undermines any potential threat emerging from more radicalized elements (Togeby, 1999; Warner and Wenner, 2006: 457). As Warner and Wenner (2006: 458) explain, '[d]espite fears of a "clash of civilizations" on European soil, religion has failed to be the unifying focal point of Muslims in Western Europe'.

Evidence that the vast majority of Muslims living in western societies utilize opportunities to seek the best from public institutions and are at least somewhat satisfied can be found on many fronts. Giry (2006: 96), for example, states that 'Muslim voters behave like other French people with similar socioeconomic backgrounds, displaying little evidence that their religious preferences have much impact on their political positions'. Lorcerie (2010: 67), similarly, explains, as we noted in Chapter Two, that Muslim immigrant families and girls in France set aside the headscarf, as required by French authorities, to attend school rather than passing up the opportunities for advancement provided by educational attainment.

Community fragmentation and persistent homeland orientations have also adversely affected the formation and electoral fortunes of Islamic parties (Ajala, 2010; Hussain, 2004: 391–392; Klausen, 2008). Islamic parties have failed to gain an electoral foothold in any of the four countries despite Muslims representing a growing and, especially at the local level, potentially powerful voting bloc. Operating from

1989 to 2006, the now defunct Islamic Party of Britain participated in elections but failed to secure more than a handful of votes (www. islamicparty.com/).

Despite the high degree of fragmentation within Muslim communities, Muslims and other ethnic minorities in all four countries have been ardent supporters of parties and individual candidates on the left (Ajala, 2010: 84; Hunger, 2001; Hussain, 2004: 390–391; Messina, 2006: 476; Saggar, 2000; Tillie, 1998; Wüst, 2002) though new evidence concludes that Muslims have gradually diversified their partisan support to parties in the centre and right of the political spectrum (see Ajala, 2010). That left parties, including Labour in the UK, the Social Democrats and to a lesser extent Greens and Left Party in Germany as well as the Socialists in France and Netherlands, are the preferred party of choice among a majority of Muslims is somewhat curious given that these parties have maintained a strong secular tradition. Nevertheless, there are at least two important reasons why Muslims have championed parties on the left. First, leftist parties have worked to embrace policies that matter to immigrants and ethnic minorities such as more inclusive integration policies, local voting rights, less restrictive naturalization laws, racial equality, public education, anti-discrimination policies (Messina, 2006: 478–480; Saggar, 2001: 78; Wüst, 2004). As Messina (2006: 478) states, 'the Labour Party is predominantly the political party of Britain's ethnic minorities because it historically has been and is the party ideologically, politically, and most publically for ethnic minorities'. Secondly, some have identified a clear overlap between religious and class identity as many Muslims are members of the working class, the core constituency of leftist parties (Ajala, 2010: 86; Hussain, 2004: 390–391; and for a contrasting view see Messina, 2006: 477, 2007; Tillie, 1998: 91).

Voluntary associations represent another channel through which Muslims mobilise. More active participation in the civic community is correlated with stronger participation and greater trust in democratic institutions (Fennema and Tillie, 1999, 2004; Theiss-Morse and Hibbing, 2005). Consultative organizations work on behalf of groups that are politically powerless (lack citizenship) or may be poorly organized and often lack local voting rights. However, these organizations are themselves often powerless, possessing only an advisory function without real decision-making power (Andersen, 1990; Budzinski, 1999: 168–170) and few immigrants are aware of their existence (Ögelman, 2003: 173).

Ethnic minorities are underrepresented in public office in Britain, France and Germany, but not in the Netherlands as a percentage of the population (Hussain, 2004: 389; Messina, 2006: 485; 2007; Togeby,

1999). Increases in representation have occurred at both the local level in Britain, France and the Netherlands and at the federal level in Britain, Germany and Netherlands but not France (Messina, 2006: 482–483). Not surprisingly the majority of these elected officials represent parties on the left (Messina, 2006: 484 and see van Heelsum, 2000). Regarding Muslims' political engagement in European states, Klausen (2008: 28–29) summarized the key elements of their strengths and limitations in this area in the following passage:

> About two dozen Muslims are currently sitting in the national parliaments with Holland, Germany, Denmark and Sweden having the largest representation. There are no elected Muslim members of the French National Assembly, but there are two senators. In the past few years a number of ministers who are Muslims have been appointed. All but one are women. France, Sweden, the Netherlands, and Britain have ministers of justice and integration who are Muslim. Few parliamentarians, if any, were elected based upon blocs of Muslim voters. In some cases, the election of Muslims has been facilitated by the concentration of immigrant voters in an electoral district but in most cases ethnicity has played no role in their election or appointment. (Klausen, 2008: 28–29)

The mounting evidence that Muslims do not vote in a bloc, but rather, like other Europeans, on the basis of their own individual concerns should not be surprising. Based on a survey of approximately 378 newly naturalized German citizens living in Heidelberg, Wüst (2002) found that Muslim identity was positively correlated with a general integration index. Their voting record, based as it appears to be on their situation as individual citizens, provides one more piece of evidence of their integration.

Muslims' trust in the political system and satisfaction with democracy

The question of Muslims' trust in public institutions is an important one, because citizens' willingness to voluntarily obey the organizational rules and laws that form the basis of government authority rests on their trust in its institutions (Doerschler and Jackson, 2010b; Keele, 2007; Tyler, 1998). Many western European states have witnessed declining levels of political trust in recent decades (Catterberg and

Moreno, 2005; Dalton, 2004; Kaina, 2008). While commitment to core principles of democracy and democratic regimes has generally remained strong, evaluations of government institutions and officials have evidenced weakened trust (Kingemann and Fuchs, 1995; Putnam, Pharr and Dalton, 2000). The stagnation of divided governments and economic uncertainty in a global economy have contributed to the loss of trust in government among the citizenries of western Europe, as well as to falling electoral turnout, and increases in protest voting and other political demonstrations of dissatisfaction (see Doerschler and Jackson, 2010b, 2011 for a complete discussion).

Considerable public and academic discussion has centred on the possibility of Muslims' lack of trust in the official agencies of Europe and its member states (cf. Baran, 2010; Goldberg, 2002; Huntington, 1996). Those who share this perspective construe the acts of terrorists and violent extremists as evidence of incompatibility between core tenets of Islam and democracy. This position has been rejected by many researchers and policy experts on the basis of data from recent surveys and interviews showing a large majority of Muslims to be very supportive of democracy (cf. Esposito and Mogahed, 2008; Inglehart and Norris, 2003; Shore, 2006). On the basis of their analysis of data from the World Values Survey, Inglehart and Norris (2003: 65) point to value differences regarding sexual liberalization and gender equality as constituting 'the real fault line' between Muslims and non-Muslims, rather than support for democracy. Terrorists who call themselves 'jihadists' often invoke Islam as a basis for their violence to infuse a sacred dimension into their ideology of violent opposition to what they see as the extension of western powers' strategic interests throughout the Islamic world at the expense of ordinary citizens (Goody, 2004: 3; Munson, 2004). But data from a recent Gallup survey of 'over 90% of the global Muslim population ... found that there was no correlation between level of religiosity and sympathy for terrorism' (Mogahed and Nyiri, 2007: 4). Furthermore, researchers in the Netherlands found that for Muslims there, frequency of visiting a mosque 'is positively related to most of the trust levels: church, army, police, parliament and civil servants in particular' (Schmeets and te Riele, 2010: 14).

There is reason to expect that Muslims' trust in the institutions and values of democracy may be on par with non-Muslims. Because immigration to Europe in the post-war era has been centred on economic gain, the immigrant background of many Muslim families may have contributed to improvement in their general standard of living. Former guest-workers and colonial subjects are likely to have left extreme poverty and massive unemployment in their countries of origin. Consequently their perspective as Europeans may be shaped by the satisfaction of having achieved economic gains in stable democracies, ensuring a better future for their children. It is not unreasonable to think that Muslims' satisfaction at these gains may frame their outlook toward the institutions in their European state, and in Europe as a whole. But feelings of trust in democratic institutions exhibited by Muslims may well go beyond their material satisfaction. For example, many members of the first generation may have experienced various forms of government persecution and corruption in their countries of origin. (See, for example, the reports from Transparency International and Amnesty International on the persecution of minorities in many sending countries including Pakistan, Morocco, Turkey and Tunisia. These reports are available at www.transparency.org/policy_research/nis/nis_reports_by_country/asia_pacific and www.amnesty.org).

Wüst (2002: 128, 131) found that among different groups of recently naturalized citizens, Muslims ranked in the middle regarding their overall satisfaction with democracy (Muslims=79%, Catholics=90%, Protestants=91% and non-Religious=71%) and their acceptance of democracy as a form of government (Muslims=78%, Catholics=90%, Protestants=93% and non-religious=77%). Similarly, Muslims expressed moderate levels of interest in politics compared to other groups (Muslims=40%, Catholics=21%, Protestants=21%, Non-religious=69%) (Wüst, 2002: 131).

Furthermore, while it appears that Muslims' voter turnout generally lags behind national rates (Ajala, 2010: 84), additional evidence concludes that it exceeds that of non-minority voters in the UK (Klausen, 2008: 28–29) and among newly minted citizens of different religious denominations in Germany (Wüst, 2002: 166). Cross-national variation in turnout is thought to be influenced by different citizenship regimes, the persistence of homeland politics and other features of the domestic political opportunity structure (Freeman and Ögelman, 1998; Hammar, 1994: 146; Koopmans and Statham, 2000; Messina, 2006: 146; Togeby, 1999). Weak participation also appears at the local level even in areas where Muslims are highly concentrated (Castles and Miller, 2009: 286).

Evidence from the European Social Survey

Voting

In rows 2 and 3 of Table 4.1 we look at the voting patterns of eligible voters in 2008 in contrast to 2002. In the Netherlands in 2008, Muslim respondents who were eligible to vote were only about 6% less likely to vote than non-Muslims (80% of Muslims in contrast to 86% of non-Muslims) and Muslims' likelihood of voting was up considerably from 2002 (when only 50% of Muslims who were eligible voted). In the UK, eligible Muslims were about 4% less likely than eligible non-Muslims to vote in both 2008 and 2002 (66% of Muslims in 2008 in contrast to 70% of non-Muslims in 2008). Seventy percent of Muslim respondents eligible to vote in Germany did so in 2008, about 14% less than non-Muslims. The likelihood of eligible Muslims voting in Germany was 25% greater in 2008 than it was in 2002 (when only 45% voted). In France eligible Muslims were about as likely to vote in 2008 as in 2002 (about 48% voted both times). In 2008 non-Muslims eligible to vote in France were about 30% more likely to vote than their Muslim counterparts (78% of non-Muslims). The lack of a decline in Muslims' likelihood of voting in France is surprising in light of the contentious minority/majority climate in the nation, during a decade of sufficient frustration on both sides to have produced rioting (most notably in 2005) outside of Paris, a ban on headscarves worn by schoolgirls, and a ban on the *niquab* in public places. Though Muslims who are eligible to vote are considerably less likely to vote than eligible non-Muslims are, the fact that the percentage of eligible Muslims voting did not decline suggests continued efforts to work within the system even in the face of the hostility and controversy surrounding riots and development of the legislation intended to limit Muslims' display of distinctive cultural norms. The question of greater concern may be why Muslims eligible to vote in France in 2008 were between 18% and 32% less likely to vote than were eligible Muslims in the other three member states. In addition, for Muslims in all four states, voting appears to be a slack resource that could be more fully utilized to place their concerns on the political agenda.

Vote choice

The bottom half of Table 4.1 indicates that Muslims are considerably more likely than non-Muslims to vote for the party on the left. That greater likelihood ranges from 20% in the UK (where 71% of Muslims voted on the left) to 45% in the Netherlands (where 82% of Muslims voted for the party on left). These differences make sense, given the left parties' more egalitarian, inclusive stances toward minorities and immigrants than the parties on the right. Muslims thus appear to be voting in their objective interests, as other European relative newcomers faced with problems of exclusion and discrimination would be expected to vote.

Table 4.1 Comparing electoral participation and vote choice of Muslims and non-Muslims

	France[1]		Germany[2]		Netherlands[3]		United Kingdom[4]	
	Muslims	Other	Muslims	Other	Muslims	Other	Muslims	Other
Voted Last Election (%)								
Cumulative	44.4 (117)	77.6 (5,916)	52.5 (99)	82.7 (10,250)	60.8 (143)	85.3 (7,215)	64.3 (185)	71.5 (6,620)
2008	47.5 (40)	78.3 (1,360)	70.0 (20)	83.8 (2,469)	80.0 (40)	86.2 (1,390)	66.2 (68)	70.5 (2,069)
2002	47.8 (23)	75.4 (1,276)	45.0 (20)	85.6 (2,640)	50.0 (40)	87.0 (2,176)	68.6 (35)	72.4 (1,867)
Party Choice (%)								
Cumulative								
Right	11.6	39.3	14.3	44.5	15.7	57.9	18.1	34.7
Left	83.7	53.2	85.7	55.5	81.9	37.0	71.3	50.6
Center	4.7 (43)	7.5 (3,693)	--- (46)	--- (7,135)	2.4 (83)	5.1 (5,892)	10.6 (94)	14.7 (3,876)
2008								
Right	16.7	39.4	9.1	47.2	18.2	54.7	9.8	35.3
Left	72.2	52.4	90.9	52.8	78.8	41.3	68.2	47.1
Center	11.1 (18)	8.3 (1,138)	--- (11)	--- (1,755)	3.0 (33)	4.0 (1,335)	22.0 (41)	17.6 (1,262)
2002								
Right	0	37.5	14.3	44.5	30.0	63.3	21.1	31.1
Left	100	54.5	85.7	55.5	70.0	30.8	73.6	51.0
Center	0 (9)	8.0 (738)	--- (7)	--- (1,968)	0 (20)	5.9 (1,820)	5.3 (19)	17.9 (1,172)

Data: ESS 2008, 2006, 2004, 2002

Note: Number of respondents contained in parentheses.

Note: French vote on first ballot of National Assembly elections, second party list vote for German elections to the Bundestag.

Note: Colomer (2008) used to aid in identifying left, right and centrist parties

[1] Parties on the right include: Front National, Mouvement des citoyens, Mouvement National Républicain, Mouvement pour la France, Rassemblement du Peuple Français, Union de la Majorité Présidentielle; parties on the left: ligue communiste révolutionnaire, Lutte ouvrière, Parti communiste, Parti Socialiste, Les Verts, Autres mouvements ecologists, Parti radical de gauche; parties on the center: Démocratie Libérale, Union pour la Démocratie Française.

[2] Right parties include the CDU/CSU, FDP (the preferred coalition partner of the CDU/CSU), the Republicans and the DVU; parties on the left include Greens, SPD and the Left Party

[3] Parties on the right include: Christian Democratic Party, Party for Freedom and Democracy, List Pim Fortuyn, Christian Union, Social Reformed Party; parties on the left: Labour Party, Green Left, Socialist Party, Party for the Animals; parties on the center: Democrats ` 66.   Liveable Netherlands a populist party with anti-establishment tendencies is excluded was difficult to discern any left-right orientation

[4] Parties on the right include: Conservative; parties on the left include: Labour, Greens; parties on the center include: Liberal Democrats

Support for democracy and political trust

The levels of trust and support for government and democracy shown in Table 4.2 provide some surprising results. In France, for example, despite the problems of minority/majority relations between Muslims and non-Muslims discussed above, Muslims look quite like their non-Muslim neighbours in their attitudes toward Parliament, politicians, EU Parliament, satisfaction with national government and interest in politics. There is no statistically significant difference between them. Where there are differences between the two groups, they are also surprising: Muslims are significantly more likely than non-Muslims to trust in the political parties, and to be satisfied with the way democracy works in France. In fact, the only area in which non-Muslims express greater trust than Muslims is with regard to the UN. There is not much difference in these areas of political trust between Muslims and non-Muslims in Germany, either: German Muslims have significantly greater satisfaction with the way democracy works in Germany than do non-Muslims, greater satisfaction with national government, and more trust in EU Parliament. Non-Muslims in Germany, as in France, have

Table 4.2: Comparing mean levels of trust, satisfaction and interest in government

	France		Germany		Netherlands		UK	
	Muslims	Other	Muslims	Other	Muslims	Other	Muslims	Other
Trust in parliament	4.09 (219)	4.02 (6,748)	4.66 (248)	4.38 (10,887)	4.84 (171)	4.87 (7,618)	5.31*** (210)	4.03 (7,105)
Trust in politicians	3.53 (218)	3.47 (6,786)	3.48 (257)	3.38 (11,037)	4.76 (174)	4.95 (7,624)	4.62*** (201)	3.58 (7,110)
Trust in political parties	3.69* (164)	3.31 (5,317)	3.60 (187)	3.31 (8,164)	4.67 (124)	5.05* (5,350)	4.75*** (160)	3.59 (5,099)
Trust in EU Parliament	4.49 (205)	4.41 (6,552)	4.85*** (228)	4.26 (10,183)	5.03 (160)	4.78 (7,139)	5.04*** (172)	3.55 (6,498)
Trust in the UN	4.26 (212)	4.98*** (6,580)	4.67 (232)	4.98* (10,360)	4.24 (169)	5.49*** (7,337)	4.66 (192)	5.17** (6,676)
Satisfaction with way democracy works in country	5.42*** (221)	4.69 (6,738)	6.05*** (256)	5.32 (10,962)	5.76 (175)	5.95 (7,555)	6.02*** (201)	4.98 (6,920)
Satisfaction with national government	4.09 (219)	4.02 (6,748)	4.26*** (235)	3.61 (10,789)	4.84 (171)	4.87 (7,616)	5.31*** (210)	4.03 (7,105)
Interest in politics	2.44 (221)	2.37 (6,820)	2.25 (268)	2.69 *** (11,122)	2.37 (178)	2.66*** (7,717)	2.47 (211)	2.46 (7,192)

Data: ESS 2008, 2006, 2004, 2002
***p<.001, **p<.01, *p<.05
Note: Number of respondents contained in parentheses.

greater trust in the UN than do Muslims; non-Muslims in Germany also have significantly more interest in politics than Muslims do. But by and large, the differences between Muslims and non-Muslims in mean level of trust in government are small in both states, suggesting that Muslims' attitude toward government is much like that of non-Muslims and, in some areas, even more supportive. The Netherlands and UK stand out at opposite ends of the spectrum: in the Netherlands, the two groups look much alike, and where there are statistically significant differences, non-Muslims are slightly more supportive of political parties and the UN and they have more interest in politics than do Muslims. In the UK, Muslims are noticeably and significantly more supportive of government than non-Muslims in several areas: trust in Parliament, politicians, political parties, EU Parliament, satisfaction with the way democracy works in the UK and satisfaction with national government. (UK non-Muslims are significantly more supportive of the UN.)

Table 4.3 demonstrates that many of the significant differences between Muslims and non-Muslims remain when we control for the respondent background differences discussed earlier. Specifically, for example, in France, Germany and the UK, Muslims still have greater satisfaction than non-Muslims with the way democracy works in their member state. In Germany and the UK, Muslims have greater trust in EU Parliament than do non-Muslims even after controls. In the UK the multivariate results suggest that Muslims have significantly greater trust and satisfaction in political institutions and values than non-Muslims in all areas measured (except for the UN).

Evidence from the German General Social Survey

Separate data sources support the findings from the European Social Survey presented above. Appendix 2 describes the data we utilized in the German General Social Survey to compare the level of political support between Muslims and non-Muslims. Details of our use of the German General Social Survey in examining trust in the political system among Muslims and non-Muslims are available in Doerschler and Jackson (2010b, 2011). In distinguishing between more diffuse, normative attitudes related to one's support for the wider community and democratic values, and more specific attitudes concerning an individual's evaluation of government institutions and public officials, we follow others in utilizing Easton's conceptual framework (Easton,

Table 4.3: Effects of Muslim ID on trust, satisfaction and interest in political institutions and values

	France		Germany		Netherlands		UK	
	Muslim	Full	Muslim	Full	Muslim	Full	Muslim	Full
Trust in parliament	-.17 (6,906)	-.20 (4,478)	.27 (11,134)	.22 (7,965)	.20 (7,805)	.26 (6,424)	1.45*** (7,304)	.75*** (5,390)
Trust in politicians	.06 (7,002)	-.09 (4,510)	.09 (11,292)	-.11 (8,006)	-.19 (7,798)	-.07 (6,406)	1.04*** (7,310)	.31* (5,406)
Trust in political parties	.38* (5,480)	.13 (4,503)	.29 (8,350)	.14 (5,870)	-.37* (5,474)	-.36* (4,536)	1.16*** (5,258)	.57** (3,837)
Trust in EU Parliament	.06 (6,756)	-.10 (4,392)	.60*** (10,410)	.39* (7,576)	.25 (7,298)	-.10 (6,077)	1.48*** (6,669)	.55** (5,076)
Trust in the UN	-.72*** (6,792)	-.96*** (4,410)	-.31* (10,591)	-.35 (7,721)	-1.26*** (7,505)	-1.24*** (6,243)	-1.09*** (6,868)	-.51** (5,204)
Satisfaction with democracy in country[1]	.73*** (6,958)	.48* (4,520)	.73*** (11,217)	.44** (8,097)	-.19 (7,729)	.17 (6,428)	1.04*** (7,121)	1.12*** (5,361)
Satisfaction with national government[1]	.06 (6,966)	-.09 (4,518)	.65*** (11,024)	.25 (8,024)	-.03 (7,785)	-.05 (6,446)	1.28*** (7,313)	.94*** (5,425)
Interest in politics	.07 (7,040)	.21 (4,518)	-.45*** (11,389)	-.08 (8,024)	-.30*** (7,895)	-.02 (6,446)	.01 (7,402)	.01 (5,425)

Data: ESS 2008, 2006, 2004, 2002
***p<.001, **p<.01, *p<.05, figures represent unstandardized OLS coefficients
Note: The number of respondents is included in parentheses.
Note: Full models control for R's level of social trust, age, gender, income, citizenship, unemployment, education, ideology, interest in politics, amount of TV watching, satisfaction with government
[1] Variables satisfaction with democracy and satisfaction with government were correlated at .563 across all cases. To reduce the effects of multicollinearity, neither variable is used as a control variable in any of the full models.

1965: 171–219; Dalton, 2004, 1999; Klingemann, 1999), illustrated below.

Diffuse   Specific

Political   Regime   Regime Norms   Regime   Political

Community Principles   and Procedures Institutions   Authorites

Easton (1965: 177) describes the community as a group of persons who despite cultural or even nationality differences participate in the broad structures and processes of the political system. Regime principles refer to a set of core values underpinning a political system. Freedom of expression, citizen representation, equality and authority are the values forming the basis of democratic systems (Easton, 1965: 194–195). Easton (1965: 200) describes regime norms as the 'operating rules' of a particular regime – the overall function of democracy. Regime institutions and political authorities link citizen attitudes to evaluations of specific institutions and public figures.

In a test of the relationship between Muslim religious identification and political trust in Germany, we examined 14 dependent variables representing different levels of trust (from specific to diffuse) following Easton's multilayered conceptual framework. (A full discussion of this project is available in Doerschler and Jackson, 2010b, 2011.) A dichotomous measure of respondents' self-identity as a Muslim is one of our two central independent variables. The second is a self-reported measure of each respondent's religiosity (coded 1–7). We include additional independent variables to test alternative theories of political trust. These control variables include two that measure social capital (a dichotomous measure of social trust and a scale of participation in five voluntary organizations); age, gender, and variables reflecting socioeconomic status (net monthly income, level of education (1–5), employment status (dichotomous), place of birth, citizenship (German or non-German), and level of post-materialism (1–4). Separate measures are included for respondents espousing extreme ideological views on the far left or far right as well as two measures identifying political winners and losers as those more likely (on a 10-point scale) of supporting the Social Democrats (SPD) and Christian Democrats (CDU), the two parties in power during the fielding of the survey. Also controlled are measures reflecting the amount of television watched in minutes per day, overall interest in politics (1–4) and respondent's evaluation of the overall performance of the government (1–6). (We utilize these controls in Table 4.4, to be discussed further on.)

Figure 4.1 indicates that Muslims and non-Muslims share approximately the same level of support for democracy as a theoretical concept; there is no significant difference between them. Muslims, however, are significantly more supportive than non-Muslims of democracy as practised in the FRG. Figure 4.2 (ALLBUS trust in institutions) provides more evidence in this direction, comparing mean levels of trust between Muslims and non-Muslims for seven political and legal institutions, with a cumulative index of institutional trust. Muslims hold significantly higher levels of trust on the cumulative index and in all of its seven dimensions.

Figure 4.1: Support for democracy in Germany

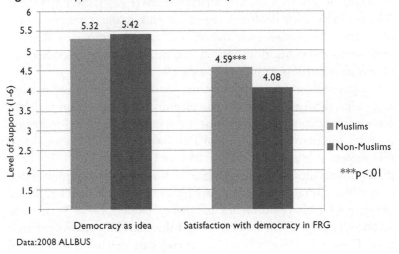

Data: 2008 ALLBUS

Figure 4.2: Trust in public institutions

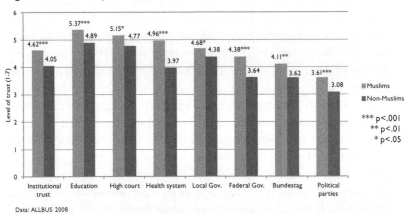

Data: ALLBUS 2008

The multivariate results in Table 4.4 indicate that Muslims exhibit significantly greater levels of satisfaction with democracy in Germany, as well as higher levels of trust in political institutions (the cumulative index) and in separate institutions including parliament, supreme court and in the health system when the control variables discussed above (and listed at the bottom of the table) are included in the multivariate equations.

Table 4.4: Effects of Muslim ID, religiosity and place of birth on dimensions of trust among German Muslims

	Full sample		Muslims only			
	Muslim ID[1]	N	Religiosity[2]	N	Born in Germany	N
Political community						
Connection to community	.33	1,297	-.08	43	-.03	93
Connection to state and its people	.22	1,296	-.06	44	.11	93
Connection to federal republic	.18	1,298	.01	44	.05	94
Connection index	.73	1,294	-.13	43	.12	94
Regime principles						
Evaluation of democracy as idea	.30	1,282	-.06	41	.31	87
Regime norms						
Satisfaction with democracy in FRG	.55*	1,299	.14	42	-.15	90
Regime institutions						
Education system	.31	1,205	-.05	37	-.08	77
Health system	.72*	1,297	.18	44	1.21**	94
Supreme court	.85*	1,224	.14	37	-.18	72
Federal government	.16	1,294	.17	40	.91	85
Parliament	.60*	1,284	.16	38	.46	78
Local government	.16	1,293	.19	43	-.17	91
Political parties	.35	1,290	.20	37	.56	81
Political institutions index	.60**	1,141	.08	30	.42	60

Data: 2008 ALLBUS
**p<.01, *p<.05
Results are unstandardized OLS regression coefficients
[1] The following variables are controlled for: social trust, participation in voluntary institutions, age, gender, income, citizenship, born in Germany, level of post-materialism, employment status, ideology, support for parties in power, interest in politics, amount of education, television viewing and evaluation of government performance.
[2] Self-reported religiosity was given to a split sample.

The bivariate relationships between Muslims' religiosity and their levels of political trust provided in the middle column of Table 4.4 demonstrate that there is no statistically significant relationship between religiosity and any measure of political trust. There is no basis for believing that Muslims' political trust is affected by their degree of religiosity. We also provide bivariate tests of whether greater exposure to German society is related to higher trust among Muslims by comparing mean levels of political trust among Muslims born abroad with those born in Germany (variable scored '1' for those born in Germany and '0' for those born abroad). The results in Table 4.4 indicate that among our 14 measures of political trust, those born in Germany displayed significantly higher levels of trust in only the health system. These results provide only very modest support, and then only at the institutional level, that earlier exposure to German society leads to greater trust.

The results from the German General Social Survey allow us to elaborate on those from the European Social Survey presented earlier in this chapter. Both surveys show that Muslims are significantly more satisfied with democracy (than non-Muslims) as it is practised in Germany. In addition, the ALLBUS (2008, Table 4.4) and ESS coefficients for about the same time period (in Table 4.3) for the effect of Muslim identification on indicators of trust in the political system and the political community are all in the same direction – positive – except for the ESS coefficient for trust in politicians) even where they are not statistically significant. For Germany, the results of both bivariate and multivariate analyses using the German General Social Survey (ALLBUS) lend strong support to the conclusion that Muslims exhibit equal or greater levels of political trust than non-Muslims. The results undermine the assumption that there are strong currents of anti-democratic sentiment among Muslims, and they are supported by data from the European Social Survey. On most indicators, there is no statistically significant difference between Muslims and non-Muslims in their trust in the political system, and where differences do appear – for example, with regard to satisfaction with democracy – Muslims are more satisfied in the political system than non-Muslims.

Evidence from the Home Office Citizenship Survey

For Britain, further support for the ESS results presented above, showing Muslims' greater political trust, is provided by data from the 2007 Home Office Citizenship survey (HOCS). HOCS, described in Chapter One, used a representative national sample of people in England and Wales. Maxwell (2010b) has conducted an extensive analysis of the

2007 HOCS data in an effort to examine the importance of migration status in trust in government among British Muslims. His findings are as follows. First, Maxwell demonstrates that 'Muslims are more likely than Christians to have trust in Parliament and in the local council. For example, 16% of Muslims have "a lot" of trust in Parliament compared to only 4% of Christians, and 16% of Muslims have "a lot" of trust in the local council compared to 7% of Christians. These same patterns hold when the two positive response categories are combined, with an especially large gap between the 62% of Muslims and 35% of Christians who either have "a lot" or "a fair amount" of trust in Parliament' (Maxwell, 2010b: 96–97). Secondly, Maxwell provides HOCS data indicating that Muslims have higher levels of satisfaction in government performance than Christians, and suggesting that it is 'the key to understanding their higher levels of trust in government' (Maxwell, 2010b: 102). Maxwell (2010b: 103) further 'claim[s] that migration status is an important mitigating factor which shapes how individuals evaluate their experiences. Therefore, even though migrants are more likely than natives to live in highly-deprived neighborhoods and are more likely to fear crime in their local community, migrants are also more likely to be satisfied in government performance.' Maxwell finds roughly similar satisfaction scores between Muslims and Christians once he takes account of migration status. In his words, 'Muslims' higher levels of satisfaction in government performance are primarily a function of their larger percentage of migrants and the general dynamic of more positive evaluations among migrants as opposed to natives' (Maxwell, 2010b: 104). Maxwell assesses the implications of his analysis of HOCS data as indicating that 'Muslims are better incorporated in British society than is commonly assumed ... Further evidence of the integrated normality of Muslim political attitudes is their relatively high levels of positive British identification, which are either close to or slightly more positive than those of Christians across the 2001, 2003, 2005, and 2007 HOCS' (Maxwell, 2010b: 105).

Data from the 2007 Home Office Citizenship Survey provide additional support for the 2008 European Social Survey findings regarding British Muslims' greater trust (than non-Muslims) in Parliament, politicians, political parties, and EU Parliament. These statistically significant ESS findings were robust, withstanding controls for citizenship, social trust, ideology, economic status, satisfaction with government and other background factors. The fact that more than one source of data collected at different, but roughly comparable, time periods in Britain, yields comparable data supports the validity of the findings about Britain, just as the ALLBUS results supported the ESS findings for Germany.

Evidence from the Statistics Netherlands Studies

With regard to additional support for the ESS findings on the Netherlands, we turn to a study presented at the Office of Economic Cooperation and Development (OECD) International Conference on Social Cohesion and Development in 2010. Schmeets and te Riele (2010), authors of this study from *Statistics Netherlands,* used data on political participation and trust from the Dutch Parliamentary Election Studies of 2006 and 2010. They integrated these data with information on social and institutionalized trust from the European Social Survey, gathered bi-annually in the 2002–2008 period, and with the Social Statistical Database (SSB), which contains longitudinal data on the Dutch population relating to gender, age, country of origin, marital status and income, in addition to data from the Labour Force Survey. Their analysis reports that about 56% of the population in the Netherlands has a religious affiliation, and about 20% go to church or mosque on a regular basis. Twenty-eight percent of the Dutch indicate that they are Catholic and 18% say they identify with one of the Protestant denominations. Schmeets and te Riele (2010) do not specify the percentage of Muslims in their analysis, but estimates generally place that figure at just under 6% of the Dutch population. They do note that 'Muslims have above average contacts with friends and neighbours … while the non-religious have lower than average contact rates with relatives and neighbours' (Schmeets and te Riele, 2010: 13). We have presented some of their findings in Table 4.5 (institutional trust in the Netherlands).

Table 4.5: Institutional trust in the Netherlands

% **Indicating trust in:**	**Muslims**	**Catholics**
Dutch Parliament	53	51
Legal system	56	55
European Parliament	44	43
Political parties	38	46
Politicians	40	45
Police	63	69

Source: Schmeets and te Riele, 2010: 16, study utilized European Social Survey (fieldwork conducted by GfK), Permanent Survey on Living conditions, Dutch Parliamentary Election Study.

Table 4.5 indicates that Muslims are 2% more likely than Catholics, the largest religious group, to trust the Dutch Parliament (53% Muslims, 51% Catholics), and 1% more likely to trust the legal system (56% Muslims in contrast to 55% of Catholics). Muslims are 1% more likely than Catholics to trust the European Parliament (44% of Muslims in contrast to 43% of Catholics). Muslims are 8% less likely than Catholics to trust the political parties (38% Muslims in contrast to 46% Catholics), 5% less likely to trust politicians (40% Muslims vs. 45% Catholics) and 6% less likely to trust the police (63% Muslims in contrast to 69% of Catholics).

Schmeets and te Riele (2010: 14) also report results from the 2009 Permanent Survey on Living Conditions (POLS 2009), indicating that 'Muslims have above average trust rates in lawyers, civil servants and the European Union'. As we noted earlier in the chapter, regarding religiosity, Schmeets and te Riele (2010: 14) indicate that POLS 2009 results support ESS in finding that the frequency of church or mosque attendance is positively related to most areas of trust, including trust in parliament and the police.

The comparison of Muslims with other religious groups in the Netherlands in terms of their trust in official institutions and agencies of authority, relying not only on data from the European Social Survey but also on data from the 2009 Permanent Survey on Living Conditions and other Dutch sources presents an unsurprising picture in light of the ESS results comparing Muslims and non-Muslims that we presented earlier in the chapter. With regard to their level of confidence toward the Dutch Parliament and the European Parliament, Muslims are about as positively disposed as other Dutch. But Muslims do have significantly less confidence in the political parties (and the UN) than others in the Netherlands.

Corroboration for our examination of data from the European Social Survey for all four states has come from data for three of the states from the German General Social Survey, the Home Office Cohesion Study as assessed by Maxwell, and Statistics Netherlands' examination of several Dutch data sources including the 2009 Permanent Survey on Living Conditions in comparison to the ESS Dutch data. Collectively, these results paint a picture of Muslims as about as supportive of political institutions as non-Muslims in their European states, and sometimes more so. Efforts to benchmark Muslims' well-being in Europe, by providing continuous data on Muslims' confidence in the institutions of the state, would undermine the negative assertions about Muslims' willingness to cooperate in the political goals and activities of Europe and its member states.

Those who say that Muslims fail to support democracy clearly have not reviewed the considerable data indicating that the opposite is true: Muslims are, by and large, more enthusiastic than their European neighbours in the institutions of democratic European states. Where exceptions are evident – for example, in Dutch Muslims' lower level of confidence in the political parties (a significant relationship in the ESS data even with the controls in the full model) – a clear rationale can be discerned from the recent platforms of the parties. In some states, like Britain, Muslims are consistently found to be more confident than non-Muslims in the state and its agencies; in others, like Germany, the findings consistently paint Muslims as more positive than non-Muslims in their satisfaction with the way democracy is practised in Germany. French Muslims too are more satisfied than non-Muslims with democracy as it is practised in France; Muslims' trust in Parliament is not significantly different from that of non-Muslims in France, but the coefficient is negative, unsurprisingly, in light of the French Parliament's passage of legislation limiting Muslims' display of religious identity in the civic arena.

Overall, these results provide an opening for political rejuvenation in European states. Whether Muslims' relative confidence in the political systems of Europe and the practice of democracy in their member state comes from experiences related to their immigrant backgrounds, their upward mobility in contrast to their previous situation (or that of their families) in the country of origin, or their greater religiosity, their trust and support present an opportunity for Europe and its member states. While there are some areas of dissatisfaction (for example, in Dutch Muslims' lack of trust in the political parties), Muslims are generally as supportive of democracy and governmental institutions as their non-Muslim neighbours, and in some areas more so. If the doors to political involvement are open to them, they are attitudinally disposed to participate and to support the institutions in which they are involved.

The political trust of Muslims deemed 'vulnerable'

The positive orientation to European governments found among Muslims, in contrast to non-Muslims, in data from the ESS, ALLBUS, HOCS and Statistics Netherlands' surveys discussed above, is widely shared by the groups of Muslims often deemed vulnerable to higher levels of dissatisfaction. Table 4.6 provides ESS data suggesting that trust and support for the political system are also characteristic of young Muslims (15–29), those who are highly religious, males, those with foreign nationality, and those who were born abroad.

Table 4.6: Average levels of political trust among vulnerable groups of Muslims

	France	Germany	Netherlands	UK
Age groups				
15-29	3.72	3.94	5.33	5.11
others	4.27	4.65*	5.07	5.50
50 and older	4.32	4.71[1]	4.88	5.92[1]
others	3.99	4.31	5.21	5.21
Religiosity				
high (7-10)	3.99	4.27	5.12	5.51
others	4.11	4.34	5.26	4.93
low (0-3)	3.98[1]	4.48[1]	5.58[2]	3.68[2]
others	4.07	4.27	5.10	5.38*
Gender				
male	3.93	4.11	5.66**	5.31
female	4.22	4.61	4.51	5.24
Citizenship				
national	3.88	3.92	4.94	5.16
foreign	4.52	4.51	6.22**[1]	6.35*[1]
Place of birth				
national	3.52	3.22	4.74	4.24
foreign	4.53**	4.73***	5.33	5.98***

Data: ESS 2008, 2006, 2004, 2002
***p<.001, **p<.01, *p<.05
[1] 10<N<30, [2] N<10

The dependent variable of this table is an index of political trust, combining five variables, all equally weighted: trust in politicians, trust in parties, trust in parliament, satisfaction with government and satisfaction with the way democracy is practised in the state. The index is best thought of as reflecting trust and satisfaction with the political system. Like the variables of which it is comprised, it forms an 11 point scale ranging from least (0) to greatest trust (10). The average levels of political trust and satisfaction are not greatly different for Muslims under 30 (15–29) than for those who are older. Only in Germany does the difference between Muslims under 30 and others reach statistical significance (with the trust index for Muslims under 30 on average less than one scale point lower than the score for older Muslims). Highly religious Muslims are not significantly different from the less religious in terms of their political trust. This finding will seem surprising to those who argue that Islam is incompatible with democracy. In fact, the only significant difference relating to religiosity in Table 4.6 indicates that in the UK, Muslims with the lowest level of religiosity have significantly lower levels of trust and satisfaction with the political system than do more religious Muslims. (The low number of cases in this cell and a few others, all indicated in the table, leads us to suggest further research before some of the findings on vulnerable groups are fully accepted.) But even for this significant difference, the average 'trust ' difference between the less religious and others is less than two points on the political trust index. Similarly, there is little divergence between Muslim males and females in terms of their degree of political trust, with the one significant difference, found in the Netherlands, in the direction of males having more trust in the political system than females. Citizenship is expected to provide more trust in the political system. Surprisingly, these data do not provide support for that assumption. In the Netherlands and the UK, Muslims who have not yet taken citizenship of the European state in which they reside have significantly more trust and satisfaction in the political system than Muslims who are nationals; and in France and Germany there is no significant difference between Muslims with and without citizenship of the European host nation. It is possible that foreign nationals expect less of government than do those with citizenship, for whom the benefits of citizenship may appear partially unfulfilled. This possibility is supported by the findings relating to place of birth: in three of the four states (not the Netherlands), those of foreign birth have significantly more trust and satisfaction with the political system than those born in the European state.

While there is some degree of variation among Muslims regarding their confidence in the state, it is not in the directions on which public concern and policy making focus. Muslims born abroad and without citizenship in the European state appear to be more supportive of European states than other Muslims; highly religious Muslims trust the political system as much as the less religious; young Muslims are by and large as supportive as older cohorts. Rather than posing a threat to democratic political traditions, Muslims born abroad or without citizenship may provide an important basis of support for European states. Similarly, religious Muslims and Muslims under 30 are also supportive of European political systems. More can easily be done by European and state agencies to capitalize on this support. Muslims in these key groups appear to be ready and willing to support the European states in which they live.

FIVE

Muslims' experiences of discrimination in public institutions

Despite European Muslims' confidence in the political and justice systems in Europe and its member states, our examination of criminal justice data in Chapter Three highlighted the religious minority's concerns about crime victimization. More than one data source indicated that Muslims were more worried than non-Muslims about the possibility of victimization and about antisocial behaviour in their neighbourhoods. Data on discrimination provided in this chapter underscore the picture of Muslims' sense of relative unease in their European homes.

In its report, *Racist Violence in 15 Member States,* the EUMC (European Monitoring Centre on Racism and Xenophobia) (2005a) provides examples of anti-foreigner violence and reviews single state studies then available regarding discrimination against ethnic groups likely to be Muslim. Due to the lack of data at the time, EUMC was not able to provide a systematic analysis of discrimination against Muslims in Europe. Joachim Brüß (2008) investigated Muslims' perceptions of discrimination in samples (drawn in 2004) of Turkish Muslims in Berlin, Bangladeshi Muslims in London, and Moroccan Muslims in Madrid. (The French research contingent 'decided not to launch the survey, as they could not define a satisfactory sampling frame for Paris because of missing information for the Muslim population' (Brüß, 2008: 892).) Brüß (2008: 886) found that in Berlin '30 percent of Turkish Muslims indicated that they felt treated respectfully and in a friendly way by the receiver society ... In contrast, in London 93 percent of Bangladeshi Muslims ... felt respectfully treated'. In London, age differences were evident in perceptions of discrimination: young Bangladeshi Muslims saw themselves as 'belonging to a discriminated minority ... reported being stopped by the police more often ... [and] felt that they were treated disrespectfully by the receiver society' (Brüß, 2008: 886–887). Brüß' (2008: 889) multivariate analysis suggests that disrespectful treatment and verbal attacks were key factors influencing respondents' perceptions of being a member of a group that is discriminated against on the part of Bangladeshi Muslims in London and Turkish Muslims in Germany respectively.

Brüß discusses the implications of these results for the social mobility of Muslims in the receiver states. In his words: 'severe and persistent forms of social exclusion can probably be tackled more thoroughly by taking Muslims' experiences seriously ... more knowledge is needed to explore ... the structure and meaning of everyday interaction between Muslims and host societies across Europe' (Brüß, 2008: 891).

While Bruß cites several limitations to his study, his results underscore the significance of discrimination for Muslims' sense of marginality: disrespectful treatment, discrimination by police and non-official members of the host society, and verbal hostility directed at Muslims increase their perception of being in a minority group that is discriminated against and are likely to reduce their optimism about the extent to which they can contribute to their European state.

We further examine Muslims' experiences of discrimination in Europe using information from two large-scale studies with data collected more recently than those gathered by Brüß: the European Minorities and Discrimination Study (EU-MIDIS, described in Chapter One and commissioned by the European Agency for Fundamental Rights), and the European Social Survey (2002–2008). The EU-MIDIS (FRA, 2009 02: 5) *Data in Focus Report* on Muslims analyses respondents' experiences of discrimination on the basis of ethnicity in nine areas: when looking for work, at work, looking for a house or apartment, by health care or social service personnel, by school personnel, at a café or restaurant or bar, entering or in a shop, or in opening a bank account or getting a loan. Summarizing the study as a whole, FRA reports that: 'overall, 51% of Muslims compared to 20% of non-Muslim ethnic minorities surveyed in the 14 EU-Member states in which Muslims were surveyed believe discrimination on grounds of religion or belief to be "very" or "fairly" widespread' (FRA, 2009 02: 10).

EU-MIDIS did not gather data on Muslims in Britain (as we explained in Chapter One); but Germany, France and the Netherlands were among the member states in which Muslim minority groups were surveyed. FRA (2009 02: 10) indicates that 'on average the majority of all Muslim respondents considered discrimination on the grounds of both ethnic or immigrant background and religion or belief to be widespread in their country. However, the responses of different Muslim groups in individual countries vary.' We look at some of these differences below for the states in our examination. Table 5.1 summarizes key results.

Table 5.1: EU MIDIS: Muslims' perceptions of discrimination and rights awareness

Muslims in:	Germany	France		Netherlands	
Ethnicity of Muslim respondents:	Turkish	North African	Sub-Saharan African	Turkish	North African
% Discrimination in one of 9 areas	31	25	26	29	30
Number of incidents	5.8	4.1	6.2	5.0	7.2
% Unaware of law against employment discrimination	45	21	15	33	50
% Stopped by police	24	44	37	27	26
% Perceived ethnic profiling during police stop	37	66	44	15	39
% Perceived ethnic profiling during border patrol stop	36	30	32	31	35

European Agency for Fundamental Rights (FRA): 2009 02: EU-MIDIS Data in Focus Report: Muslims. No data on Muslims in the United Kingdom were gathered for EU-MIDIS.

In Germany 31% of self-identified Turkish Muslim respondents indicate that they have been *discriminated against in one of the nine areas in the past 12 months* (close to the 30% overall average for Muslim minorities). The number of incidents of discrimination reported by Turkish Muslims in Germany was 5.8, below the 14 state overall average of 7.7 (FRA, 2009 02: 6). Forty-five percent of Turkish Muslims in Germany reported that they were unaware of a law forbidding 'discrimination against people on the basis of their ethnicity/immigrant background when applying for a job' compared to 37% of Muslims in the survey overall (FRA, 2009 02: 10). Twenty-four percent of Turkish Muslims surveyed in Germany indicated that they had been *stopped by the police* in the past 12 months (compared to 25% of Muslims in the comparative survey overall). Thirty-seven percent of Turkish Muslims surveyed in Germany *perceived ethnic profiling* when stopped by the police in the last 12 months (compared to 40% of Muslims in the comparative survey overall). Thirty-six percent of Turkish Muslims surveyed in Germany perceived ethnic profiling when they were *stopped by the border control* (similar to the 37% average for Muslims in the comparative survey overall). The EU MIDIS (FRA, 2009 02) survey results suggest that Turkish Muslims perceive blocked access in many areas of social interaction and endeavour in Germany and that this is true for other categories of Muslims in the other European states examined.

In France, where self-identified Muslims in the North African and Sub-Saharan African respondents provided the Muslim sub-sample, 25% and 26% of respondents respectively *reported discrimination in the past 12 months* in one of the nine areas examined by the survey, indicating that there had been 4.1 and 6.2 discriminatory incidents respectively. Twenty-one percent of North African and 15% of Sub-Saharan African Muslims in France reported no awareness of a law forbidding 'discrimination against people on the basis of their ethnicity/ immigrant background when applying for a job' compared to 37% of Muslims in the survey overall (FRA, 2009 02: 10). Higher numbers of those identified as Muslims in France had been **stopped by the police** in the last 12 months than in Germany: 44% of North African respondents in France and 37% of Sub-Saharan African respondents indicated they had been stopped by the police (in contrast to 24% of Turkish Muslim respondents in Germany, as noted above). The French Muslims surveyed were much more likely than those in Germany to have **perceived ethnic profiling when stopped by the police** in the last 12 months: 66% of the French Sub-Saharan Africans and 44% of the French North Africans perceived ethnic profiling (in contrast to 37% of the Turkish Muslims surveyed in Germany, as noted above). These figures suggest a contentious relationship between Muslim minorities and the police in France, a picture that has received considerable support in the last decade, but especially after the riots near Paris in 2005. Interestingly, though, Muslims identified as Sub-Saharan Africans or North Africans in France were not more likely than Turkish Muslims in Germany to perceive **ethnic profiling when stopped by the border control**: 30% of Sub-Saharan African and 32% of North African Muslim respondents in France indicated that they perceived ethnic profiling by border control, in contrast to 36% of Turkish Muslim respondents in Germany (as noted above).

EU-MIDIS Muslim respondents in the Netherlands were members of Turkish and North African ethnic groups. They indicated **having experienced discrimination in the last 12 months** in one of the nine areas examined at a rate of 29% and 30% respectively, close to the Muslims surveyed in Germany, but 4–5% more likely to report discrimination than those in France. Turkish and North African respondents in the Netherlands reported 5 and 7.2 incidents of discrimination in the last 12 months. The two groups also differed in their **awareness of laws forbidding discrimination** on the basis of ethnicity and immigrant background when applying for a job: 50% of North African Muslims surveyed in the Netherlands reported that no such law existed, while 33% of Turkish Muslims surveyed in the Netherlands thought there was no such law. The French Muslim groups surveyed were most likely to be aware of such laws (with only 15% Sub-Saharan African or 21% North African indicating there was no such law), suggesting that anti-discrimination efforts have reached them in France more effectively than they have reached Muslim minorities in either the Netherlands or Germany. Muslims in the North African and Turkish groups surveyed in the Netherlands were less likely than French Muslims surveyed to report that they had been ***stopped by the police*** (26% of North Africans and 27% of Turkish in the Netherlands, compared to figures 10–18% higher for the Muslim groups surveyed in France, as noted above). Thirty-nine percent of North African and 15% of Turkish Muslim respondents in the Netherlands perceived ***ethnic profiling when stopped by the police***, the difference between them perhaps reflecting the greater visibility of North Africans. Thirty-five percent of North African and 31% of Turkish Muslims surveyed in the Netherlands ***perceived ethnic profiling*** when stopped by the border control, placing them close to the Muslim respondents from the selected ethnic groups in France and Germany, as noted above. Regarding rights awareness, 45% of Turkish Muslims in Germany reported that they were unaware of a law forbidding 'discrimination against people on the basis of their ethnicity/ immigrant background when applying for a job' (compared to 37% of Muslims in the survey overall). In the Netherlands, 50% of North African Muslims were unaware of such a law. French Muslims had the highest rate of rights awareness, with between 15% and 21% unaware.

Data from the ESS (2002–2008) in Table 5.2 permit us to compare Muslims and non-Muslims in their perceptions of discrimination. In the UK, for example, Muslims are over 16% more likely than non-Muslims to say that they are a member of a group discriminated against in their country of residence. In Germany, the difference is 29%, with Muslims again more likely than non-Muslims to indicate that they are in a group that faces discrimination. Slightly greater differences exist between Muslims and non-Muslims in France (33% difference) and the Netherlands (37% difference) in likelihood of reporting membership in a group that is the target of discrimination.

Religious discrimination is the greatest source of difference between Muslims and non-Muslims in the UK and Germany: in the UK, Muslims are 23.6% more likely than non-Muslims to report being a member of a group that faces religious discrimination. In Germany, the difference between the two groups is over 16%, with Muslims more likely to report religious discrimination of their religious group. Dutch Muslims are 29% more likely than non-Muslims to report that they are in a group that is the target of religious discrimination, while French Muslims are 15% more likely than non-Muslims to indicate religious discrimination of their group.

Table 5.2: Percentage of Muslims identifying with discriminated groups

	France		Germany		Netherlands		UK	
	Muslims	Other	Muslims	Other	Muslims	Other	Muslims	Other
Member of a group discriminated against in this country	41.6 (219)	8.6 (6,794)	33.5 (254)	4.0 (11,100)	43.6 (172)	6.5 (7,702)	29.1 (203)	12.7 (7,155)
Discrimination of respondent's group: religion	15.8 (221)	0.8 (6,821)	16.7 (269)	0.3 (11,135)	30.1 (180)	1.2 (7,722)	26.1 (211)	2.5 (7,198)
Discrimination of respondent's group: color or race	24.4 (221)	1.5 (6,821)	3.3 (269)	0.2 (11,135)	13.3 (180)	1.3 (7,722)	15.6 (211)	3.4 (7,199)
Discrimination of respondent's group: nationality	15.4 (221)	0.7 (6,821)	22.3 (269)	0.6 (11,136)	22.8 (180)	1.1 (7,722)	7.6 (211)	1.7 (7,199)
Discrimination of respondent's group: ethnicity	10.0 (221)	0.3 (6,821)	10.0 (269)	0.6 (11,136)	12.8 (180)	0.4 (7,722)	9.9 (212)	1.0 (7,199)

Data: ESS 2008-2002
Note: Number of respondents indicated in parentheses

Figure 5.1 depicts the ESS (2002–2008) results for all four states from the last table, regarding perceptions of Muslims and non-Muslims on the source of discrimination. The graph also displays the relative importance of **religion, race** and **nationality** as the source of the discrimination experienced by Muslims in each state.

Figure 5.1: Comparing Muslims' and non-Muslims' source of discrimination (%)

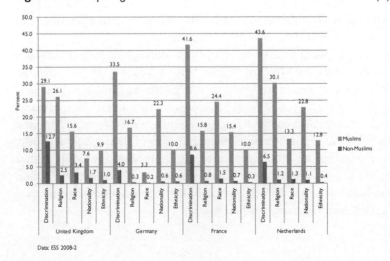

Data: ESS 2008-2

We compared the states in terms of Muslims' and non-Muslims' experiences of religious discrimination above. Regarding **race** as a trigger of discrimination against Muslims, in the UK Figure 5.1 indicates that Muslims are 12% more likely than non-Muslims to indicate racial discrimination against their group. In France, Muslims are 23% more likely than non-Muslims to report that their group faces racial discrimination, while the difference is 12% for the Netherlands. **Nationality** is the trigger of discrimination cited most often by Muslims in Germany, with Muslims about 22% more likely than non-Muslims to indicate discrimination on the basis of the nationality of their group. In France and the Netherlands, the differences were 15% and 22% respectively. The visibility of race in France and nationality in Germany to those who discriminate may reflect the states' expectations for integration by their largest minorities, who are the legacy of guest-worker recruiting from North Africa (in France) and Turkey (in Germany). While state policy is not drafted to promote discrimination, indications that visible minorities are not measuring up to official standards for integration can be utilized by those who discriminate to justify their behaviour.

Figure 5.2 shows an increase in the discrimination faced by Muslims in Europe during the first decade of the twenty-first century. The graph demonstrates the difference in Muslims' experience of discrimination between 2002 and 2008, ranging from an increase of over 11% in France to a smaller increase of 2.6% in the UK. Increases in Muslims' perceptions of discrimination for the Netherlands and Germany are 6.7% and 4.2% respectively.

Figure 5.2 Percentage of Muslims claiming membership in discriminated group

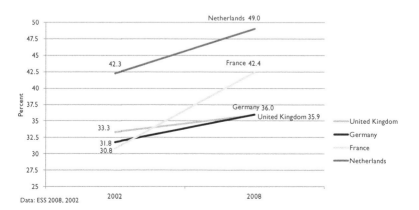

Growth in the pervasiveness of discrimination faced by Muslims in Europe reflected in these data may well have been triggered in part by the securitization of police and immigration policies related to Muslim minorities in Europe during this decade. In France, Germany and the Netherlands, the first decade of the twenty-first century saw the development of immigrant integration contracts reflective of perceptions of a threat posed by non-western minorities, especially Muslims, to European culture (cf. Guiraudon, 2008; Huysmans, 2006). The French reaction to perceptions of a 'Muslim threat' may have been most evident, with the highly publicized 2004 ban on headscarves in public schools (followed up later by the *niqab* or Islamic face veil ban that went into effect in April 2011), and the widespread belief that the 2005 riots reflected a failure of Muslim integration, rather than the socioeconomic and political exclusion of the religious minority. (See, for example, *The Washington Post*, 2005).

The multivariate results examining the impact of Muslim religious identification on respondents' reported membership in a group that is discriminated against are shown in Table 5.3, with results from the cumulative file containing respondents from all four years of ESS administration (2002, 2004, 2006, 2008) and individually for 2002 and 2008. (We present beginning and endpoint data in this section to demonstrate that while discrimination against Muslims grew during the decade, it was already significant early in the twenty-first century.) In all four states, Muslims are significantly more likely than non-Muslims to report that their group is discriminated against in both 2002 and 2008, even when we control for respondent's age, gender, income, citizenship, religiosity, unemployment, education, ideology, and satisfaction with government.

Data from two different data sources, gathered in multiple European states, over several different time periods during the last decade, present a consistent picture of discrimination against Muslims in key areas of life including employment, health care, housing, school, shopping and social life. The data also suggest that discrimination has increased throughout the decade. As we discussed in Chapter One, EU-MIDIS data were gathered by Gallup-Europe for the European Agency for Fundamental Rights. The European Social Survey was funded through the European Commission's Framework Programmes, the European Science Foundation, and national funding bodies in each of the 30 participating countries. The results urgently call for programmes to reduce the discrimination faced by Muslims. In its special report on multiple discrimination, discussed below, FRA points out that Muslims

Table 5.3: Effects of Muslim ID on respondents' reported membership in discriminated group

	France		Germany	
	Muslim	Full	Muslim	Full
Cumulative	.33***	.30***	.30***	.15***
	(7,012)	(4,540)	(11,353)	(8,042)
2008	.34***	.21***	.32***	.31***
	(2,066)	(1,734)	(2,730)	(2,080)
2002	.22***	.13***	.28***	.17***
	(1,489)	(1,381)	(2,897)	(2,611)
	Netherlands		United Kingdom	
	Muslim	Full	Muslim	Full
Cumulative	.37***	.32***	.16***	.12***
	(7,873)	(6471)	(7,358)	(5,363)
2008	.43***	.35***	.23***	.14**
	(1,769)	(1,494)	(2,338)	(1,764)
2002	.36***	.31***	.21***	.24***
	(2,355)	(2,192)	(2,038)	(1,821)

***p<.001, **p<.01, *p<.05, figures represent unstandardized OLS coefficients
Data: ESS 2008-2002
Note: Number of respondents indicated in parentheses
Full models control for R's age, gender, income, citizenship, religiosity, unemployment, education, ideology, satisfaction with government

are particularly vulnerable to discrimination triggered by more than one aspect of their identity.

Multiple discrimination

'Multiple discrimination' is a special focus of the European Union Agency for Fundamental Rights. (See FRA, 2010 05.) Discussion of the need for a 'Horizontal Directive' (FRA, 2010 05: 5) and the 'Genderace' project of the Seventh Framework Programme (European Union, 2010) both highlight the problem of multiple discrimination and the 'intersectionality' (European Union, 2010: 272) of axes of discrimination. The Genderace report (European Union, 2010: 32) cites Kimberlé Crenshaw as coining the term intersectionality in 1989 'to define a situation in which there is a specific type of discrimination, in which several grounds of discrimination interact concurrently. For instance, minority women may face specific types of discrimination, not experienced by minority men, because they are exposed to specific types of prejudices and stereotypes'. This report (European Union, 2010) follows the European Commission's (EC) 2007 study, *Tackling*

Multiple Discrimination: Practices, Policies and Laws, in which the problem of multiple discrimination and the significance of intersectionality on the impact of discrimination are examined. The 2007 EC report examines EU case law on this topic and compares it to the related legal terrain in Canada, Australia and the United States. Questionnaires were given to representatives from European member-state ministries, equality bodies and NGOs in preparation for related round-table discussions. The report ends with a series of recommendations for policy changes at the European and national levels. These recommendations urge research, legislative change, awareness raising, and the promotion of 'multiple ground NGOs' promoting the interests of groups whose members are the targets of intersectional discrimination (cf. European Commission, 2007: 53–56).

EU-MIDIS (FRA, 2010 05), the *Data in Focus Report on Multiple Discrimination*, compares EU-MIDIS results regarding experiences of multiple discrimination to the findings from the European Commission's *Special Eurobarometer* on discrimination (Number 296). Identical questions were asked in the two surveys, but, as the EU-MIDIS Multiple Discrimination report notes (FRA, 2010 05: 10), 'data collection for EU-MIDIS was mainly carried out in urban areas while the *Eurobarometer* surveys are based on nationwide samples of respondents; therefore the results have to be cautiously interpreted as reflecting the locations where the two surveys were conducted'.

The *Eurobarometer 296* results provide a glimpse of the general population's perceptions of the prevalence of discrimination in Europe. Overall, FRA (2010 05: 8) explains:

> more respondents from the majority population, who were interviewed for *Special Eurobarometer 296,* considered discrimination to be *widespread* [emphasis in text] across all six grounds asked about. Strikingly, 62% of the general population thought that discrimination on the basis of ethnic origin was widespread in comparison with 55% of the ethnic minority and immigrant respondents, **and 45% of the majority population in comparison with 33% of minority interviewees considered that discrimination on the basis of religion or belief was widespread**. (emphasis ours).

Neither EU-MIDIS (FRA, 2010 05) nor *Eurobarometer 296* permits us to compare the perceptions of Muslims in Europe to what FRA refers to as the 'general population' (phrase used in quote above) examined in *Eurobarometer 296*. We can, however, consider (as FRA, 2010 05: 9 does), the degree to which the minorities surveyed in EU-MIDIS perceive the extent of discrimination in Europe to be greater than does the *Eurobarometer's* 'general population'. This comparison suggests that the majority and the minority population most likely to be Muslim do not differ greatly about the level of discrimination in their member state. For example, in Germany 56% of *Eurobarometer's* general population indicated that discrimination based on ethnic or immigrant origin was very or fairly widespread, while 52% of the Turkish population in Germany did. The French North African and Sub-Saharan African populations were 88% and 87% in agreement with this statement, not far from the 76% figure for the French general population surveyed by *Eurobarometer*. In the Netherlands, EU-MIDIS (FRA, 2009 02: 9) found that the Turkish population had the most self-identified Muslims. In EU-MIDIS (FRA, 2010 05: 9), 61% of Turkish respondents in the Netherlands indicated that discrimination based on ethnic or immigrant origin is very or fairly widespread, less than the *Eurobarometer's* general population in the Netherlands, 79% of whom agreed with the statement. In the UK, 69% of the *Eurobarometer's* general population agreed with the statement; there was no Muslim ethnic group sampled for EU-MIDIS in the UK.

Overall, these comparisons underscore the agreement between majority and minority group members in perceptions of how widespread the discrimination is against those groups most likely to be Muslim. These results on the agreement regarding the extensiveness of discrimination against Muslim minorities provide a political basis for both national and European action to reduce it.

Specifically regarding multiple discrimination, EU-MIDIS reports that for the member state populations involved in its study, 14% of the ethnic minority and immigrant respondents (clustered in urban areas) were discriminated against on multiple grounds, and 23% of respondents were discriminated against on one ground. The *Eurobarometer* results, based on nationwide surveying of majority group members in the EU-27, are somewhat lower: only 3% reported having been discriminated against on multiple grounds, and 12% on one ground (FRA, 2010 05: 10). Citing these discrepancies as evidence, FRA reports that the findings 'indicate that minority respondents interviewed in EU-MIDIS experienced what they considered to be discrimination on the basis of a single ground and on multiple grounds more often than the majority population interviewed in *Special Eurobarometer* survey 296' (FRA, 2010 05: 10).

Examining those EU-MIDIS respondents who reported having been discriminated against on multiple grounds, FRA (2010 05: 13) reports that for both males and females, 93% were discriminated against on the basis of *ethnic or immigrant origin*. For this same group of respondents reporting multiple discrimination, *'religion or belief'* was a trigger for discrimination for 72% of males and 56% of females. *Age* was next in importance as a trigger for discrimination in this group (30% of males, and 29% of females), with 'other reasons' (21% males, 15% females), 'disability' (13% males, 9% females), and 'sexual orientation' (11% males, 9% females) following in importance.

FRA offers the following explanation of the importance of these findings on multiple discrimination for Muslim respondents, highlighting the salience of religion as an aspect of personal identity.

> In particular, Muslim respondents indicated that religion was either 'very' or 'fairly' important in their lives – 91% of North Africans and 85% of Turkish respondents indicated this to be the case – while 90% of Sub-Saharan Africans, coming from a mixture of different religious backgrounds, also indicated that religion was important to them. This suggests that identity – encompassing factors such as ethnicity and religion – can be experienced as intersectional discrimination by many minority ethnic groups in Europe, meaning that different grounds of discrimination interact and are hard to distinguish from each other. This interpretation is useful to keep in mind when looking to understand high levels of reported discrimination on multiple grounds by specific aggregate groups. (FRA, 2010 05: 12)

Slightly more men than women reported multiple discrimination (53% of men, 47% of women) on all of the grounds examined, except with regard to gender. Women were almost twice as likely as men to report having been discriminated against on the basis of gender (44% of women vs. 24% of men). But men experienced greater levels of multiple discrimination than women, and FRA stresses the importance of this finding for economically active males. FRA indicates that 'most respondents who said they had been discriminated against indicated that this occurred most often when looking for work and when at work' (FRA, 2010 05: 12), and that 'respondents who are more exposed to multiple discrimination tend to come from socially disadvantaged backgrounds ... since as many as 46% of them were located in the lowest income quartile recorded in the survey ... with 21% of the unemployed reporting discrimination on more than one ground compared with 12% of those who were employed' (FRA, 2010 05: 13). In addition, FRA reports that '[w]hen looking at the age of respondents reporting discrimination on the basis of ethnicity/immigrant origin for the different areas of everyday life asked about, a pattern of heightened exposure to discrimination emerges among younger respondents .. younger people, namely those in age categories 16–24 and 25–34 years, generally experience higher levels of discrimination ... [especially with regard to ethnicity/ethnic origin]' (FRA, 2010 05: 15).

While all of the findings in the EU-MIDIS study (FRA, 2010 05) on multiple discrimination do not apply exclusively to Muslims, the religious minority is singled out by FRA as particularly vulnerable to experiencing discrimination triggered by several sources (religion, ethnicity, gender, age), and Muslim youth are the subject of a related study by FRA (2010). In the next section we look within the Muslim population at those demographic groups of Muslims seen as most vulnerable to dissatisfaction in Europe to consider the extent to which these personal characteristics influence the sense of being in a group that is discriminated against. We further examine the perspective of Muslim youth with regard to their situation in Europe in Chapter Six, focused on general well-being.

Perceptions of membership in a group that is discriminated against among Muslims deemed 'vulnerable'

Table 5.4 continues the examination (using ESS data) begun in the preceding table (5.3) by investigating respondents' reported membership in a group that is discriminated against. While Muslims were significantly more likely than non-Muslims to indicate membership in a group that is discriminated against throughout the first decade of the twenty-first century (as reported in Table 5.3 above), Table 5.4 allows us to begin assessing the impact of this perception within the Muslim population. Young Muslims (15–29) are more likely than others to indicate that they are in a group targeted by discrimination: 11% more likely in France, 13% more likely in Germany, close to 13% more likely in the Netherlands, and close to 9% more likely in the UK. These differences underscore the critical importance of member state and European efforts to reduce barriers imposed by discrimination and thereby smooth the path toward full involvement in the society not only for Muslims in general, but particularly for those under 30.

Table 5.4: Percentage of Muslims in vulnerable groups claiming membership in discriminated group

	France	Germany	Netherlands	UK
Age groups				
15-29	48.8	40.7	51.6	33.7
Others	37.3	27.2	38.9	25.0
50 and older	30.0	23.7	43.5[1]	27.6
Others	44.4	34.0	43.6	29.5
Religiosity				
High (7-10)	37.1	36.5	47.9	29.1
Others	47.1	29.2	32.0	28.6
Low (0-3)	60.0	35.1	28.6[2]	14.3[1]
Others	39.0	33.7	45.2	29.6
Gender				
Male	47.8	33.3	34.7	25.0
Female	34.6	33.3	54.5	34.1
Citizenship				
National	46.4	20.0	46.0	31.3
Foreign	30.9	39.9	32.4	12.0[1]
Place of birth				
National	52.0	37.1	53.3	45.3
Foreign	32.5	32.1	38.7	20.2

Data: ESS 2008-2002
[1] 10<N<30   [2] N<10

It is unlikely that they can fully develop their talents and contribute their abilities to states in which they are the target of discrimination.

There is considerable variation among the states in our study with regard to the relationship between high religiosity and perception of being in a group that faces discrimination. Muslims who are highly religious in France are 10% less likely to report that they are in a group targeted by discrimination. In fact, the least religious are most likely to report discrimination in France by a wide margin: they are over 21% more likely than other Muslims to feel part of a group that is discriminated against. The reasons for this finding are not clear, but one possibility is that, in France, the politicization of religious symbols in the public arena has been interpreted by the least religious Muslims as directed at stigmatizing Islam in France. More religious Muslims in France may be less concerned about their place as citizens in the state than are the least religious. Those Muslims who are highly religious in France may feel that the doors are open to practising Islam, while for the least religious French Muslims the practice of Islam may seem less important than the right to display one's religious identity in the civic arena. This explanation receives further support in the findings for the other three states, none of which have gone as far as France in legally suppressing expressions of religious group membership in public institutions. In the UK, for example, there is no difference between highly religious Muslims and others in their sense of being in a group that is highly discriminated against, a finding that may reflect the relatively open policy toward religiously identifying garb still in place in the UK, despite recent political controversy over face veils in the public arena. In Germany and the Netherlands, highly religious Muslims are more likely to feel that they are in a group that is the target of discrimination: highly religious Muslim respondents are 7% more likely in Germany and close to 16% more likely in the Netherlands to make this claim. In both Germany and the Netherlands, there is considerable discussion of religiosity as leading toward 'seductive fundamentalism' (cf. Heitemeyer, Müller and Schröder, 1998; Sarrazin, 2010) and 'parallel societies' (De Wijk, 2006; Jackson and Parkes, 2007). But neither of these states has a uniform policy banning religious garb for all school children and face veils in any public institutions, and this lack of uniformity may soften the sense of discrimination among less religious Muslims in these states, in contrast to their counterparts in France.

The importance of the politicization of religious identity fostered by recent French policies may also be reflected in the gender differences in identification with a group that is discriminated against. In France, Muslim male respondents are about 13% more likely than women to feel part of such a group. Despite the fact that the dress codes apply to Muslim women, Muslim men are more likely to feel victimized by discrimination. This is not the case in the other three states. There is no difference between men and women in perceptions of discrimination in Germany; in the Netherlands, Muslim women are about 20% more likely to feel part of a group targeted by discrimination, and in the UK 9% more likely. One of the unintended consequences of recent state policy implementing Muslim dress codes in public in France might be the sense of alienation of Muslim men, who are more likely than those in the other states to feel that their group is discriminated against. In addition, the French policy permitting random police checks for identity documentation targets young minority men, no doubt contributing to Muslim young men's sense of being part of a group that is discriminated against.

In three of the four states, citizenship is not a protective factor in reducing the impact of discrimination. In France, for example, Muslim citizens are 16% more likely to feel part of a group targeted by discrimination; in the Netherlands, they are 14% more likely, and in the UK, 19%. Only in Germany does citizenship appear to provide protection from the sense of discrimination. This is a positive sign for Germany, especially in light of their recently more open citizenship policies implemented in 2001, enabling Muslims of immigrant background to choose that option for themselves and their children. Birth in the member state does not appear to reduce the sense of discrimination for Muslims; Muslims born in the state are between 5% and 25% more likely to feel part of a group facing discrimination than those born elsewhere. In the UK, those born abroad are least likely to feel part of a targeted group, but those born in the UK are closer to their peers in the other three member states in feeling part of a group that is discriminated against. In Germany, the difference between groups is smallest, only 5%, but still in the direction of those born in the state more likely to claim discrimination of their group.

This look at perceptions of discrimination within the Muslim population provides several important clues for policy makers regarding the impact of state policy toward Muslims. Policies focused on keeping manifestation of religious identity out of the public arena, and the associated hostility toward those at whom such policies are targeted may serve to exclude Muslims from full membership in European states. To some extent, the impact that these policies have on non-Muslims may be the heart of the problem: such policies may send a signal that Muslims do not belong, making interactions between Muslims and non-Muslims more likely to reflect that attitude.

SIX

The general well-being of Muslims in Europe

The well-being of European Muslims is key to their ability to fully develop and apply their talents to the advantage of Europe and its member states. State level efforts to assess well-being have been promoted by David Cameron (Mulholland and Watt, 2010) and Nicholas Sarkozy (Stiglitz, Sen and Fitoussi, 2009), and are also evident in Germany (Gjoksi, 2010) and the Netherlands (de Jonge, 2009), as we discussed in Chapter Two. These are being considered in tandem with the European benchmarking discussions (European Parliament, 2007). In the spirit of these projects, we examine in this chapter the life satisfaction and general happiness of Muslims in Europe along with their well-being in several specific key areas of life (European Parliament, 2007), including income, health, education, employment, awareness of political information, and access to information sources.

Muslim youth

The attitudes and achievements of young Muslims may be the best indicator of the general well-being of the religious minority in Europe. A 2008/9 survey commissioned by the European Union Agency for Fundamental Rights with youth 12–18 years old provides a glimpse of the background and life chances of Muslim young people in comparison to their non-Muslim counterparts in two of the states we are examining, France and the UK (FRA, 2010). (Spain was also included in the study.) Noting 'the absence of evidence about the experience of young Muslims in EU Member States' and the extent to which it frustrates policy development, FRA (2010: 16) requested this research from 'a consortium of three academic institutions experienced in the area of survey research with young people ... from minority backgrounds ... the Universidad de Castilla-La Mancha ... the lead university; ... Université de Bordeaux; and the University of Edinburgh' (FRA, 2010: 16). The research team in each of the states surveyed 1,000 youths aged 12–18 years old in the member state, equally representing Muslims and non-Muslims, as well as males and females, 'to explore the experiences, attitudes and behaviours of Muslim and non–Muslim youths' (FRA, 2010: 16).

Table 6.1 summarizes some of these results (FRA, 2010). The vast majority of Muslim youth were born in their European country of residence (81% of those in France, 73% of those in the UK; ESS results compare favourably), and in that regard are quite similar to their non–Muslim counterparts (who were not more than 10% more likely to have been born in the European state) (FRA, 2010: 25). (In the ESS 2002–08 sample, among French Muslims aged 15–18, 100% (N=16) were born in France; 66.7% (N=24) of German Muslims aged 15–18 were born in Germany; 89.3% (N=28) of Dutch Muslims aged 15–18 were born in the Netherlands; 81.0% (N=21) were born in the UK.)

Table 6.1 Background characteristics of youth 12–18, FRA Comparative Study (%)

	France		UK	
	Muslims	Non-Muslims	Muslims	Non-Muslims
Employment (in work)				
Father	68	86	75	79
Mother	54	83	23	74
(Care for family)	29	9	61	14
Born in residence country	81	91	73	81
Dominant language				
(spoken all/most)	50	61	42	50
Unfairly picked on	28	22	25	25
Discrimination by adults when out w/ friends	18	10	5	10
Interest in national politics				
(very or quite)	50	48	45	38
Level of concern state of world				
(very or quite worried)	80	81	80	75
Degree life affected by world		·		
(many or some ways)	62	58	82	80

Source: European Agency for Fundamental Rights, 2010 (p. 24, 25, 28, 36, 57-59)

Muslim youth are also within 11% as likely as non–Muslim 12–18-year-olds to speak the dominant language of their European state all or most of the time. About half of Muslim youth in France speak French all or most of the time (in comparison to 61% of non–Muslim youth), and about 42% of Muslim youth in the UK usually speak English (in contrast to 50% of non–Muslim youth) (FRA, 2010: 28). The language-use statistics provided in the FRA study of Muslim young people suggest that any problems of host nation language acquisition in France and Britain have little to do with the presence of Muslims: Muslim youth represent a small proportion of the French and UK populations, and they are about as likely to communicate in the European host language as their non-Muslim counterparts.

Table 6.1a: Muslims' dominant language usage by age

	France		Germany		Netherlands		UK	
	15-20	21+	15-20	21+	15-20	21+	15-20	21+
Percentage of Muslims speaking country's chief language as primary language spoken at home	72.5	63.7	44.7	40.1	63.2	59.3	67.5	41.5
Percentage of Muslims speaking country's chief language as secondary language spoken at home	0	11	55.3	54.6	10.8	19.4	4.7	6.5
Total percentage	72.5	74.8	100	94.7	74	78.7	72.2	48

Data: ESS 2008, 2006, 2004, 2002

Table 6.1a, providing ESS data on Muslims' dominant language usage by age, supports the FRA survey results discussed above, and indicates that for all four states in our analysis the majority of Muslim 15–20-year-olds speak the primary language of the European state at home. For the 15–20-year-old age group (slightly older than the data available in the FRA survey) in France, French is the primary language spoken at home for about close to 73% of Muslims. In the UK, about 68% of Muslims aged 15–20 speak English as the primary language at home and another 5% or so speak English as the secondary language at home. With ESS we can also look at Germany, where all of the Muslim respondents aged 15–20 speak German at home as either the primary (45%) or secondary (55%) language, and the Netherlands, where 63% of the 15–20-year-old Muslims speak Dutch as the primary language at home, and another 11% converse in Dutch as the secondary language at home. The total percentage figures indicate that in all four states, close to three-quarters or more of Muslims in the 15–20-year-old age group converse in the chief language of their European nation at home. In the UK, 15–20-year-old Muslims are 24% more likely to speak English at home than those who were 21 or over (48% of whom speak English at home); the differences between 15–20-year-olds and those 21 and over were not as great in the other states, ranging from 2–5%, varying in direction. Germany stands out in two ways: first, Muslim

15–20-year-olds are 19–28% *less* likely than their counterparts in the other three states to make the chief language of their European nation their primary language at home and, secondly, they are 44–55% *more* likely than youth in the other states to use the chief language of their European nation as the secondary language at home. In Germany young Muslims do not differ greatly from Muslims aged 21 and over in language usage, so we cannot suggest that the young are accommodating their parents' language abilities at home. Rather, it appears that while most Muslims in Germany learn the national language, over half of them choose to use it at home only on a secondary basis. In light of the fact that it was difficult for those not of German blood to obtain German citizenship until implementation of the new naturalization law in 2001, the language preference data may reflect a tentative identification with Germany on the part of Muslims because of their uncertain welcome. It is not fair to say that Muslims in Germany fail to learn German; they are more likely to speak it at home than are Muslims in the other three states. But they are also more likely to choose it as a secondary language at home.

Regarding the difficulties of youth, FRA (2010) results (in Table 6.1) suggest that Muslim 12–18-year-olds experience them at levels not dramatically different from that of their non-Muslim peers: in France, 28% of Muslim young people indicated in response to the survey that they were 'unfairly picked on' (in comparison to 22% of non-Muslim youth). In the United Kingdom, 25% of both Muslim and non-Muslim youth responded that they were unfairly picked on. (See discussion in FRA, 2010: 36.) But closer examination of these data underscores a problem that FRA and the European Commission refer to as 'multiple discrimination' (cf. European Commission, 2007; FRA, 2010 05), and that it places a greater burden on Muslim than on non-Muslim youth. In data not shown here, the three most commonly cited 'reasons given for being picked on' by Muslim youth in both the French and UK surveys are 'cultural background' (46% France, 36% UK), 'religion' (31% France, 44% UK), and 'skin colour' (26% France, 45% UK). For non-Muslim youth in both states, religion is not a commonly cited factor in their discrimination. (See FRA, 2010: 36 for further discussion of these results.) FRA (2010: 37) also examined the extent to which 12–18-year-olds experienced discrimination by adults when out with friends. (See Table 6.1.) Muslim youth in France were 8% more likely to have encountered the problem than were non-Muslim youth. In the UK, though, Muslim youth were 5% less likely than non-Muslim young people to report discrimination by adults as a problem. (In Chapter Three, we reported that Muslim 15–29-year-old ESS respondents in France were significantly less likely to trust the police (Table 3.5) than were older Muslims, and that young UK Muslims had greater trust in the police than their older counterparts. Both the FRA and ESS data paint the same picture of young Muslims' interactions with police or adults in public. In results reported in the FRA study but not shown here, school/college appears to be a 'safe' zone for Muslims, when it comes to differential treatment by adults. In France, for example, about 10% of Muslim young people felt that they experienced 'worse' treatment than others by adults in school/college, just under the figure for non-Muslim youth. Similar results characterize the UK (FRA, 2010: 38).

Most of the Muslim youth surveyed in the FRA (2010) study were in households where their father (or 'male carer') was employed. In the UK, there was little difference between Muslim and non-Muslim youth in this regard, with 75% of the fathers of Muslim youth employed, and 79% of those of non-Muslim youth. Muslim youth in France were 18% less likely than non-Muslim youth to report that their father was working (68% of Muslim youths' fathers were working, in contrast to 86% of those of non-Muslims). The mothers of Muslim youth were less likely to be working than those of non-Muslim youth. In France, for example, just over half of the mothers of Muslim youth were employed, in contrast to 83% of the mothers of non-Muslim youth. The mothers of UK 12–18-year-olds were 51% less likely to be working than those of non-Muslim youth. (Twenty-three percent of UK Muslim youths' mothers were working in contrast to 74% of the mothers of non-Muslim youth.) In addition, Muslim youth were more likely to report that their mother 'cares for the family' than were non-Muslim youth. Twenty-nine percent of Muslim youth in France (in contrast to 9% of non-Muslim youth), and 61% of Muslim youth in the UK (vs. 14% of non-Muslim youth) indicated that their mother 'cares for the family'. Whether this difference between Muslim and non-Muslim youth in the likelihood of their mothers working is due to mothers' greater preference to remain at home or to their inability to obtain work is not examined in the survey.

Muslim young people in France and the UK express a great deal of interest in national politics and world affairs. (See FRA, 2010: 57–59.) In both states Muslim 12–18-year-olds are slightly more likely than non-Muslim youth to indicate that they are very or quite interested in national politics (50% of Muslim youth in France, vs. 48% of non-Muslim youth; 45% of Muslim youth in the UK, in contrast to 38% of non-Muslim youth). With regard to their level of concern about the state of the world, about 80% of both groups of youth in France are very or quite worried; in the UK, Muslim youth are 5% more likely than non-Muslim young people to be very or quite worried about the state of the world (with 80% of Muslim young people very or quite worried in contrast to 75% of non-Muslims). Similarly, there is little difference between Muslim young people and non-Muslim youth in terms of their perception of the extent to which their lives are affected by the state of the world today: 62% of Muslim youth in France, in contrast to 58% of non-Muslim youth there, indicated that their life was affected by things going on in the world in some or many ways. This figure was higher in the UK, with 82% of Muslim youth, and 80% of non-Muslim youth indicating that their life was affected in some or many ways by things going on in the world today. In results not shown here, both groups were quite similar in their list of top global social issues of great concern to them. In France, for example, both groups rated *poverty, racism, global warming* and *conflict between different cultures* as the top four global social issues that they are most worried about. Unlike the non-Muslim respondents, Muslim youth placed *racism* ahead of *global warming* as second in their indications of concern. The list of top concerns was also quite similar for youth in the UK, with Muslims rating *conflict between cultures, terrorist attacks, global warming/climate change* and *racism* as the top concerns; non-Muslim youth placed global warming first in the frequency of concerns cited, followed by *terrorist attacks, poverty, disease and illness, racism* and *conflict between different cultures*.

Overall, the results of the FRA study suggest that Muslim youth in France and the UK are at least as willing and able as their non-Muslim counterparts to contribute to the advancement of the member state in which they live, and to support the European project. Muslim youth may also be attitudinally well-placed to help European states move forward politically and socially: they are slightly more interested in national politics than their non-Muslim peers and are a bit more likely to recognize the impact of globalization on their lives. They are as concerned about the 'state of the world' as their non-Muslim peers, but not much more so. The image of Muslim youth as transfixed by foreign policy, uninterested in national politics, or alienated by the unfairness of their peers, adults and school officials toward them is not at all supported by these data. Muslim youth in France and the UK, as reflected in the survey, appear ready to take advantage of those educational, employment and other opportunities for success that become available to them in their member states.

To directly assess the level of alienation and isolation among Muslim youth, FRA used a version of the Multidimensionality Personality

Questionnaire (Tellegen, 1982), adapted for use with young people (Smith et al., 2001). The six-item scale examines several aspects of 'alienation, social isolation and feelings of persecution' (FRA, 2010: 39). In results not shown here, FRA (2010: 39) found 'no significant difference in average alienation scores between the Muslim and non-Muslim youths' in France and the UK and that most of the young people in the study 'did not feel highly alienated'. In an additional analysis, FRA (2010: 38) sought to measure the contentment of 12–18-year-olds in the study by asking 'how happy they are with their lives as a whole at that moment in time'. The results indicated that

> the vast majority of young people ... felt either 'very' or 'quite' happy with their lives ... [and that] there was no significant difference between Muslim and non-Muslim respondents in ... the United Kingdom in response to this question. In France, the only difference between the groups was that Muslim respondents were more likely to report being 'very happy' and less likely to be 'quite happy' compared to non-Muslims. (FRA, 2010: 38–39)

All available evidence indicates that Muslim youth are at least as happy in their European homes as their non-Muslim counterparts. We move from this consideration of Muslim young people to consider all age groups within the Muslim population, as reflected in the European Social Survey for the states we are investigating. We reconsider youth at the end of the chapter, in consideration of the well-being of those groups within the Muslim population most commonly thought of as vulnerable to dissatisfaction in Europe.

Happiness and life satisfaction of Muslims

We look now again at all age groups within the Muslim population. ESS data allow us to compare Muslims to non-Muslims on several dimensions of general well-being: happiness and life satisfaction, education, employment, income, health and information. Tables 6.2 and 6.3 demonstrate that while Muslims are slightly less happy and satisfied than non-Muslims, the gap is not as wide as the literature would suggest, and it is not statistically significant once respondents' background characteristics are controlled (in Table 6.3, with controls for age, gender, income, citizenship, religiosity, unemployment, years of education, ideology, satisfaction with government and urban residence). Though Muslims are perceived as 'part of the underclass of Europe'

Table 6.2: Comparison of Muslims and non-Muslims on indicators of general well-being and health

	France		Germany		Netherlands		UK	
	Muslims	Others	Muslims	Others	Muslims	Others	Muslims	Others
Average life satisfaction	5.99 (221)	6.39* (6,814)	6.62 (268)	6.89 (11,108)	7.01 (180)	7.64*** (7,708)	7.11 (211)	7.13 (7,179)
Average happiness	7.06 (221)	7.26 (6,815)	6.82 (268)	7.16** (11,091)	7.35 (180)	7.81*** (7,709)	7.39 (212)	7.56 (7,192)
Average monthly household income	5.41 (126)	6.61*** (4,650)	5.36 (188)	6.32*** (8,617)	5.26 (152)	7.09*** (6,647)	5.92 (158)	6.86*** (5,841)
Feelings about income (%)								
Living comfortably on present income	9.2	21.4	9.8	29.2	14.1	50.6	24.5	40.3
Coping on present income	40.4	49.4	51.1	55.4	46.3	39.3	49.1	44.4
Difficult on present income	39.9	23.6	30.5	11.8	27.7	8.2	21.2	12.5
Very difficult on present income	10.6 (218)	5.6 (6,686)	8.6 (266)	3.6 (11,020)	11.9 (177)	1.9 (7,636)	5.2 (212)	2.8 (7,115)
General health	3.87 (221)	3.76 (6,820)	3.83** (267)	3.66 (11,119)	3.71 (180)	3.87** (7,719)	4.07 (212)	3.98 (7,188)
Current state of health care in respondents' country	6.88*** (221)	5.93 (6,805)	6.22*** (265)	4.63 (10,999)	6.48*** (176)	5.78 (7,654)	6.08*** (211)	5.37 (7,160)
Hampered in daily activities by health (%)								
Yes, a lot	6.3	6.1	4.1	5.6	3.3	5.7	5.2	8.0
Yes, to some extent	10.0	16.3	14.5	21.4	19.5	19.6	5.7	15.0
No	83.7	77.6	81.4	73.0	77.2	74.7	89.1	77.0

Data: ESS 2008, 2006, 2004, 2002 ***p<.001, **p<.01, *p<.05
Note: Number of respondents indicated in parentheses

Table 6.3: Impact of Muslim religious identification on indicators of general well-being and health in bivariate and full multivariate models

	France		Germany		Netherlands		UK	
	Muslim	Full	Muslim	Full	Muslim	Full	Muslim	Full
Life satisfaction[1]	-.40* (7,034)	-.38 (4,521)	-.27 (11,376)	-.09 (8,037)	-.63*** (7,887)	-.25 (6,450)	-.03 (7,389)	.24 (5,425)
Happiness[1]	-.21 (7,035)	-.05 (4,521)	-.34** (11,358)	-.28 (8,027)	-.46*** (7,888)	-.14 (6,442)	-.17 (7,430)	.07 (5,429)
Household income[2]	-1.20*** (4,775)	-1.06*** (4,552)	-.96*** (8,804)	-.53* (8,038)	-1.83*** (6,797)	-1.04*** (6,453)	-.94*** (5,998)	-.93 (5,432)
Living comfortably on present income[1][3]	-.98*** (6,906)	-.78* (4,569)	-1.33*** (11,300)	-.53 (8,190)	-1.81*** (7,830)	-.96*** (6,520)	-.72*** (7,344)	-.35 (5,547)
General health[1]	.11 (7,040)	-.02 (4,522)	.17** (11,368)	-.09 (8,033)	-.16** (7,898)	-.21** (6,451)	.09 (7,399)	.13 (5,426)
Current state of health care[1]	.95*** (7,025)	.42* (4,517)	1.59*** (11,263)	.63** (8,004)	.70*** (7,830)	.57*** (6,417)	.71*** (7,369)	.44* (5,411)
Hampered in daily activities by health[1][3]	.02 (7,039)	.14 (4,570)	-.38 (11,382)	-.08 (8,191)	-.50 (7,902)	-.03 (6,533)	-.48 (7,396)	-.67 (5,547)

***p<.001, **p<.01, *p<.05, figures are unstandardized OLS regression coefficients unless noted
Data: ESS 2008-2
Note: Number of respondents indicated in parentheses
[1] Full models control for R's level of age, gender, income, citizenship, religiosity, unemployment, years of education, ideology, satisfaction with government and urban residence
[2] Full models control for R's level of age, gender, citizenship, religiosity, unemployment, years of education, ideology, satisfaction with government and urban residence
[3] Logistic Regression

(Cesari, 2009: 9), overall they do not fall far from non-Muslims on either of these ESS measures of general well-being. The findings support the image of Muslims portrayed by results in the previous chapters where Muslims' trust in the justice system and its agencies, as well as in the political system, was for the most part close to that of non-Muslims, and sometimes greater. The image of Muslims as dissatisfied with Europe does not fit these data.

The indicators of specific aspects of well-being in Tables 6.2 and 6.3 allow us to provide more detailed comparisons of the general well-being of Muslims and non-Muslims in the European member states. Household income from all sources is on average greater for non-Muslims than for Muslims (a decile or so greater on average in France, Germany, and the UK, and almost two deciles greater in the Netherlands). These differences in average income are statistically significant, even after controls have been imposed (see Table 6.3), and are reflected in respondents' attitude about income (in Table 6.2). In France, for example, about half of Muslim respondents indicate that it is difficult or very difficult to live on their present income, in contrast to 29% of non-Muslims. About 39% of Muslims in Germany find it difficult or very difficult to live on the present income, in comparison to 15% of non-Muslims. Dutch respondents show the greatest difference between Muslims and non-Muslims in this category, with about 40% of Muslims reporting that they find life on their current income difficult or very difficult in contrast to 10% of non-Muslims. The UK difference is about 11%, with 26% of Muslims and 15% of non-Muslims placing themselves in the categories of greatest difficulty. These differences between groups on comfort with ability to live on present income (with Muslims reporting more difficulty than non-Muslims) are statistically significant after controls have been imposed in all states but Germany.

Muslims' appraisal of their general health is generally more positive than that of non-Muslims in three of the four European states. The differences between the two groups are not large, and are statistically significant only in Germany (where Muslims are more positive) and the Netherlands (where Muslims are less positive about their health) in both the bivariate relationship (Table 6.2) and in the multivariate models (in Table 6.3) which control for the full set of individual background characteristics.

Not surprisingly, in light of the findings in previous chapters, Muslims also appraise more positively the state of their European country's health system than do non-Muslims. These differences are statistically significant in the multivariate equations where the full set of controls for individuals' background characteristics are imposed (Table 6.3). Whether Muslims' perception of the national health care systems in Europe are more positive than that of non-Muslims because these systems compare favourably to those experienced by previous generations of their family before immigration to Europe, or because Muslims have a more positive outlook overall than non-Muslims is not clear from these data. But even with controls (for respondents' age, gender, income, citizenship, religiosity, unemployment, years of education, ideology, and satisfaction with government) Muslims in these European states rate the state of the health care system better than do their non-Muslim counterparts. Tables 6.2 and 6.3 indicate that in all four states Muslims are also less likely to feel hampered by their health, though the contrast with non-Muslims is not statistically significant.

Table 6.4 shows that the average level of education between Muslims and non-Muslims is not significantly different in the UK and France, a pattern that is explained further below in discussion of Cesari's analysis; but in Germany and the Netherlands the ESS data show notable differences between the religious minority and others. For these two states, the greatest differences can be seen in the percentage of the population in each group with less than a lower secondary education. In Germany, Muslims are about six times as likely as non-Muslims to be in this category (about 18% in contrast to about 3% of non-Muslims); in the Netherlands Muslims are just over twice as likely (about 21% as opposed to 10% of non-Muslims). Furthermore, in all of the states but Britain, Muslims indicate that they have not improved their knowledge or skills during the last 12 months. Yet it appears that Muslims' positive

Table 6.4: Comparison of Muslims and non-Muslims on indicators of education

	France		Germany		Netherlands		UK	
	Muslims	Other	Muslims	Other	Muslims	Other	Muslims	Other
Average years of education	12.45 (215)	12.23 (6,740)	10.53 (262)	13.19*** (10,993)	11.38 (179)	12.97*** (7,674)	12.93 (203)	13.04 (7,138)
State of education in country	5.19 (220)	4.99 (6,711)	5.84*** (250)	4.43 (10,687)	6.28*** (176)	5.77 (7,280)	6.26*** (209)	5.54 (7,005)
Level of education (%)								
Less than lower secondary education	19.5	18.4	17.9	3.2	20.7	10.2	24.3	27.0
Lower secondary education completed	18.6	14.3	30.4	11.8	37.4	31.9	18.6	24.2
Upper secondary education completed	35.7	40.1	40.3	53.2	23.5	27.7	23.3	13.6
Post-sec., non-tertiary education completed	0	0.2	6.1	6.8	6.1	6.2	---	---
Tertiary education completed	26.2 (221)	27.1 (6,815)	5.3 (263)	25.0 (11,096)	12.3 (179)	23.9 (7,709)	33.8 (210)	35.1 (7,084)
Improve knowledge, skills last 12 months (%)								
Yes	24.4	28.8	21.3	31.1	28.3	37.8	37.6	36.8
No	75.6 (221)	71.2 (6,811)	78.7 (267)	68.9 (11,108)	71.7 (180)	62.2 (7,686)	62.4 (210)	63.2 (7,162)

Data: ESS 2008, 2006, 2004, 2002
***p<.001, **p<.01, *p<.05
Note: Number of respondents indicated in parentheses

evaluation of state agencies extends to those providing education: in all four states Muslims rate the 'state of education in the country' more favourably than do non-Muslims, and these relationships are statistically significant in all but one of the states (France).

The data in Table 6.5 show that Muslims are less likely than non-Muslims to have responsibility for supervizing others at work in all of the states. Muslims report that they are contracted to work roughly as many hours (excluding overtime) as non-Muslims, but in two of the states (the UK and France), non-Muslims report working three and four hours less respectively on average per week, and these differences are statistically significant. They are also more likely to have been unemployed and seeking a job for over three months, a difference that is not great in the UK, but ranges from 15% to over 20% in the other three states. In the Netherlands, for example, Muslims are about 16% more likely than non-Muslims to be in this category of unemployment (33% as opposed to 17% for non-Muslims). In France, Muslims are 24% more likely than non-Muslims to have experienced this long-term unemployment (56% of Muslims as opposed to 32% of non-Muslims); in Germany, they are 15% more likely to have faced it (42% of Muslims, vs. 27% of non-Muslims); and in the UK, Muslims are only about 3% more likely than non-Muslims to have experienced long-term unemployment while seeking work (25% of Muslims in contrast to 22% of non-Muslims). Results for the question on main activity indicates that Muslims are about twice as likely as non-Muslims to be in full-time education in France (19% of Muslims as opposed to 8% of non-Muslims), and close to that in Germany and the Netherlands. The difference is even greater in the UK, with about 20% of Muslims and 8% of non-Muslims in full-time education.

Despite their higher levels of unemployment, and their lower income levels, Muslims in three of the four states (all but the Netherlands) are slightly (and significantly) more likely to report higher levels of satisfaction with the economy. Even in the Netherlands, where the difference is in the other direction, non-Muslims report greater satisfaction on average of only about one point on the 10 point scale of measure used by ESS for this question. Overall, Muslims are much like their non-Muslim neighbours in their evaluation of the state of the economy.

There is also very little difference between Muslims and non-Muslims in areas related to acquisition of information. As Table 6.6 indicates, Muslims look like other members of their European state in terms of their understanding of politics, as well as their attention to news and political coverage on television, radio and in the newspaper. In

Table 6.5: Comparing Muslims' and non-Muslims' employment status and household size

	France Muslims	France Others	Germany Muslims	Germany Others	Netherlands Muslims	Netherlands Others	UK Muslims	UK Others
Average satisfaction with present state of economy	3.93*** (215)	3.48 (6,749)	4.16** (255)	3.76 (10,987)	4.60 (176)	5.51*** (7,651)	5.32*** (206)	4.56 (7,001)
Average hours contracted to work per week, no overtime	33.92 (169)	35.61* (5,782)	35.52 (193)	35.50 (9,651)	31.72 (152)	30.60 (6,705)	33.09 (154)	33.96 (6,640)
Average hours normally worked per week	36.12 (173)	39.62** (5,999)	39.09 (197)	39.37 (9,845)	34.16 (152)	34.20 (7,102)	34.95 (157)	37.40* (6,748)
Responsibility for supervizing others (%)	30.3 (178)	37.4 (6,207)	17.7 (209)	32.2 (10,162)	27.5 (160)	39.9 (7,315)	30.6 (160)	40.2 (6,868)
Member trade union (%)	5.0 (221)	7.0 (6,820)	7.1 (266)	12.2 (11,098)	11.7 (180)	19.3 (7,699)	3.8 (211)	16.0 (7,178)
Attended course/lecture/conference last 12 months to improve skills (%)	24.4 (221)	28.8 (6,811)	21.3 (267)	31.3 (11,108)	28.3 (180)	37.8 (7,686)	37.6 (210)	36.8 (7,162)
Main activity (%)								
paid work	47.0	51.9	43.4	48.8	48.0	51.9	45.8	54.4
education	19.5	8.1	16.6	8.9	14.7	8.2	19.8	7.6
unemployed, looking for job	13.0	3.8	9.4	4.5	9.6	1.2	10.4	3.1
unemployed, not looking for job	3.3	1.5	2.6	1.6	4.5	.8	.9	1.1
permanently sick or disabled	2.3	2.7	1.5	1.5	5.1	4.0	2.8	4.4
retired	3.7	26.0	7.5	23.1	2.8	14.4	5.7	20.7
community or military service	0	0	0	.2	0	0	0	.1
housework, looking after children, others	11.2 (215)	6.0 (6,747)	18.9 (265)	11.4 (10,939)	15.3 (177)	19.5 (7,466)	14.6 (212)	8.7 (7,121)
Ever unemployed and seeking job for over 3 months (%)	55.9 (220)	32.4 (6,814)	42.1 (266)	26.8 (11,079)	32.8 (180)	16.7 (7,693)	24.6 (211)	21.8 (7,179)
Average number of regular members in household	3.93*** (221)	2.75 (6,821)	3.67*** (267)	2.56 (11,118)	3.95*** (180)	2.88 (7,722)	4.47*** (211)	2.73 (7,186)

Data: ESS 2008, 2006, 2004, 2002

***p<.001, **p<.01, *p<.05

Note: Number of respondents indicated in parentheses

Table 6.6: Comparing Muslims' and non-Muslims' acquisition of information

	France		Germany		Netherlands		UK	
	Muslims	Other	Muslims	Other	Muslims	Other	Muslims	Other
Politics too complicated to understand	3.08 (219)	3.03 (6,793)	3.29*** (265)	3.00 (11,078)	3.25*** (173)	3.05 (7,662)	3.19 (208)	3.23 (7,161)
Total time watching TV on average weekday	4.03 (213)	4.27 (6,521)	4.69*** (268)	4.23 (11,129)	4.74* (180)	4.36 (7,716)	4.36 (212)	4.94*** (7,195)
Total time watching politics/ news/ current events on TV on average weekday	2.19 (212)	2.03 (6,516)	1.60 (257)	1.81** (10,779)	1.88 (173)	2.15** (7,533)	2.07 (199)	2.08 (7,030)
Total time listening to radio on average weekday	2.38 (221)	2.71* (6,817)	2.26 (268)	3.29*** (11,125)	1.58 (180)	3.05*** (7,714)	1.66 (210)	3.15*** (7,195)
Total time listening to politics/ news/ current events on radio on average weekday	1.37 (163)	1.52 (5,442)	1.15 (171)	1.55*** (9,637)	1.20 (87)	1.57* (6,020)	1.40 (118)	1.61 (5,715)
Total time reading newspaper on average weekday	.93 (221)	1.05 (6,819)	1.19 (268)	1.52*** (11,132)	1.17 (180)	1.56*** (7,713)	1.37 (212)	1.58* (7,195)
Total time reading about politics/ news/ current events in newspapers on average weekday	1.06 (138)	1.15 (4,137)	1.01 (192)	1.25* (9,116)	1.09 (128)	1.28** (6,180)	.94 (146)	1.13 (5,226)
Internet use (%)								
no internet access	22.8	28.4	43.4	30.6	21.7	16.6	26.4	27.7
use internet everyday	37.2 (145)	39.6 (3,909)	23.7 (198)	26.7 (8,288)	35.0 (180)	38.5 (7,716)	28.3 (212)	30.1 (7,197)

Data: ESS 2008, 2006, 2004, 2002
***$p<.001$, **$p<.01$, *$p<.05$
Note: Number of respondents indicated in parentheses

Germany, Muslims are about 13% less likely to have internet access than non-Muslims; in France and the Netherlands Muslims are about 5% less likely to have internet access, and in the UK the difference is just over 1%. But the differences in daily use of the internet are not more than 3% in all four states. Here again, Muslims act like their non-Muslims neighbours.

The European Social Survey results above give a new perspective on Muslims in Europe, in that they show so many similarities between Muslims and other Europeans. They do not contradict the well-documented socioeconomic marginalization of European Muslims. The ESS comparisons support the gaps in income, education, and employment that have been elaborated on by others. Jocelyn Cesari (2009: 9–10), for example, buttresses her depiction of the underclass status of Muslims in Europe by citing several European agency and international NGO reports: a study by the European Monitoring Centre on Racism and Xenophobia (EUMC, 2003) provides statistics on the higher unemployment rates of ethnic groups likely to be Muslim in the UK (Pakistanis and Bangladeshis), Germany (Turkish), France (immigrants), and the Netherlands (non-western immigrants). Data from the Organization for Economic Co-operation and Development (OECD) paint a complicated picture of Muslims' educational achievement in Europe. In France, for example, those whose ancestry is from a majority Muslim country are 10% more likely to have a secondary education or less (56% vs. 46% in the wider population). But '[h]igher degrees are more equally distributed in France' (Cesari, 2009: 10), and this phenomenon is likely reflected in the ESS data we presented above, in that averages within France portray Muslims and non-Muslims as not significantly different in terms of educational achievement. Cesari (2009: 10) notes that a similar pattern is presented by the OECD statistics for the Netherlands, where less than a secondary education characterizes half of those with ancestry likely to be Muslim, while those with likely Muslim ancestry are more likely than others to have an advanced degree. Figures for the UK suggest a roughly equal level of educational attainment for Muslims and non-Muslims, again as we found above in the ESS data. In Germany, however, Cesari indicates that OECD data show those with ancestry from majority Muslim nations are 45% more likely to have a secondary education or less (70% vs. 25% of the 'rest' of the nation), and 14% less likely to have an advanced degree (5% vs. 19% of the 'broader' population) (Cesari, 2009: 10). Cesari cites another report from the European Monitoring Centre on Racism and Xenophobia (EUMC, 2006) as providing evidence in Germany of spatial segregation of minorities in 'poorer quality housing' and a similar situation in France. The Netherlands and UK are cited as offering more effective public housing supports, but 'exclusionary violence' has been reported in the Netherlands (Cesari, 2009: 10, citing EUMC, 2006).

Despite the support provided by ESS data for the picture painted by the reports of the OECD, EUMC and scholars, the ESS data demand recognition of an under-appreciated aspect of the situation of European Muslims: they are not isolated and they are not dissatisfied with the major state institutions within which they conduct their lives. Their confidence in the educational, health and economic systems of their European state is not much different from that of their European neighbours, and in many areas is more positive. Muslims use the internet as much as their non-Muslim neighbours despite the fact that in most states they are less likely to have access to it. They pay attention to politics about as much as their non-Muslim neighbours, and follow the news on television, in the newspaper and on the radio at levels that do not distinguish them greatly from the rest of the country. These data provide little support, if any, for the belief that Muslims are isolating themselves in Europe. Like their non-Muslim neighbours, Muslims support the institutions of the state, follow politics and the news, and utilize the internet. These attitudes and habits reflect their integration into Europe, not self-segregation into parallel societies.

The general well-being of Muslims perceived as 'vulnerable' to dissatisfaction in Europe

Tables 6.7 to 6.11 allow us to examine with ESS data aspects of general well-being for specific groups within the Muslim population in our four European states of focus. We see in Tables 6.7 and 6.8 that there is little difference between the young group of ESS respondents (15–29) and older Muslims. The only statistically significant differences are in the direction of slightly greater happiness (in Germany and the Netherlands) and satisfaction with life (in the Netherlands) on the part of the Muslim young cohort (15–29) in contrast to older Muslims. We have noted already that ESS data indicate little difference between Muslim and non-Muslim Europeans in terms of life satisfaction and happiness, and these results for young adult Muslims reinforce this finding for the age group seen as most vulnerable to dissatisfaction in Europe. This finding complements those of the FRA-commissioned study discussed at the beginning of this chapter, finding little difference in happiness between Muslim and non-Muslim young people (12–18) in France and the UK, except for slightly greater happiness on the

Table 6.7: Average life satisfaction among vulnerable groups of Muslims

	France	Germany	Netherlands	UK
Age groups				
15-29	6.38	6.84	7.54**	7.09
others	5.74	6.52	6.68	7.16
50 and older	4.87	6.65	6.70[1]	6.59
others	6.24**	6.64	7.06	7.22
Religiosity				
high (7-10)	6.45**	6.60	7.26**	7.33*
others	5.48	6.65	6.37	6.74
low (0-3)	4.75	6.42	4.58[2]	6.33[1]
others	6.18**	6.68	7.10**	7.15
Gender				
male	5.64	6.19	6.86	7.21
female	6.38*	7.14**	7.21	6.98
Citizenship				
national	5.96	6.66	7.21**	7.16
foreign	6.06	6.60	6.18	6.75[1]
Place of birth				
national	6.24	6.55	7.66**	6.96
foreign	5.78	6.65	6.69	7.18

Data: ESS 2008, 2006, 2004, 2002
***p<.001, **p<.01, *p<.05
[1] 10<N<30, [2] N<10

Table 6.8: Average happiness among vulnerable groups of Muslims

	France	Germany	Netherlands	UK
Age groups				
15-29	7.24	7.35**	7.72*	7.37
others	6.94	6.58	7.13	7.47
50 and older	6.68	6.62	6.62[1]	7.15
others	7.14	6.93	7.46*	7.47
Religiosity				
high (7-10)	7.46**	6.74	7.61**	7.56
others	6.61	6.94	6.67	7.12
low (0-3)	6.53	6.49	6.84[2]	6.79[1]
others	7.13	6.89	7.33	7.42
Gender				
male	6.87	6.64	7.18	7.54
female	7.27	7.64	7.55	7.21
Citizenship				
national	7.04	7.08	7.41	7.43
foreign	7.09	6.70	7.06	7.15[1]
Place of birth				
national	7.24	7.20	7.80*	7.18
foreign	6.90	6.68	7.12	7.51

Data: ESS 2008, 2006, 2004, 2002
***p<.001, **p<.01, *p<.05
[1] 10<N<30 [2] N<10

part of Muslim youth in France in contrast to their non–Muslim counterparts.

The ESS results for highly religious Muslims also run counter to stereotypes. In terms of life satisfaction and happiness, to the extent that highly religious Muslims differ at all significantly from those who are less religious, the highly religious are, on average, more optimistic. The fact that highly religious Muslims in Europe are to a great degree as satisfied with their lives as less religious Muslims will no doubt come as a surprise to those who are suspicious of religiosity on the part of Muslims as giving rise to a critical stance toward life in Europe. Furthermore, while female Muslims, those Muslims who are citizens of the European state, and Muslims who were born in the European state in which they are now residing do not differ greatly from their counterparts (males, non–citizens and those born abroad) in average

Table 6.9: Average household income among vulnerable groups of Muslims

	France	Germany	Netherlands	UK
Age groups				
15-29	5.58	5.49	5.16	6.21
others	5.33	5.32	5.30	5.69
50 and older	5.83[1]	5.50	4.43[1]	4.58[1]
others	5.31	5.36	5.42*	6.17*
Religiosity				
high (7-10)	5.06	5.45	5.50*	5.74
others	5.71	5.26	4.65	6.18
low (0-3)	5.70[1]	4.58[1]	3.92[2]	4.73[1]
others	5.35	5.49*	5.31	6.04
Gender				
male	5.58	5.35	5.31	5.81
female	5.20	5.38	5.19	6.06
Citizenship				
national	5.67*	5.60	5.47*	5.83
foreign	4.82	5.23	4.41	6.41[1]
Place of birth				
national	5.73	6.07**	5.47	6.66*
foreign	5.18	5.08	5.18	5.53

Data: ESS 2008, 2006, 2004, 2002
***p<.001, **p<.01, *p<.05
[1] 10<N<30, [2] N<10

life satisfaction or happiness, they report in some states significantly more satisfaction or happiness.

The global life satisfaction and happiness indicators suggest that within the Muslim population, the integration of those groups about which European state-level policy makers are most concerned is not recognisably different from that of other Muslims. We turn now to the data for three specific indicators of well-being: household income, hours worked and education. Table 6.9 indicates that, for the most part, regarding income there are not large differences between the groups of Muslims expected to have the most difficult time in Europe, and other Muslims. Highly religious Muslims do not, on average, have lower income than others. Rather, the income of the highly religious is roughly the same, and, in the case of the Netherlands, significantly higher on average than that of their less religious counterparts. Table 6.10 indicates that those who classify themselves as having lower levels of religiosity do, however, report slightly higher levels of education than other Muslims, a difference that is statistically significant only in France.

Table 6.10: Average years of education among vulnerable groups of Muslims

	France	Germany	Netherlands	UK
Age groups				
15-29	13.02	11.50**	11.80	13.44
others	12.07	9.91	11.14	12.47
50 and older	12.18	8.30	7.65[1]	10.93
others	12.51	10.92***	11.98***	13.28**
Religiosity				
high (7-10)	11.48	10.10	11.11	12.48
others	13.55**	11.12*	12.09	13.75
low (0-3)	15.10**	11.63	13.25[2]	13.86[1]
others	12.00	10.35	11.31	12.86
Gender				
male	12.84	11.29***	11.09	13.52*
female	12.02	9.59	11.76	12.24
Citizenship				
national	13.32***	12.00***	11.50	12.74
foreign	10.42	9.82	10.92	14.28[1]
Place of birth				
national	13.05	12.05***	11.84	13.46
foreign	11.91	9.92	11.15	12.63

Data: ESS 2008, 2006, 2004, 2002
***p<.001, **p<.01, *p<.05
[1] 10<N<30, [2] N<10

As we would expect, older respondents, over 50, have less education than others, a difference that is statistically significant in three of the four states (all but France). (The lack of a significant educational difference in France between Muslims over and under 50 in Table 6.10 is explained by the relatively higher level of education of the over-50 group – in comparison to their counterparts in the other three states – rather than to lack of educational achievement by younger Muslims. France and the UK have the highest average educational levels for all categories of Muslims in this table.) Finally, the data in Table 6.11 allow us to examine one of the benefits of insider status in these European states: the ability to work overtime. We compare those in the 20–29-year-old age group to others in considering the effect of youth (since those who are under 20 years old are unlikely to have a steady job), and we find

Table 6.11: Average hours worked including overtime among vulnerable groups of Muslims

	France	Germany	Netherlands	UK
Age groups				
15-29	29.78	35.07	26.49	31.21
others	39.26***	41.08**	37.83***	38.23**
20-29[3]	32.61	38.12	33.59	33.84
others	39.26**	41.08	37.83	38.23
50 and older	37.41	43.06	42.13[1]**	37.33[1]
others	35.79	38.32	32.89	34.42
Religiosity				
high (7-10)	36.36	37.65	32.30	34.13
others	35.92	40.73	38.60**	35.99
low (0-3)	35.64[1]	44.22*	37.75[2]	43.05[1]*
others	36.21	38.07	34.00	34.13
Gender				
male	37.96*	42.97***	40.49***	37.37**
female	33.63	32.89	26.08	30.27
Citizenship				
national	36.33	37.63	33.37	35.46
foreign	35.69	39.86	37.29	31.50[1]
Place of birth				
national	34.59	37.00	26.61	34.48
foreign	37.29	39.78	37.76***	35.23

Data: ESS 2008, 2006, 2004, 2002
***p<.001, **p<.01, *p<.05
[1] 10<N<30, [2] N<10
[3] We created a separate category of Muslim respondents aged 20-29 with the recognition that many younger respondents may not be fully employed. Among all Muslims in the four countries, 45.6% are engaged in paid work compared to 51.4% of others. Conversely, 40.5% of Muslims 15-29 are involved in education compared to 42.2% of others.

that while young Muslims get less overtime, they are not doing much worse than their older counterparts in getting overtime work. Those who are 50 and over, as expected, get the most overtime.

The highly religious are comparable to the less religious on the indicator of hours of overtime worked, though in the Netherlands the highly religious work significantly less overtime (on average about six hours less). The general expectation would be that male Muslims would work more overtime than women, and they do. Muslim women work about four hours of overtime less than Muslim men in France, 10 hours less in Germany, 14 hours less in the Netherlands, and seven hours less in the UK. These differences might not be as large as most would expect, since women in European states are still more likely to accept greater responsibility for home and family than men, leaving less time for overtime work. While it is likely that Muslim women take on even greater responsibility for home and family than non-Muslim women in Europe, the sex-role distinction in overtime hours worked for Muslim women and men could be seen as rather modest given prevailing views of Muslim women as much more traditional than other European women.

Throughout our examination of groups of Muslims expected to have the greatest difficulty succeeding in Europe, we find few differences that distinguish them greatly from other Muslims. Young adult Muslims are at least as happy and satisfied as other Muslims, and they are doing about as well economically. The happiness and life satisfaction of highly religious Muslims can only be distinguished from that of other Muslims in that it is in some states slightly greater. Highly religious Muslims are about as well educated as other Muslims, though sometimes a bit less so. Muslim women work overtime, though less so than Muslim men. These data do not paint a picture of vulnerability with regard to these special groups within the Muslim population. Rather, they suggest that the young, the highly religious and women among the Muslim populations of these states are doing as well as other Muslims on key indicators of well-being. We turn now to the concluding chapter, where we assess the policy implications of our effort to benchmark Muslim well-being, and consider its fruitfulness for reducing disparities and polarizations between Muslims and others in Europe.

SEVEN

Reducing disparities and polarizations in Europe

Setting up a System of Benchmarking to Measure the Success of Integration Policies in Europe (European Parliament, 2007) proposes an effort to build on the strengths of Europe by protecting diversity and fostering greater equality. Whether or not a Europe-wide benchmarking system is actually put into place, states and European agencies are moving in this direction as they develop complex sets of indicators alternative to the Gross Domestic Product (GDP). We have applied the goals and strategies of the benchmarking concept to the task of examining the well-being of Muslims in four European states, focusing on the eight key areas of life specified by the Council of Europe (2003). In these states, as in Europe as a whole, Muslims represent a significant and salient dimension of the population politically, socially, economically, culturally and demographically. Without a reconsideration of official data gathering strategies, steps toward benchmarking minority integration in Europe will founder. Efforts to improve the well-being of minorities will ignore the special problems of Muslims in many European states for lack of conceptualization of the religious group as a minority in need of protection, and the resulting absence of accurate information about them. From their actual percentage of the population, to their trust in the justice and political systems, official data tell us little about Muslims in most European states.

Recognition of the European religious minority

Our look at several existing data sources suggests that much is to be learned by benchmarking Muslim well-being in Europe, and that what is learned is likely to undermine prejudices. The goal of the benchmarking process is to reduce disparities and polarizations within European populations, and thereby promote well-being in the key areas of life (Council of Europe 1997, 2003, 2004, 2005). Using unofficial, quasi-official and official data sources gathered within France, Germany, the Netherlands and the United Kingdom, we have demonstrated the utility of benchmarking in comparing Muslims and non-Muslims on these key areas of life.

The strength of our examination lies in the multiplicity of our data sources, which include: the European Agency for Fundamental Rights (FRA) and its investigative agencies comprising the Racism and Xenophobia Network (RAXEN) and National Focal Points (NFPs); the European Commission for Racism and Intolerance (ECRI); the European Social Survey (ESS); the Office for National Statistics (ONS) of the United Kingdom; the German General Social Survey (ALLBUS); Statistics Netherlands and others. Some of the studies conducted by these agencies – including FRA's EU-MIDIS undertaken by Gallup Europe; and the *Home Office Community Cohesion Study*, as well as the reports focused on ethnicity and religion by the UK Office for National Statistics (2004, 2006) and the Home Office (Jansson et al., 2007) – already offer direct comparison of Muslims and non-Muslims in terms of discrimination (provided by EU-MIDIS), and attitudes toward the political (provided by ONS) and justice systems (provided by the Home Office). But except for data gathered by the UK Office for National Statistics (for which 2001 is the most recent UK Census available during the preparation of this book) and the Home Office, it is difficult to assess the extent to which the sampling process and data gathering strategies utilized in these surveys provided a selection of respondents fully representative of the Muslim population in each of the three member states (all but the UK) without a Census question asking about religious identity. In fact, as we considered in Chapter Two, a look at the sources of estimates of the percentage Muslim in France, Germany and the Netherlands leaves room for doubt as to the accuracy of prevailing assumptions about even the relative size of the Muslim population in European states that do not gather these data as part of the Census. We also considered (in Chapter Two) the extent to which the visibility of Muslims is enhanced by the general population's predominant lack of identification with any religious denomination in these four states, and the low levels of religiosity on the part of non-Muslim Europeans who do identify with a religion. (See also Tausch et al., 2006: 47–57 for data on the non-denominational majority and low levels of religious observance in European states.)

The results in Table 7.1 suggest some differences between Muslims and non-Muslims on topics that may relate to the religious/secular divide, as well as several areas of agreement on topics that would surprise many observers of the heated minority inclusion political debate throughout Europe. On the basis of the ESS data, Muslims can be characterized as having rather conservative social values and a strong sense of social justice on economic and quality of life issues. With regard to the former, Muslims are two to five times less likely than non-Muslims to respond that they have ever lived with a partner without being married. Close to a third of non-Muslims in each of the four European states indicate that they have done so; in the UK only 6% of Muslims have, with only slightly larger likelihoods of living with a partner without marriage for Muslims in the Netherlands (10%), Germany (12%), and France (15%).

Muslims are also less likely than non-Muslims to have been divorced. In the UK, for example, about 13% of non-Muslim respondents report having been divorced, in contrast to 5% of Muslims. In Germany, about 11% of non-Muslims have been divorced, but only 1% of Muslims. The differences between the two groups are smaller in France and the Netherlands. A 2008 Gallup survey analysis of results from Berlin, Paris and London (Rheault and Mogahed, 2008) similarly suggested that Muslims in these capital cities and non-Muslims in the general populations of these countries differ in their opinions on moral issues, in particular abortion, pornography and sex outside of marriage. The ESS results in Table 7.1 discussed above support this conclusion.

In three of the states (but not in France), Table 7.1 suggests that Muslims are slightly (and statistically significantly) more likely to agree that men should have the right to a job over women. The differences between Muslims and non-Muslims on this five-point scale are not great. (The differences between the average levels of support for this statement between groups never reach the next rung on the scale.) Similarly, Muslims' scores average slightly (and statistically significantly) lower than those of non-Muslims on the five-point scale indicating agreement with the statement that gays and lesbians are free to live as they wish. Here again, the difference between the two groups never reaches the next rung on the scale.

Muslims are considerably more likely than non-Muslims to indicate support for the idea that it is 'important to behave properly': in the United Kingdom, for example, 74% of Muslims indicated support for this statement, in contrast to 54% of non-Muslims. In the other three states, the direction of the differences was the same, with magnitudes ranging from 9% (in France) to about 15% (in Germany and the Netherlands).

Some of the results in Table 7.1 would not be expected given the public debate about the failure of integration policies in these four states: Muslims' responses suggest that they are supportive of equality and do not eschew capitalist goals. Muslims are more likely than non-Muslims to indicate that it is 'important that people be treated equally and have equal opportunities'; they are more likely to agree that it is important for government to be strong and ensure safety; Muslims are

Table 7.1: Comparing cultural values between Muslims and non-Muslims

	France		Germany		Netherlands		UK	
	Muslims	Others	Muslims	Others	Muslims	Others	Muslims	Others
Average agreement that gays and lesbians free to live life as they wish	3.47 (216)	4.19*** (6,768)	2.97 (258)	3.90*** (11,004)	3.44 (174)	4.31*** (7,688)	3.08 (209)	3.91*** (7,151)
Average agreement that government should reduce differences in income levels	4.25* (221)	4.11 (6,791)	3.63* (250)	3.47 (10,875)	3.57* (175)	3.41 (7,658)	3.72** (203)	3.48 (7,103)
Average agreement that men should have right to job over women when jobs are scarce[1]	2.26 (91)	2.13 (3,458)	3.22*** (130)	2.37 (5,417)	2.53* (79)	2.22 (3,556)	2.91*** (131)	2.31 (3,767)
Lived with partner without being married (%)	15.0	34.4	12.4	29.6	10.1	29.3	6.3	29.7
Ever been divorced (%)	5.0	7.5	1.2	10.7	6.5	8.4	5.0	13.5
Percent agreeing that person being described is very much like me								
important to live in safe and secure place	65.9	51.8	60.5	59.0	62.3	45.5	71.5	62.4
important to be rich, have money, expensive things	13.1	6.2	23.6	10.6	20.0	7.1	27.9	12.9
important that people treated equally	85.5	78.2	76.1	72.2	86.9	73.6	89.0	69.4
important to understand different people	74.8	61.5	64.5	67.7	76.0	59.6	65.6	64.2
important to make own decision and be free	61.2	55.2	65.3	76.0	74.9	72.3	75.9	69.6
important to help people/care for others' well-being	72.9	55.6	69.5	66.2	74.1	64.5	81.2	71.0
important gov. is strong and ensures safety	66.4	51.4	64.3	59.1	62.2	46.5	75.9	61.2
important to behave properly	57.9	48.5	57.1	42.9	59.0	44.4	74.0	54.1
important to care for nature and environment	62.6	66.7	57.0	69.6	66.5	66.5	71.7	64.3

Data: ESS 2008, 2006, 2004, 2002

***p<.001, **p<.01, *p<.05

[1] 2008 ESS only

Note: Number of respondents indicated in parentheses

more likely to agree that it is important to help people and care for others' well-being; Muslims are also more likely to indicate that it is 'important to be rich, have money and expensive things'.

In three of the four states, Muslims are more likely to indicate that it is important to understand different people. (The exception is in Germany, where Muslims are about 2% less likely than non-Muslims to agree with this statement.) Muslims' values may in some ways be more toward the left than those of non-Muslims when it comes to equality and income distribution: Muslims are slightly more likely to feel that government should reduce differences in income levels, as Table 7.1 indicates.

The lack of accurate information about Muslims leaves unrecognized key aspects of their cultural orientation, and reduces awareness of some areas of general agreement (for example, with regard to non-Muslims thinking there is more discrimination in their member state than Muslims do, as reported in the *Special Eurobarometer* and discussed in Chapter Five). The absence of reliable information about Muslims leaves the door open to misunderstanding, impeding efforts to foster greater equality in Europe and protect diversity.

The 'politics of statistics' (Geddes and Wunderlich, 2009: 196) preventing official data collection on Muslims' well-being in three of the member states we examined (all but the UK) is largely supported with reference to 'the national model of integration'. As we discussed in the first chapter, the civil rights of Muslims have not been the focus of efforts to include them in European states: rather, Muslims have been viewed in terms of an *immigration and security threat* framework. With information specifically about Muslims, European and state-level efforts to benchmark and otherwise measure well-being could change that perspective, in that they would provide data facilitating the examination of structural barriers to the religious minority's achievement in the host society. Measuring Muslim well-being in Europe would yield information underscoring the permanence of Muslims in the European religious and political landscape, thereby opening a constructive dialogue.

Widespread discussion of Muslims' 'failure' to integrate into European societies rests on the assumption that members of the religious minority were born abroad, that they are not citizens and are ethnic minorities, and that these groups do not support European values and institutions. Seen as a diaspora, Muslims appear to have a weak claim to their European homes. Yet we have examined data from several highly credible sources and it all suggests that Muslims are at home in Europe: they trust the criminal justice system and its officials, including police, magistrates and the courts, often to a greater degree than do non-Muslims. Where there are exceptions to this finding (as in French Muslims' distrust of the police), we have only to look at official policy (the French minority identity check and stop and search policy currently being examined by the French and European courts for constitutionality) to understand why.

Results from Gallup polls in Europe provide firm support for our findings: examination of Gallup survey data for France, Germany and the UK comparing responses from Muslims in the capital cities (Paris, Berlin and London) to respondents in the nation as a whole indicated no statistically significant difference between Muslims and non-Muslims in their identification with the country, except for the fact that in the UK Muslim respondents were 9% more likely to identify with the country than were respondents in the nation at large (Nyiri, 2007).

Policies protecting the national integration model are ineffective in reducing disparities and polarizations

Political focus on the national model of integration, on the relationship between religion and the state, and on the degree of prominence of state over individual identity has not provided the key to assuring equality and protecting diversity in Europe. *Laïcité*, for example, described as central to the French national model of integration, appears to be irrelevant in explaining Muslims' lower level of trust in the police or their continued trust in the justice system; it does not explain their greater (than non-Muslims') satisfaction with the way democracy works in France, or their attendance at school. Despite the ban on *schoolgirls' headscarves*, for example, Muslim families send their daughters to public schools, and Muslims are as likely as non-Muslims to evaluate the state of education in the country positively. Policies that deny Muslims the same stake in the system as other Europeans in their member state may weaken the religious minority's sense of belonging to the state, but not their satisfaction with the system. An example is provided through consideration of the German practice of disallowing Muslims the right to contribute through their taxes to the social service activities of their mosques – as provided for other religions through the German '*church tax*'. It is possible that such policies have weakened Muslims' trust in the political parties and their interest in politics; but they apparently have not undermined Muslims' satisfaction with the way democracy works in Germany, because they are more satisfied than their non-Muslim neighbours.

Fetzer and Soper (2005) laid the groundwork for recognition of the irrelevance of the official church-state relationship on public opinion. While their research supported the hypothesis that church-state structural arrangements influence state responsiveness to Muslims in social policy, the results of their public opinion surveys led them to question the assumption of a link between respondents' views on church-state arrangements and their attitudes toward extending state accommodations to Muslims. In Fetzer and Soper's (2005: 143) words:

> in France and Germany ... the data provide no support for the mass-level version of our church-state structure theory. French devotés of *laicite* were no more likely to oppose the wearing of the *hijab* than were those who rejected French separatism. German respondents likewise showed no propensity to link support for *Kirchensteuer* (tax collection for churches designated as public corporations) to sympathy for Islamic instruction in public schools.

On the level of public opinion, then, it appears that existing patterns of church-state relations are not an insurmountable barrier to change, though some political leaders and groups might utilize them in justifying their unwillingness to respond to Muslims' demands for accommodation.

There are some lacunae in our survey instruments. We do not have survey questions, for example, on attitudes about state involvement in the funding of religious organizations (like the church tax in Germany, for example), or on the requirement that women present themselves in secular attire in state institutions (the ban on headscarves in public schools in France, for example, as well as the ban on veils covering the face in state institutions there). It is likely that these policies find weak support among Muslims who are affected by them. But despite such institutional procedures marginalizing the presence of the religious minority in Europe, several data sources indicate that Muslims are at least as satisfied with the way democracy works in the European country in which they live as non-Muslims are (as supported by ESS and ALLBUS data); and that Muslims identify with their European country at levels equal to or higher than those of non-Muslims in the state (as supported by Gallup data).

Hotly contested policies intended to change Muslims in directions that make them more 'European' may be superfluous. The emphasis on language acquisition and limits on family reunification for non-western applicants found in *civic integration contracts*, for example, may be irrelevant to the process of integration and the degree of trust in state institutions. In the UK – where only about half of Muslims report that they use English as the primary or secondary language at home (reported in Table 2.1), where 65% of Muslims report being born abroad, and where 74% indicate that they are a member of an ethnic minority (Table 2.3) – Muslims had higher levels of trust than non-Muslims in Parliament, politicians, political parties and in the criminal justice system, and greater satisfaction with the national government and the way democracy works in the UK. In further investigation with ESS data, we also found an inconsistent, sometimes insignificant impact of Muslims' host nation language ability on several indicators of trust, education, life satisfaction and general happiness, suggesting that further research should be directed in this area before the success of related policies is assumed.

Table 7.2 summarizes the comparisons between Muslims and others in specific areas of well-being shown in data from the European Social Survey and the German General Social Survey (ALLBUS). (While the preceding chapters also offered inter-group well-being comparisons from additional sources – including FRA, ONS and the Home Office – including them all in the table would make it unwieldy.) In Table 7.2 for each state we provide a summary sign for each indicator showing whether Muslims' level of well-being is greater than (+1), less than (-1), or not significantly different (0) from that of other respondents in the full multivariate models. For the most controversial aspects of well-being – trust and concern about Justice/Crime/Victimization and in public institutions, for discrimination, and for life satisfaction – we have provided multivariate models and these are summarized in Table 7.2; bivariate relationships offered in other areas of well-being, and discussed particularly in Chapter Six, suggest fruitful paths for further multivariate study in areas for which there was not sufficient space in this book.

Several important findings can be quickly summarized with reference to Table 7.2. Though Muslims feel part of a group that is discriminated against in all four states, for example, they do not have less trust in the legal system or parliament of their European state. In fact, the multivariate findings suggest that in the UK, Muslims have greater trust in these institutions than others do. In addition, in three of the four states, Muslims are more likely to be satisfied with democracy as it is practised in the country than are others, and in the fourth state (the Netherlands) Muslims are not significantly less satisfied with democracy than others. The multivariate results also indicate that Muslims are not significantly less happy or satisfied than others in their European state.

Table 7.2: Effects of Muslim ID on select indicators of well-being

	France		Germany		Netherlands		UK	
	Muslim	Full	Muslim	Full	Muslim	Full	Muslim	Full
Justice/crime/victimization								
Trust in legal system	0	0	0	0	0	0	+1	+1
Trust in judiciary[1]	---	---	+1	0	---	---	---	---
Trust in police	-1	-1	0	0	0	0	+1	0
Trust in police[1]	---	---	0	0	---	---	---	---
Safety walking alone after dark	+1	0	-1	0	-1	-1	0	0
Worried about home being burgled[2]	0	0	0	0	0	0	+1	0
Worried burglary effects quality life[2]	0	0	0	0	-1	-1	-1	-1
Worried About being victim of violent crime[2]	+1	0	-1	0	0	0	-1	0
Worried being victim has effect on quality life[2]	0	0	-1	0	-1	-1	-1	-1
Public institutions								
Trust in Parliament	0	0	0	0	0	0	+1	+1
Trust in politicians	0	0	0	0	0	0	+1	+1
Trust in political parties	+1	0	0	0	-1	-1	+1	+1
Trust in EU Parliament	0	0	+1	+1	0	0	+1	+1
Trust in the UN	-1	-1	-1	0	-1	-1	-1	-1
Satisfaction with democracy in country	+1	+1	+1	+1	0	0	+1	+1
Satisfaction with national government	0	0	+1	0	0	0	+1	+1
Interest in politics	0	0	-1	0	-1	0	0	0
Connection index[1]				0				
Trust in political institutions index[1]				+1				
Discrimination								
Reported membership in discriminated group	-1	-1	-1	-1	-1	-1	-1	-1
General well-being								
Life satisfaction	-1	0	0	0	-1	0	0	0
Happiness	0	0	-1	0	-1	0	0	0
Monthly household income (all sources)	-1	-1	-1	-1	-1	-1	-1	0
Living comfortably on present income	-1	-1	-1	0	-1	0	-1	0
General health	0	0	+1	0	-1	-1	0	0
Current state of health care	+1	+1	+1	+1	+1	+1	+1	+1
Hampered in daily activities by health	0	0	0	0	0	0	0	0
Totals	-1	-3	-3	+2	-11	-7	+3	+4

[1] ALLBUS 2008. All other indicators ESS

[2] ESS 2008-2006. All other ESS indicators use the full sample 2008-2. Key: +1 (vulnerable group has statistically higher averages than comparison group), 0 (groups have statistically equal levels), -1 (vulnerable group has statistically lower levels)

By both objective and subjective measures (*monthly household income, living comfortably on present income,* respectively), the socioeconomic position of Muslims is weaker than that of others. But the outlook of Muslims is sometimes more positive. Specifically, for example, they report greater satisfaction in the health care system, even when we have controlled for their income level.

The bivariate results (discussed previously in Chapter Six, not presented in Table 7.2) similarly suggested a positive outlook on the part of Muslims in Europe, and point the direction for further investigation. Muslims are more *satisfied with the present state of the economy* than non-Muslims in three of the four states examined (all but the Netherlands), and are more satisfied in the state of education (except in France where there is no significant difference between them and others in satisfaction). The difficulty of categorizing Muslims as predisposed toward parties of the left or right emerges in consideration of these bivariate results: Muslims are more likely, for example, to indicate that government policy should work to reduce income differences, even while they are less likely to support the lifestyle of gays and lesbians and more likely (in three states) to feel that men have the right to a job over women. Interestingly, Muslims overwhelmingly support parties on the left, despite these parties' secular traditions. No doubt multivariate investigation of these results will indicate the importance of the personal characteristics of Muslims in support of these views and in other areas that we have not yet fully investigated. But, after all, that is the most important implication of our results so far: European Muslims, like other Europeans, cannot be categorized simply on the basis of their religious orientation.

At the bottom of Table 7.2, we offer a summary 'well-being' score for each state calculated on the basis of those results for which we have presented full multivariate models. (For each state an initial summary score for the bivariate relationships between Muslim religious identification and the well-being indicators is also presented. This bivariate summary score demonstrates the well-being of Muslims without taking account of their background personal characteristics, as we did in the multivariate equations.) The utility of these scores lies only in their summary capacity. The UK score (+4) reflects the fact that Muslims in the UK often report greater levels of political trust and satisfaction than others – for example, in their trust in the legal system, in Parliament, politicians, political parties, satisfaction with democracy as it is practised in the country, and in the national government. Muslims are also more satisfied with the state of health care in the UK. The positive well-being score for Muslims in the UK does not at all suggest that their situation could not be improved. Rather, it suggests that they are at least as engaged in supporting the state and its agencies as others are. As we noted earlier, they do have important areas of unease. Muslims are more concerned than others about the effect on their lives of worry about crime victimization, and are more likely to feel that they are members of a group that is discriminated against. These concerns – about crime and discrimination – bring down their total well-being score relative to that of non-Muslims. But overall, these results for the UK suggest that Muslims can be relied upon to support politicians and political agencies, and could be enlisted especially in promoting efforts to reduce bias and improve neighbourhood safety. The surprising aspect of these results is that they do not at all fit the stereotypical images of alienation and dissatisfaction often attributed to Muslims in Britain.

The well-being score for Muslims in Germany, '+2', reflects the fact that they are for the most part as satisfied with state agencies as others are in Germany. Muslims in Germany trust the legal system, the police, Parliament and political parties as much as others do, and have greater trust in the EU Parliament and greater satisfaction with democracy as it is practised in Germany than do other Germans. Results for the political trust index created with ALLBUS suggest that Muslims in Germany have even greater trust in the political system than other Germans. In terms of their concerns about crime, Muslims in Germany have the same feelings as their German neighbours, and Muslims have a more optimistic evaluation of the state of health care in Germany than do other Germans. The full multivariate models indicate that Muslims in Germany have lower well-being in terms of discrimination, and in terms of income.

In France, lower trust in the police on the part of Muslims is one of the elements reducing their overall well-being summary score to '-3'; in addition, French Muslims are alone among Muslims in the four states in reporting that they have difficulty living comfortably on their present income once we have controlled for background factors in the full model. We noted earlier that Muslims in France, unlike those in the UK and Netherlands, do not report that unease about being victimized by crime influences their quality of life. We attributed this difference to their relative segregation in the *banlieues*, because previous research supporting a structural theory of 'fear of crime' has demonstrated that segregation reduces fear of crime (Liska, Lawrence and Sanchirico, 1982). Since Muslims in France perceive themselves as members of a group that is discriminated against, the unease in their own neighbourhoods reflected by 'fear of crime' may be reduced by the physical segregation from groups recognized to be biased toward them. We do not argue that this is a positive phenomenon; rather, we note that it may explain the fact that alone among Muslims in the four states, French Muslims are not uneasy about crime in their neighbourhoods. Like Muslims in the other three European states, French Muslims do not distrust the legal system (though they do distrust the police, as noted above and explained earlier in this book). They are also as likely to support Parliament, politicians and political parties and are more likely to indicate satisfaction with democracy in France than are other French. It is fair to say that Muslims are largely satisfied with public institutions in France, and are as happy with their lives as other French, even while they have great difficulty living on their income, face discrimination and distrust the police.

The overall well-being score for Muslims in the Netherlands, '-7' is reflective of several problems faced by the religious minority there. While they are as likely to support the legal system and police as other Dutch, Muslims in the Netherlands do not feel safe walking alone after dark in their neighbourhoods; and they report concern about the effect of worry about becoming a victim of crime on the quality of their life. They also report being a member of a group that is discriminated against. The multivariate results indicate that while Muslims trust Parliament and politicians as much as other Dutch, they do not trust the political parties. Since there are no areas in which Dutch Muslims have higher trust or satisfaction scores than other Dutch, the negative aspects of their situation are not thereby counterbalanced in the summary score for well-being. Muslims in the Netherlands have lower monthly income than other Dutch, though in the multivariate model Muslims are as likely as others to report that they live comfortably on their present income. Despite these concerns, Muslims in the Dutch state indicate that they are as satisfied with their lives and as happy as others, once background indicators are controlled in the multivariate equations.

This review of the overall situation of Muslims in each of these four European states provides no support for the influence of national integration models on the well-being of minorities in comparison to others in the state. The UK and the Netherlands diverged considerably in the overall well-being of Muslims living there. Yet both of these states are usually viewed as characterized by some degree of multiculturalism and weaker state imposition of uniform policies regarding public presentation of the civic self, in contrast to the religious self, in state institutions. The ESS data we examined were from the 2002–2008 period, so more recent highly publicized efforts to move the Dutch state away from multiculturalism are not even reflected in the attitudes of respondents.

Adding France and Germany to our comparisons leads us in the same direction: the evidence about them provides no significant support for the influence of the national integration model on the well-being of Muslims and the level of disparity between the religious minority and others in the state. Despite the strength of the French state in marginalizing the presence of Muslims in the civic sphere, Muslims in France are as likely to support political institutions and agencies (except for the police) as are Muslims in Germany, where the state has not imposed a uniform policy with regard to displaying the religious self in public.

These comparisons suggest that the national model of integration itself – with its associated structure of state/religion coordination and degree of state control in stipulating the requirements of integration – is not central to the well-being of Muslims in Europe or to the disparities between Muslims and others in European states. Individual state policies themselves, regardless of the conceptual integration models from which they come, may hold the most promise for reducing disparities and polarizations between Muslims and others in Europe. It is also not fair to say that the integration model drives state policy, since states with quite different integration models have, to some extent, gone in similar policy directions in areas related to immigrant integration (cf. Joppke, 2007). The integration models themselves do not seem to influence the degree of polarization between groups: ESS indicates that in all four states, even with the controls for respondent background factors imposed in the multivariate models, Muslims were significantly more likely than non-Muslims to feel that they were members of a group that is discriminated against, despite the fact that the states have different official integration models.

State policy supports discrimination

While Muslims indicate that religion is a key trigger of the discrimination they face in Europe, they often find that their race, nationality, and ethnicity direct discrimination toward them as well. Multiple discrimination, as explained by FRA (2010) and demonstrated by ESS data, is a problem faced by Muslims in Europe to a much greater degree than by non-Muslims. ESS data also indicate that discrimination against Muslims has grown over the first decade of this century in all four states. Thus it is surprising that Muslims have retained their positive outlook toward the state and its institutions and that they are more enthusiastic about them than are non-Muslims.

While the data indicate that Muslims in Europe are supportive of the state and its institutions, and that they are also supportive of the European Union, our analyses – and those by FRA, ECRI and the British Home Office – indicate that discrimination and crime are two problems that make Muslims uneasy in their European homes. It is unlikely that they can achieve their potential in the midst of the uncertainty created by these conditions. EU-MIDIS reported discrimination in nine areas of life relating to Muslims' interaction with public, private and commercial institutions and organizations. ESS results indicated discrimination triggered by several characteristics besides religion directed at those who are likely to be Muslim – their religion, race, nationality and ethnicity. The Home Office reported Muslims' concern with anti-social behaviour (for example public drunkenness and rubbish) in their neighbourhoods, as well as their greater likelihood of worry (than Christians) about violent crime, burglary and car crime.

Further examination of ESS data indicates that social trust (the belief that most people can be trusted, see Appendix 1 for the indicators) is negatively related to worry about crime. Currently Muslims' levels of political trust are at least as high on most measures as those of non-Muslims in the four states we examined. But failure by the state to attend to the circumstances causing Muslims' worry about the impact of crime concerns on their lives may lead to a reduction in Muslims' political trust, through the erosion in their social trust. Similarly, increases in social trust may reduce feelings of concern about crime. We found that among Muslims in Germany, Netherlands and the United Kingdom social trust was a negative and significant predictor of individual feelings of being a victim of a crime. In other words, the greater one's level of social trust, the less worried one is of being a victim of a crime. This same relationship did not hold in the case of France.

Without institutional change directed by state policy, the conditions of uncertainty faced by Muslims in Europe will lead the best among them to avoid the doors closed by discrimination and bias. Muslims in Europe are likely to conform to institutional policy where it will advance their children, as French Muslim families have demonstrated in sending their daughters to public schools despite the headscarf ban. But official state policies embolden bigots and racist organizations by suggesting that symbols (such as the headscarf) and habits (such as a preference for halal food) favoured by Muslims threaten European traditions. By requiring civil servants to practise institutional bias when they deny Muslims the right to these symbols and habits, states reinforce wariness about Muslims. Several areas of state policy teach citizens to be suspicious of their Muslim neighbours: these include the exclusion of Muslims' religious organizations from the existing system of church-state relations (for example, in the case of the German church tax), the implementation of civic integration contracts primarily for those from largely Muslim countries of origin, the failure to include education about Islam in school curricula that provide education about other religions, as well as the focus on what Muslim women prefer to wear in setting institutional dress codes. Greater inclusiveness could be provided in each of these policy areas if states actively sought to develop it: compromises could be reached on all of these institutional practices enabling Muslims to fully engage in Europe and signalling to other Europeans that Muslims belong.

Making a place for Muslims in Europe is a job for the state; the discrimination Muslims currently experience signals a failure of state policy. States have reacted to perceptions of Muslims as threatening to the security and culture of Europe by developing policies that reinforce those perceptions. States have permitted fears of the threat posed by Muslim terrorists to extend to widespread worry about Muslims in general. State policy should instead affirm that religious and other ideologies are unjustifiably appropriated by 'Muslim' terrorists to provide a seemingly significant rationale for violent objectives, as is recognized for 'Christian' and 'right-wing' terrorists (such as those who assassinate abortion providers and bomb their clinics, or set fires to homes perceived to be occupied by asylum seekers).

Xenophobic concerns about religiosity

Discrimination and bias against Muslims triggered by their religion are particularly significant problems given the importance of religion to their identity. In fact, as we discussed earlier, it may be that their visibility to other Europeans rests largely on this one difference between the two groups. As we discussed in Chapter Two (and demonstrated in Tables 2.1 and 2.4), ESS results indicate that Muslims on average rate themselves as two or three points more religious along the religiosity scale (which runs from 0–10) than do non-Muslims. Muslims are also noticeably more likely to engage in weekly religious services and to pray daily apart from religious services. Gallup's (Nyiri, 2007) survey of Muslims in Paris, London and Berlin found that Muslims in each of these capital cities were two to three times more likely than the general populations of their European country to indicate that religion was an important part of their lives. Muslims also indicated no conflict between their religious and national identities, and (as we discussed above) were at least as likely (more in the UK) to identify with their European state as were those in the general population of the country.

Non-Muslim Europeans' focus on the religiosity of their Muslim neighbours (cf. Sarrazin, 2010: 268) may obscure from their view Muslims' identification with the state. Studies consistently demonstrate that, in general, Europeans are not religious. In self-report data that Gallup collected for the European Commission's *Eurobarometer* and the European Social Survey, for example, fewer than 10% of French and German respondents indicated that they attend church weekly, and only 10–15% of citizens attend weekly in the Netherlands and UK (Manchin, 2004). These figures contrast sharply with Muslims' likelihood of weekly religious observance and offer the same picture of the religiosity divide between Muslims and other Europeans that we presented in Chapter Two.

It may be this religiosity divide that is most threatening to non-Muslims (cf. Sarrazin, 2010), even while religious freedom is a basic tenet of Europe and its member states. Those who know little about a religion may construe it to be dangerous. Those who have largely sidelined religion in their own lives might find it difficult to relate to others who make a regular effort to organize their lives around their religious identity. Greater attention to education about the principles and practices of all religions, including Islam, in public schools and in cultural venues would go a long way toward bridging this divide. To the extent that animosity between religious groups is based on ignorance, it is the responsibility of the state to marshal policy development in the direction of widespread education about religious differences and beliefs.

In these four countries, in particular, the educational task could be accomplished. While they have differing degrees of involvement in and control over setting the terms of minority integration, all four nation states are actively involved in establishing educational standards, even when they are implemented by administrative agencies below the national level. In countries where it is possible to ban the headscarf and other religious symbols worn by students in school, or forbid female civil servants from wearing headscarves to work, or require a certain level of host nation language competency to qualify for permanent residence, it is entirely within the power of the state and its administrative divisions to bridge the religious divide through education. So far, where this education occurs, it is one-sided – directed at religious minorities and focused on the religious and secular traditions of the host nation. To bridge the divide between Muslims and non-Muslims in European states, education would also have to be directed at non-Muslims, and focused on the important elements of Islam as it influences the daily lives and aspirations of their Muslim neighbours.

The cultural orientation and overall well-being of Muslims perceived to be 'vulnerable' to dissatisfaction in Europe

The age, religiosity, gender, citizenship and place of birth of individual Muslim Europeans are perceived to place special requirements on their situation. Young Muslims are often assumed to be most vulnerable to radicalization: males toward violent extremism, and females toward gender subordination and the tacit support for anti-western extremist political agendas that headscarves signify to many non-Muslim Europeans. Highly religious Muslims stand out in a largely non-denominational or non-religious European context, and are expected to be vulnerable to radical fundamentalism. Muslims with foreign citizenship and those with foreign birthright are viewed with suspicion and concern, assumed to present a threat to the cultural and physical security of Europe and its member states.

The preconceptions about these demographic categories of Muslims rest on the assumption that their attitudes and habits are less supportive of Europe than those of other Muslims and of Europeans in general. Our look within the Muslim population, at the young, the highly religious, males, females, and those with foreign citizenship or birthright does not support the supposition that they offer a different picture attitudinally in terms of their satisfaction with Europe and its institutions, or their sense of happiness and general well-being. Unwarranted preconceptions about 'vulnerable' groups within the Muslim population in Europe – specifically in France, Germany, the Netherlands and the UK – foster prejudice and discrimination toward them. The resulting wall of resistance toward them prevents young male Muslims, for example, from developing their talents through the informal mentoring processes available to other Europeans. Widespread negative and bureaucratic reactions triggered by young women's headscarves, for example, prevent women who wear them from contributing their skills and abilities to the institutions of their European member state. Resistance to those Muslims perceived to be highly religious or dangerous, perhaps because of their membership in cultural organizations or because of their formal clothing or demeanour, prevents those Muslims to whom the bias is directed from giving the best of themselves to Europe.

Table 7.3 offers ESS data suggesting that the influence of state policy with regard to tolerance is not lost on the groups of Muslims perceived by many to be most likely to be dissatisfied in Europe. Young adult Muslims in the UK, the Netherlands, and Germany expressed greater agreement than other Muslims with the statement that 'gays and lesbians should be free to live life as they wish'. (The UK difference was statistically significant.) In addition, Muslims born in the European member state in which they reside expressed more support for gays and lesbians on this question than did those born abroad, and the differences were statistically significant in the Netherlands and the UK. The impact of state policies positively disposed toward preventing bias might be seen in these results, along with the willingness of Muslims born in Europe to accept the guidance of the state. Muslims' trust in the state and its political institutions, demonstrated in several studies and with

Table 7.3: Average agreement among vulnerable groups that gays and lesbians are free to live as they wish

	France	Germany	Netherlands	UK
Age groups				
15-29	3.18	3.18	3.67	3.50***
others	3.65*	2.86	3.31	2.71
50 and older	3.45	2.57	2.73[1]	2.88
others	3.47	3.06*	3.56***	3.12
Religiosity				
high (7-10)	3.08	2.79	3.39	2.89
others	3.88***	3.22*	3.58	3.38**
low (0-3)	3.95	3.28	3.46[2]	3.46[1]
others	3.39	2.92	3.45	3.05
Gender				
male	3.27	3.00	3.17	2.90
female	3.69*	2.94	3.79**	3.29*
Citizenship				
national	3.55	3.06	3.45	3.10
foreign	3.28	2.93	3.42	2.93
Place of birth				
national	3.57	3.20	3.71*	3.56***
foreign	3.38	2.88	3.31	2.81

Data: ESS 2008-2002
***p<.001, **p<.01, *p<.05
[1] 10<N<30, [2] N<10

considerable data in Chapter Four, enables policy makers to exert great influence on their attitudes in areas such as discrimination and bias.

Considerable attention has been focused on the radicalizing potential of the marginality created by many Europeans' unwillingness to fully open public institutions to Muslims in their states. The attitudes of Muslims presented in the previous chapters, on the basis of several different data sources, suggest that it is unlikely that fundamentalist radicalization will be the primary response of young or religious Muslims to their exclusion by their European neighbours from full participation in the state. In data that we cited above, those who are young, those who are religious, those who were born abroad all espouse European values – trust in public institutions, belief in social justice, confidence in criminal justice agencies – and indicate that they are more satisfied with many of these institutions than their European neighbours, despite the fact that they are part of a group that is marginalized in terms of discrimination, income, education and other indicators.

Table 7.4 summarizes our multivariate findings from ESS and ALLBUS regarding the well-being of groups of Muslims seen as particularly vulnerable to dissatisfaction in European states. We code differences and similarities between these specific demographic groups of Muslims and other Muslims as we did in our summary examination of the well-being of all Muslims in contrast to others (above, in Table 7.2): '+1' designates that the vulnerable group has a statistically higher average than the comparison group; '-1' indicates that the vulnerable group has a statistically lower level of well-being than the comparison group; and '0' indicates statistically equal levels between the vulnerable and comparison groups. The results are again organized separately for each European state.

In France, the lower levels of trust in the police and in the legal system on the part of Muslim 15–29-year-olds stand out. We discussed the reasons for it in Chapter Three, demonstrating that several European agencies, NGOs and scholars have indicated that the treatment of French Muslim youth by police and the justice system in France merits distrust. The attitudes of French Muslim youth contrast notably with the greater level of trust in the police expressed by the same age group in the UK, and the lack of difference between the young and others in trust in the legal system in all states but France. German Muslim young adults (15–29) similarly have lower trust in the police than others, but they trust the legal system as much as Muslims who are older do. French Muslim young adults' overall well-being score, -2, is low not only because of their distrust in the police and legal systems, but also

Table 7.4: Summary results of vulnerable groups of Muslims

	Youth	Older	Low religiosity	High religiosity	Women	Foreign citizenship	Foreign born
France							
Trust in the police	-1	0	0	0	0	+1	+1
Trust legal system	-1	+1	0	0	0	+1	+1
Political trust	0	0	0	0	0	0	+1
Life satisfaction	0	+1	-1	+1	+1	0	0
Happiness	0	0	0	+1	0	0	0
Household income	0	0	0	0	0	-1	0
Years of education	0	0	+1	-1	0	-1	0
Hours worked[1]	-1	0	0	0	-1	0	0
Totals	-2	+2	0	+1	0	0	+3
Germany							
Trust in the police	-1	0	0	0	+1	0	0
Trust legal system	0	0	0	0	0	0	0
Political trust	+1	0	0	0	0	0	+1
Life satisfaction	0	0	0	0	+1	0	0
Happiness	+1	0	0	0	0	0	0
Household income	0	0	-1	0	0	0	-1
Years of education	+1	-1	0	-1	-1	-1	-1
Hours worked[1]	0	+1	+1	0	-1	0	0
Totals	+2	0	0	-1	0	-1	-1
Netherlands							
Trust in the police	0	0	0	0	0	0	0
Trust legal system	0	0	-1	0	0	0	0
Political trust	0	0	0	0	-1	+1	0
Life satisfaction	+1	0	-1	+1	0	-1	-1
Happiness	+1	-1	0	+1	0	0	-1
Household income	0	-1	0	+1	0	-1	0
Years of education	0	-1	0	0	0	0	0
Hours worked[1]	0	+1	0	-1	-1	0	+1
Totals	+2	-2	-2	+2	-2	-1	-1
UK							
Trust in the police	+1	0	0	0	0	+1	0
Trust legal system	0	0	0	0	0	+1	+1
Political trust	0	0	-1	0	0	+1	+1
Life satisfaction	0	0	0	+1	0	0	0
Happiness	0	0	0	0	0	0	0
Household income	0	-1	0	0	0	0	-1
Years of education	0	-1	0	0	+1	0	0
Hours worked[1]	0	0	+1	-1	-1	0	0
Totals	+1	-2	0	0	0	+3	+1

Data: ESS 2008-2002
Key: +1 (vulnerable group has statistically higher averages than comparison group), 0 (groups have statistically equal levels), -1 (vulnerable group has statistically lower levels)
[1] Youth are represented by all Muslims 15-29 for all indicators except hours worked where youth are 20-29.

because they have fewer hours worked than other Muslims in France, a problem that is not apparent for Muslims in the same 20–29-year-old age group in the other three states (where the score of '0' for this item indicates that they have about as many hours worked as other Muslims in the country).

There is no statistical difference between French Muslim women and men in terms of their trust in the police and the legal system (as indicated by the scores of '0' in this column, indicating no difference between Muslim women and their comparison group, men). In France, though, women indicate more life satisfaction than men (as indicated by the score of +1), and this is also true in Germany.

Those with high religiosity report more life satisfaction in France, the Netherlands and the UK; in Germany they have the same amount of life satisfaction as other Muslims. As we noted in Chapter Six, the highly religious have lower levels of well-being on the key indicators of 'years of education' in France and Germany, and 'hours worked' in the Netherlands and the UK. In other areas they do not differ negatively from less religious Muslims, and on the key indicators of happiness and life satisfaction often report more favourable well-being. Muslims with low levels of religiosity report less life satisfaction in France and the Netherlands, and less political trust in the UK. Muslims with low religiosity are more like other Europeans in that they too have low religiosity. Less religious Muslims may feel relatively deprived, in that they are more like other Europeans in terms of religiosity, but do not feel that they are treated as such. This is certainly the case in France, where the least religious Muslims were most likely to feel that they are a member of a group that is discriminated against, as we discussed in Chapter Five. We reported earlier, in Chapter Four, that foreign-born Muslims had greater trust in some elements of the political or justice system in three of the states (all but the Netherlands) suggesting that these states could do more for Muslims born in the state. The last column of Table 7.4 summarizes those findings.

Our examination of the well-being of these special demographic groups of Muslims perceived to be more vulnerable to dissatisfaction in Europe suggests the benefits of data for policy development. Institutional changes in policing appear to be warranted in France and Germany to improve young Muslims' trust in the police, for example. Related policies in the UK might provide useful examples, since Muslim youth in the UK had greater trust in the police than other Muslims in the 2002–2008 period examined by ESS. French men and Dutch women are much more likely than their gender opposites to report that they are a member of a group that is discriminated against, as we discussed in Chapter Five. Structural aspects of their situation should be examined to determine the basis of their greater sense of vulnerability.

The data provide no basis for concern about the disaffection of those Muslims with high religiosity: they do not differ from other Muslims in terms of their trust in the state and agencies of justice. The data also suggest that those Muslims with foreign citizenship or born abroad have higher well-being in Europe than do Muslims with the citizenship of their European state, or who were born there. Examination of areas in which the state can provide greater accommodation to the needs of its nationals who are Muslim would seem to be warranted.

Support for adults guiding Muslim youth

Widespread concern that Muslim youth won't fit into European states has not been based on analysis of data about them. Data from ESS and commissioned by FRA described earlier demonstrate that young Muslims in these four European states mirror the optimism of their elders, and, like them, express trust in the political system, trust in the legal system (in all states but France, where the activities toward Muslim youth are currently under outside scrutiny), and are at least as happy and satisfied as other Europeans. Our data also fail to support concerns that the Muslim highly religious are dissatisfied with Europe. While both young adults and the highly religious are very likely to report that they are members of a group that is discriminated against, they are not unhappy in Europe. Yet their satisfaction with life in Europe, despite their struggles to move forward, has not been taken into account by political or civic leaders. It is an untapped resource for the improvement of the communities and states within which they live. Muslims are generally as satisfied as other Europeans, and sometimes more so. These data suggest that they are attitudinally well placed to help Europe and its member states go forward.

Much has been made of the likelihood of radicalization emerging from Muslims' marginalization in Europe. Far more likely than the radicalization of Muslim youth and the Muslim highly religious is the possibility that they will focus on their own cultural organizations, rather than on the European agenda or that of its member states. Several aspects of Muslims' social organization and patterns of behaviour reflect both the permanence and the marginality of the religious minority in Europe. These include language-of-origin use at home, the continuing pull of homeland politics, the choice of homeland marriage partners, the attraction of newspapers and television shows from the 'old country', and economic ties to the homeland in the form of remittances. The fact that older Muslims are also happy and satisfied with their situation in Europe – and with the institutions of their member state – supports the hunch that they will guide their youth in directions that steer them clear of trouble, but allow them to prosper to the extent possible in Europe. Older Muslims, after all, sought opportunities for themselves and their families by coming to Europe. They are unlikely to look the other way if their young fail to prosper in Europe, but these parents and grandparents are also unlikely to encourage radicalization. ESS data demonstrate their trust and satisfaction in the institutions of their European state and their belief in the importance of behaving properly; the Home Office data for the UK indicate Muslims' greater concern than others about anti-social behaviour in their neighbourhoods. To the extent that they can, Muslims will keep their young close, sometimes using cultural organizations and symbols from the country of origin to give them a sense of identity where their European identity is not respected or where their Muslim identity is not respected within Europe. Parents and grandparents will do their best to guide their youth toward legitimate avenues of achievement, even if they cannot fully develop or utilize their talents for Europe.

Where the doors to youths' achievement are shut by bureaucratic regulations or bias, Muslim adults will lead their young to focus on their status within cultural organizations reflecting the family's religion and country of origin. Supervizing mosques' educational programmes, organizing symposia about Muslims' identity in Europe, developing *niche* businesses catering to the needs of the Muslim minority – all of these are opportunities open to women who choose to wear headscarves, to Muslim graduate students who are passed over for university positions or employment in research organizations, and to entrepreneurs or tradesmen (for example, butchers who will not cut pork) whose religious requirements reduce their appeal to employers. While non-Muslim Europeans do not think of these activities as mainstream – and may even feel threatened by them – it is hard to argue that they do not reflect the permanence of Muslims in Europe, their desire to lead the young toward legitimate avenues of achievement, and their initiative in contributing to the economy productively.

We do not deny the likelihood that Europe will find radicals who use Islam to support violent causes, but they will not be guided toward radicalism by their Muslim parents and grandparents in Europe. Violent extremists who claim the protection of Islam will have more in common with violent radicals who claim the protection of Christianity or of right wing ideology than with the Muslim youth or Muslim highly religious in Europe. As we have shown, several sources of data consistently suggest that Muslims in Europe seek to participate in and benefit from its democratic institutions, not to destroy them.

Accurate information provides key support for policy making in a low-trust political environment

The lower level of trust in political and justice institutions found among non-Muslim Europeans (than for Muslims) will make it more difficult for leaders to move in the direction of reducing discrimination and bias toward the religious minority on the institutional and individual level. Perceptions of minority group threat are difficult to dispel, even if they are unfairly attributed. Both accurate information and official support for its veracity are key in undermining inaccurate assumptions about minority populations. Benchmarking Muslim well-being in national and European examinations of happiness, life satisfaction and the key areas of life would provide a firm basis of knowledge pointing the way toward greater equality and protection of the religious diversity that Muslim Europeans represent.

ESS data indicate, for example, that Muslims in all four states, despite their positive outlook toward European and state institutions, are slightly uneasy in Europe about discrimination and crime. It is likely that both the bias reflected in discrimination against them and the reduction in social trust that is related to worry about crime reduce their ability to fully contribute their talents economically and socially. The processes of assessing well-being under development in individual states (for example; Gjoksi, 2010; de Jonge, 2009; Mulholland and Watt, 2010; Stiglitz, Sen and Fitoussi, 2009), as discussed in Chapter Two, include examination of the negative impact of discrimination, disparities in equality, political voice and social connectedness. Yet these data gathering plans do not currently propose to assess the degree to which such problems can be consequences of the structural segmentation of Muslims – as it develops, for example, from exclusionary church tax policies, bans on headscarves in public institutions, the strict language and family reunification limitations of civic integration contracts, and from multiple discrimination triggered by religious identification.

To the extent that they fail to gather data specifically on the situation of Muslims, efforts to benchmark well-being in Europe will limit their effectiveness in reducing disparities and polarizations, and in opening the door to the full utilization of talent across the member states. In the absence of these data, policy makers intent on reducing both the divide between religious groups and the marginalization of

Muslims will be without the key support that accurate information can provide. These data are necessary to convince electorates to move in the direction of greater inclusion of the needs of European Muslims in the bureaucratic regulations and institutional processes of the state and its agencies. The talents and abilities of European Muslims, like those of other newcomers, will then accrue to the benefit of Europe and its member states.

Appendix I ESS variables

Question	Coding
Religion	
Current religious denomination (RLGDNM)	1=Islam, 0=other religions and no affiliation
How religious are you (RLGDGR)	0-10, 10=very religious
How often pray apart from religious services (PRAY)	1-7, 1=every day, 7=never
How often attend religious services apart from special occasions (RLGATND)	1-7, 1=every day, 7=never
Overall Well-Being	
Satisfaction with life (STFLIFE)	0-10, 10=extremely satisfied
Overall happiness (HAPPY)	0-10, 10=extremely happy
Housing	
Important to live in secure and safe surroundings (IMPSAFE)	1-6, 6=very much like me, 1=not like me at all
Number of people living as regular members of household (HHMMB)	1-22 members
Urban-Rural (DOMICIL)	1=big city, 2=suburbs or outskirts of city, 3=town or small city, 4=country village, 5=farm or home in countryside
Education	
Highest level of education (EDULVL)	1-5, 5=highest level of education (tertiary education completed)
Years of full-time education completed (EDUYRS)	0-56 years
State of education in country (STFEDU)	0-10, 10=extremely good

Question	Coding
Employment and Income	
How satisfied with present state of economy in country (STFECO)	0-10, 10=extremely satisfied
Total number of hours contracted to work, overtime excluded (WKHCT)	0-168 hours
Total hours worked per week in main job, overtime included (WKHTOT)	0-168 hours
Ever unemployed and seeking work for more than 3 months (UEMP3M)	1=yes, 0=no
Responsibility for supervizing others (JBSPV)	1=yes, 0=no
Main source of household income (HINCSRCA)	
Household income, all sources (HINCTNTA)	R placed in percentile (1-10%, 11-20%...)
Feeling about household's income (HINCFEL)	1-4, 1=very difficult on present income, 4=living comfortably
Member of trade union (MBTRU)	1=yes, 0=no
Improve knowledge/skills: course/lecture/conference, last 12 months (ANTCRSE)	1=yes, 0=no
Ever had a paid job (PDJOBEV)	1=yes, 0=no
Main activity last 7 days (MNACTIC)	1=paid work, 2=education, 3=unemployed and looking for job, 4=unemployed and not looking for job, 5=permanently sick or disabled, 6=retired, 7=community or military service, 8=housework, looking after children
Health Care	
Subjective general health (HEALTH)	1-5, 5=very good
State of health services in country (STFHLTH)	0-10, 10=very good
Hampered in daily activities by illness/disability (HLTHHMP)	1=yes, a lot, 2=yes to some extent, 3=no

Question	Coding
Information	
Politics too complicated to understand (POLCMPL)	1-5, 5=frequently
TV, total time watching on average weekday (TVTOT)	0-7, 7=more than 3 hours
TV, total time watching news/politics/current affairs on average weekday (TVPOL)	0-7, 7=more than 3 hours
Radio, total time listening on average weekday (RDTOT)	0-7, 7=more than 3 hours
Radio, total time listening to news/politics/current events on average weekday (RDPOL)	0-7, 7=more than 3 hours
Newspaper, total reading time on average weekday (NWSPTOT)	0-7, 7=more than 3 hours
Newspaper, total time reading news/politics/current events on avg. weekday (NEWSPPOL)	0-7, 7=more than 3 hours
Use of internet (NETUSE)	0-7, 7=every day
Culture (interpreted as value statements)	
Gays and lesbians free to live life as they wish (FREEHMS)	1-5, 5=strongly agree
Men should have right to job over woman when jobs are scarce (MNRGTJB)[1]	1-5, 5=strongly agree
Ever lived with partner without being married (LVGPTNE)	1,0 1=yes
Ever been divorced (DVRCDEV)	1,0 1=yes
Government should reduce differences in income (GINCDIF)	1-5, 5=strongly agree
Basic public functions (equality, anti-discrimination and self-organization)	
Respondent or Household Member victim of Burglary/Assault last 5 years (CRMVCT)	

Question	Coding
Feeling of safety of walking alone in local area after dark (AESFDRK)	1-4, 4=very unsafe
How often worried about home being burgled (BRGHMWR)[1]	1-4, 4=never
Worry that home burgled has effect on quality of life (BRGHMEF)[1]	1-3, 3=no real effect
How often worry about being victim of violent crime (CRVCTWR)[1]	1-4, 4=never
Worry that victim of violent crime has effect on quality of life (CRVCTEF)[1]	1-3, 3=no real effect
Member of a group discriminated against in this country (DSCRGRP)	1=yes, 0=no
Discrimination of Respondent's Group: Religion (DSCRRLG)	1=yes, 0=no
Discrimination of Respondent's Group: Colour or Race (DSCRRCE)	1=yes, 0=no
Discrimination of Respondent's Group: Nationality (DSCRNTN)	1=yes, 0=no
Discrimination of Respondent's Group: Ethnicity (DSCRETN)	1=yes, 0=no
Discrimination of Respondent's Group: Gender (DSCRGND)	1=yes, 0=no
Political trust	
Most people can be trusted or you can't be too careful (PPLTRST)	0-10, 10=most people can be trusted
Trust in Parliament (TRSTPRL)	0-10, 10=highest level of trust
Trust in legal system (TRSTLGL)	0-10, 10=highest level of trust
Trust in police (TRSTPLC)	0-10, 10=highest level of trust
Trust in politicians (TRSTPLT)	0-10, 10=highest level of trust
Trust in political parties (TRSTPRT)[1]	0-10, 10=highest level of trust

Question	Coding
Trust in European Parliament (TRSTEP)	0-10, 10=highest level of trust
Trust in United Nations (TRSTUN)	0-10, 10=highest level of trust
Voted in last national election (VOTE)	1=yes, 0=no
Party voted for in last election (Germany) (PRTVDE2, PRTVADE2, PRTABDE2)	category of parties
Party voted for in last election (France) (PRTVTBFR, PRTVTAFR, PRTVTFR)	category of parties
Party voted for in last election (UK) (PRTVTGB, PRTVTAGB)	category of parties
Party voted for in last election (NL) (PRTVTCNL, PRTVTBNL, PRTVTANL, PRTVTNL)	category of parties
How interested in politics (POLINTR)	1-4, 4=highest interest
How satisfied with national government (STFGOV)	0-10, 10=highest satisfaction
How satisfied with the way democracy works in country (STFDEM)	0-10, 10=highest satisfaction
Controls	
Placement on left right scale (LRSCALE)	0-10, 10=farthest right
Citizen of country (CTZCNTR)	1=yes, 0=no
Citizenship (CTZSHIP)	nominal with multiple categories
Born in country (BRNCNTR)	1=yes, 0=no
Country of birth (CNTBRTHB)	nominal with multiple categories

Question	Coding
Language(s) at home: first mentioned (LNGHOMA) , second mentioned (LNGHOMB)	
Belong to minority ethnic group in country (BLGETMG)	1=yes, 0=no
Gender (GNDR)	1=female, 0=male
Age of respondent, calculated (AGEA)	scale, 15 (lowest age)-98 (highest age)
Urban-Rural (DOMICIL)	1=large city, 0=others

[1] Present only in 2008

[2] Present only in 2002

[3] Used in construction of age variable in 2002.

Appendix 2: Descriptives of variables from ALLBUS (2008)

Independent Variables	Muslims				Non-muslims			
	Min	Max	Mean	Sd	Min	Max	Mean	Sd
Religiosity (v709)	1	7	4.91	1.43	1	7	3.32	1.82
Born in Germany (v156)	0	1	0.14	0.34	0	1	0.87	0.33
Social trust (v126)	0	1	0.14	0.35	0	1	0.20	0.40
Participation voluntary organizations (v615–v619)	1	3	1.34	0.46	1	5	1.47	0.63
Net monthly income (v386)	200	3,000	1,094.78	511.32	1	8,000	1,302.35	817.78
Age (v154)	18	69	37.67	11.79	18	97	50.72	17.82
Gender (Female) (v151)	0	1	0.40	0.49	0	1	0.51	0.50
Level of education (v173)	1	5	2.78	1.36	1	5	3.11	1.19
Unemployed (v219)	0	1	0.18	0.38	0	1	0.06	0.24
German citizenship (v4)	0	1	0.30	0.46	0	1	0.97	0.18
Post-materialism (v105)	1	4	1.86	0.97	1	4	2.47	1.00
Extreme right ideology (v106)	0	1	0.10	0.31	0	1	0.08	0.27
Extreme left ideology (v106)	0	1	0.19	0.40	0	1	0.20	0.40
Supported CDU (v131)	1	10	3.59	2.88	1	10	5.33	3.40
Supported SPD (v132)	1	10	6.52	3.04	1	10	5.42	2.94

	Muslims				Non-muslims			
	Min	Max	Mean	Sd	Min	Max	Mean	Sd
Independent Variables								
Minutes watching TV per day (v12)	0	720	170.05	118.80	0	1200	149.52	94.39
Interest in politics (v100)	1	5	2.45	1.07	1	5	3.08	1.01
Evaluation of gov performance (v95)	1	6	3.90	1.20	1	6	3.35	1.20
Dependent Variables								
Connection to community (v501)	1	4	2.86	0.78	1	4	2.98	0.82
Connection to state and its people (v502)	1	4	2.73	0.78	1	4	2.95	0.79
Connection to Federal Republic (v505)	1	4	2.79	0.71	1	4	2.90	0.74
Evaluation of democracy as idea (v93)	1	6	5.32	0.75	1	6	5.42	0.86
Satisfaction with democracy in FRG (v94)	1	6	4.59	1.10	1	6	4.08	1.21
Trust in education system (v78)	1	7	5.37	1.15	1	7	4.89	1.23
Trust in health system (v71)	1	7	4.96	1.53	1	7	3.97	1.50
Trust in supreme court (v72)	1	7	5.15	1.50	1	7	4.77	1.53
Trust in Federal government (v79)	1	7	4.38	1.62	1	7	3.64	1.40
Trust in Parliament (Bundestag) (v73)	1	7	4.11	1.60	1	7	3.62	1.39
Trust in local government (v74)	1	7	4.68	1.50	1	7	4.38	1.45
Trust in political parties (v81)	1	7	3.61	1.48	1	7	3.08	1.31
Trust in judiciary (v75)	1	7	4.86	1.50	1	7	4.18	1.51
Trust in police (v80)	1	7	5.03	1.61	1	7	4.78	1.36

References

Ager, A. and Eyber, C. (2002) Indicators of Integration: A Review of Indicators of Refugee Integration. *Report to the Home Office on behalf of Michael Bell Associates.*

Ager, A. and Strang, A. (2004a) *Indicators of Integration: Final Report.* London: Home Office.

(2004b) The Experience of Integration: A Qualitative Study of Refugee Integration in the Local Communities of Pollokshaws and Islington. *Home Office Online Report 55/04.* London: Home Office.

(2008) Understanding Integration: a Conceptual Framework. *Journal of Refugee Studies* 21 (2): 167–191.

Ajala, I. (2010) The Muslim Vote and Muslim Lobby in France: Myths and Realities. *Journal of Islamic Law & Culture* 12 (2): 77–91.

Amiraux, V. (2000) Unexpected Biographies: Deconstructing the National Welfare State in M. Bommes and A. Geddes (eds) *Immigration and Welfare: Challenging the Borders of the Welfare State.* London: Routledge, pp. 227–247.

(2010a) From Empire to Republic, the French Muslim Dilemma in A. Triandafyllidou (ed.) *Muslims in 21st Century Europe.* London: Routledge, pp. 135–159.

(2010b) Crisis and New Challenges? French Republicanism Featuring Multiculturalism in A. Silj *European Multiculturalism Revisited.* London: ZED Books, pp. 65–104.

Amiraux, V. and Simon, P. (2006) There are No Minorities Here: Cultures of Scholarship and Public Debate on Immigrants and Integration in France. *International Journal of Comparative Sociology* 47: 191–215.

Andersen, U. (1990) Consultative Institutions for Migrant Workers in Z. Layton-Henry (ed.) *The Political Rights of Migrant Workers in Western Europe.* London: Sage Publications, pp. 113–126.

Argun, B. E. (2003) *Turkey in Germany: The Transnational Sphere of Deutschkei.* New York: Routledge.

BAMF (2009) (Bundesamt für Migration und Flüchtlinge, Federal Office for Migration and Refugees) *Muslimisches Leben in Deutschland* (Muslim Life in Germany) (Prepared by S. Haug, S. Musig and A. Stichs). Berlin: Bundesministerium des Innern (Ministry of the Interior) (BMI).

Baran, Z. (ed.) (2010) *The Other Muslims: Moderate and Secular.* New York: Palgrave.

BBC News. (2006) The Legacy of the Brixton Riots by Cindi John [Online] Available at http://newsvote.bbc.co.uk/mpapps/pagetools/print/news.bbc.co.uk/2/hi/uk_news/4854556.stm

(2009) Q&A Identity Cards [Online] Available at http://news.bbc.co.uk/2/hi/uk_news/politics/3127696.stm

Beckford, J. A., Joly, D. and Khosrokhavar, F. (2005) *Muslims in Prison*. Basingstoke: Palgrave.

Begag, A. (2007) *Ethnicity and Equality*. Lincoln, NE, USA: University of Nebraska Press.

Bell, M. (2009) 'Benchmarking Standards in Anti-Discrimination Law and Policy', in J. Niessen and T. Huddleston (eds), *Legal Frameworks for the Integration of Third-Country Nationals*. Leiden: Martinus Nijhoff Publishers, pp 141-58.

Bennhold, K. (2006) Sarkozy Turns France to Talk of Immigration. *International Herald Tribune*.

Bertossi, C. (2010) *What if National Models of Integration Did Not Exist?* Paper presented at the Annual Meeting of the American Sociological Association, Atlanta, Georgia, USA.

Bigo, D. (1994) The European Internal Security Field in M. Anderson and M. den Boer (eds) *Policing Across National Boundaries*. London: Pinter, p. 164.

(2002) Immigration and Security. *Alternatives* 27: 63–92.

Bird, K., Saalfeld, T. and Wüst, A. (eds) (2010) *The Political Representation of Immigrants and Minorities: Voters, Parties and Parliaments in Liberal Democracies*. London: Routledge.

Bleich, E. (2003) *Race Politics in Britain and France*. Cambridge: Cambridge University Press.

Boelhouwer, J. (2010) *Wellbeing in the Netherlands*. The Netherlands Institute for Social Research (SCP). The Hague: Textcetera. [Online] Available at www.scp.nl/english/Publications/Publications_by_year/Publications_2010/Wellbeing_in_the_Netherlands

Brubaker, R. (1992) *Citizenship and Nationhood in France and Germany*. Cambridge, MA, USA: Harvard University Press.

Brüß, J. (2008) Experiences of Discrimination Reported by Turkish, Moroccan and Bangladeshi Muslims in Three European States. *Journal of Ethnic and Migration Studies* 34 (6): 875–894.

Budzinski, M. (1999) *Die Multikulturelle Realitat: Minderheitsherrschaft und Minderheitenrechte*. Gottingen: Lamuv Verlag.

Buijs, F. (2006) *Muslims in NL*. Institute for Migration and Ethnic Studies, University of Amsterdam.

Cahn, C. (2004) Void at the Centre. *Roma Rights Quarterly* 1: 30–37. [Online] Available at www.errc.org/cikk.php?cikk=1942)

Castles, S. (1995) How Nation-States Respond to Immigration and Ethnic Diversity. *New Community* 21 (3): 293–308.

Castles, S. and Miller, M. J. (2009) *The Age of Migration: International Population Movements in the Modern World*. Fourth edition. New York: Guilford Press.

Catterberg, G. and Moreno, A. (2005). The individual Bases of Political Trust: Trends in New and Established Democracies. *International Journal of Public Opinion Research* 18 (1): 31–48.

CBS (2008) See Statistics Netherlands (2004).

Centre for Comparative Social Surveys (2010) *European Social Survey: Monitoring Attitude Change in Over 30 Countries.* London: Centre for Comparative Social Surveys.

CERD-UN (2008) (Committee on the Elimination of Racial Discrimination) Consideration of Reports Submitted by State Parties Under Article 9 of the Convention. Concluding Observations of CERD. Germany (Seventy-third session).

Cesari, J. (2004) *When Islam and Democracy Meet*. New York: Palgrave Macmillan.

(2009) The Securitization of Islam in Europe Research Paper 15 *The Changing Landscape of European Liberty and Security: An Integrated Project Financed by the Sixth EU Framework Programme.* [Online] Available at http://aei.pitt.edu/10763/1/1826.pdf

Colomer, J. M. (ed.) (2008) *Comparative European Politics*. Third edition. London: Routledge.

Communities and Local Government (2011) Future Cancellation of the Citizenship Survey [Online] Available at www.communities. gov.uk/communities/research/citizenshipsurvey/surveycancellation

Council of Europe (1997) *Measurement and Indicators of Integration.* Strasbourg: COE.

(2003) *Proposed Indicators for Measuring Integration of Immigrants and Minorities with a View to Equal Rights and Opportunities for all.* MG-IN Strasbourg: 7.

(2004) *Immigrant Integration Policy in the European Union.* Brussels 14615/04 (Presse 321). [Online] Available at www.consilium.europa. eu/uedocs/cms_data/docs/pressdata/en/jha/82745.pdf

(2005) *Concerted Development of Societal Cohesion Indicators: Methodological Guide.* Council of Europe Publishing. Strasbourg [Online] Available at www.coe.int/t/dg3/socialpolicies/socialcohesiondev/source/ GUIDE_en.pdf

(2008) Towards an Active, Fair and Socially Cohesive Europe. *Report of the High Level Task Force on Social Cohesion.* Council of Europe: Strasbourg [Online] Available at www.coe.int/t/dg3/default_en.asp

Crowley, J. (1993). Paradoxes in the Politicisation of Race: A Comparison of Britain and France. *New Community* 19 (4):627–643.

Dalton, R. J. (1999).Political Support in Advanced Industrial Democracies in P. Norris (ed.) *Critical Citizens: Global Support for Democratic Governance.* Oxford: Oxford University Press, pp. 57–77.

(2000a) The Decline of Party Identification in R. J. Dalton and M. Wattenberg (eds) *Parties without Partisans: Political Change in Advanced Industrial Democracies.* Oxford: Oxford University Press, pp. 19–36.

(2000b) Value Change and Democracy in S. J. Pharr and R. D. Putnam (eds) *Disaffected Democracies.* Princeton: Princeton University Press, pp. 252–269.

(2004) *Democratic Challenges, Democratic Choices: The Erosion of Political Support in Advanced Industrial Democracies.* Oxford: Oxford University Press.

(2005) The Social Transformation of Trust in Government. *International Review of Sociology* 15 (1): 133–154.

Dalton, R. J. and Weldon, S. A. (2005) Public Images of Political Parties: A Necessary Evil? *West European Politics* 28 (5): 931–951.

Davies, W. (2010) David Cameron to Introduce National Well-Being Measure in the UK, *Positive Psychology Digest.* [Online] Available at www.science20.com/positive_psychology_digest/david_cameron_introduce_national_wellbeing_measure_uk

de Jonge, T. (2009) *The State of Play in Measuring SWB in the Netherlands.* Statistics Netherlands. Paper presented at ISQOLS Conference: Measures and goals for the progress of societies. Satellite Meeting on Measuring Subjective Well-Being: An Opportunity for National Statistical Offices? [Online] Available at www.isqols2009.istitutodeglinnocenti.it/Content_en/Measuring%20SWB%20in%20The%20Netherlands%20v2RGED%20with%20cover%20page.pdf

Der Spiegel (2002) Basbakanimiz Schröder, 3: 40–41.

de Wijk, R. (2006) The Multiple Crisis in Dutch Parallel Societies. in A. S. Boubekeur, R. de Wijk and A. Maleshenko *Between Suicide Bombing and the Burning Banlieues: The Multiple Crises of Europe's Parallel Societies.* Working Paper 22 of the European Security Forum, pp. 7–15. [Online] Available at www.ceps.eu/book/between-suicide-bombings-and-burning-banlieues-multiple-crises-europes-parallel-societies

Diehl, C., Urbahn, J. and Esser, H. (1998) *Die soziale und politische Partizipation von Zuwanderen in der Bundesrepublik Deutschland,* Bonn: Friedrich-Ebert Stiftung.

Doerschler, P. and Jackson, P. I. (2010a) Host Nation Language Ability and Immigrant Integration in Germany: Use of GSOEP to Examine Language as an as an Integration Criterion. *Democracy and Security* 6: 147–182.

(2010b) Do Muslims in Germany Really Fail to Integrate? Muslim Integration and Trust in Public Institutions *Forum 21* (6): 110–117. [Online] Available at www.coe.int/t/dg4/youth/resources/forum_21/forum_EN.asp

(2011) Do Muslims in Germany Really Fail to Integrate: Muslim Integration and Trust in Public Institutions. *Journal of International Migration and Integration,* 1–21. [Online] Available at https://springerlink3.metapress.com/content/183x06469w833u76/resource-secured/?target=fulltext.pdf&sid=xisxzx3sqrwxk3ougzku2c3b&sh=www.springerlink.com

Dogan, M. (2005) Erosion of Confidence in Thirty European Democracies. *Comparative Sociology* 4 (1–2): 11–53.

Dutch News.nl (2011) School Muslim headscarf ban, only if education under threat Feb. 9. http://www.dutchnews.nl/news/archives/2011/02/school_muslim_headscarf_ban_on.php

(accessed April 5, 2012).

Dutch News.nl (2011) School Muslim headscarf ban, only if education under threat Feb. 9. http://www.dutchnews.nl/news/archives/2011/02/school_muslim_headscarf_ban_on.php (accessed April 5, 2012).

Duyvendak, J. W. and Scholten, P. W. A. (2010) Beyond the Dutch 'Multicultural Model': The Coproduction of Integration Policy Frames in the Netherlands. *International Migration and Integration.* [Online] Available at www.springerlink.com/content/653675h748u26875/fulltext.pdf

Easton, D. (1965) *A Systems Analysis of Political Life.* New York: John Wiley & Sons, Inc.

Economist (2007) France's suburbs, pp. 64–65, 10 November.

(2008) Happiness is a warm baguette? 13 January [Online] Available at www.economist.com/blogs/freeexchange/2008/01/happiness_is_a_warm_baguette

(2011) Quis custodiet? 63–64, 18 June [Online] Available at www.economist.com/node/18836258

ECRI (2000) European Commission against Racism and Intolerance General Policy Recommendation Number 5 On Combating Intolerance and Discrimination Against Muslims (adopted on 16 March 2000) [Online] Available at www.coe.int/t/dghl/monitoring/ecri/activities/gpr/en/recommendation_n5/Rec5%20en21.pdf

Reports on France (1998, 2000, 2005, 2010) [Online] Available at www.coe.int/t/dghl/monitoring/ecri/Country-by-country/France/France_CBC_en.asp

Reports on Germany (1998, 2000, 2004, 2009) [Online] Available at www.coe.int/t/dghl/monitoring/ecri/Country-by-country/Germany/Germany_CBC_en.asp

Reports on Netherlands (1998, 2001, 2008) [Online] Available at www.coe.int/t/dghl/monitoring/ecri/Country-by-country/Netherlands/Netherlands_CBC_en.asp

Reports on UK (1999, 2001, 2005, 2010) [Online] Available at www.coe.int/t/dghl/monitoring/ecri/Country-by-country/United_Kingdom/UnitedKingdom_CBC_en.asp

Englemann, B. and Muller, M. (2008). *Brain Waste. Die Anerkennung von auslandischen Qualifikationen in Deutschland.* Augsburg: Tur an Tur Integrationsprojekte gGmbh, pp. 54–59 (see chapter 3.1.3) [Online] Available at www.berufliche-anerkennung.de/brain%20waste.pdf

Esposito, J. and Mogahed, D. (2008) *Who Speaks for Islam? What a Billion Muslims Really Think.* New York: Gallup Press.

ESS (2008) European Social Survey Round 4 Data. Data file edition 3.0. Norwegian Social Science Data Services, Norway.

(2012) The European Social Survey [Online] Available at http://ess.nsd.uib.no/

Esser, H. and Korte, H. (1985) The Policy of the Federal Republic of Germany in T. Hammar (ed.) *European Immigration Policy: A Comparative Analysis.* Cambridge: Cambridge University Press, pp. 165–205.

EU MIDIS 2009 01, 02, 03; 2010, 05. See FRA (European Agency for Fundamental Rights)

European Commission (2005) A Common Agenda for Integration. Framework for the Integration of Third Country Nationals in the European Union. [Online] Available at http://eur-lex.europa.eu/LexUriServ/LexUriServ.do?uri=CELEX:52005DC0389:EN:NOT

(2007) *Tackling Multiple Discrimination: Practices, Policies and Laws.* [Online] Available at http://ec.europa.eu/social/main.jsp?catId=738&furtherPubs=yes&langId=en&pubId=51

EUMC Reports of the European Monitoring Centre on Racism and Xenophobia

(2003) Comparative Report: Migrants, Minorities and Employment. [Online] Available at http://fra.europa.eu/fraWebsite/research/publications/publications_by_date/previous_publications/pub_cr_migrantsemployment_en.htm

(2005a) Racist Violence in 15 EU Member States. [Online] Available at www.fra.europa.eu/fraWebsite/attachments/CS-RV-main.pdf

(2005b) EUMC Migrants, Minorities and Housing 2005 (December). [Online] Available at http://fra.europa.eu/fraWebsite/material/pub/comparativestudy/CS-Housing-en.pdf.

(2006) Muslims in the European Union. [Online] Available at www.fra.europa.eu/fraWebsite/attachments/Manifestations_EN.pdf.

(2008) Migrants, Minorities and Housing. [Online] Available at www.libertysecurity.org/auteur655.html

European Parliament (2007) Committee on Civil Liberties, Justice and Home Affairs. (J. Niessen and T. Huddleston, authors.) *Setting Up a System of Benchmarking to Measure the Success of Integration Policies in Europe.* Brussels.

European Parliament and Council (1995) Directive 95/46/EC. [Online] Available at www.cdt.org/privacy/eudirective/EU_Directive_.html

European Union (2010) Seventh Framework Programme. *Genderace: The Use of Racial Antidiscrimination Laws.* [Online] Available at http://genderace.ulb.ac.be/rapports/GENDERACE%20FINAL%20REPORT%20sent.pdf

Faas, D. (2010a) Muslims in Germany: from Guest Workers to Citizens? in A. Triandafyllidou (ed.) *Muslims in 21st Century Europe.* London: Routledge, pp. 59–77.

(2010b) Negotiating Political Identities: Multiethnic Schools and Youth in Europe. Surrey, England: Ashgate.

Favell, A. (1998a) Multicultural Race Relations in Britain: Problems of Interpretation and Explanation in C. Joppke (ed.) *Challenge to the Nation State: Immigration in Western Europe and the United States.* Oxford: Oxford University Press, pp. 319–350.

(1998b) *Philosophies of Integration: Immigration and the Idea of Citizenship in Britain and France.* London: Macmillan.

Federal Office for Migration and Refugees (2009). See BAMF.

Feilzer, M.Y. (2009) 'Not Fit for Purpose. The (AB)Use of the British Crime Survey as a Performance Measure for Individual Police Forces'. *Policing*, 3(2), pp 200-211.

Feldblum, M. (1999) *Reconstructing Citizenship.* Albany, NY: State University of New York Press.

Fennema, M. and Tillie, J. (1999) Political Participation and Political Trust in Amsterdam Civic Communities and Ethnic Networks. *Journal of Ethnic and Migration Studies* 25 (4): 703–726.

(2004) Do Immigrant Policies Matter? Ethnic Civic Communities and Immigrant Policies in Amsterdam, Liege and Zurich in R. Penninx, K. Kraal, M. Mortiniello and S. Vertovec (eds) *Citizenship in European Cities: Immigrants, Local Politics and Integration Policies*. Aldershot, England: Ashgate, pp. 85–106.

Fermin, A. (1997) *Nederlandse politieke partijen over minderhedenbeleid 1977–95*. Amsterdam: Thesis Publishers.

Fetzer, J. S. and Soper, J. C. (2005) *Muslims and the State*. Cambridge: Cambridge University Press.

Finkielkraut, A. (2003) *Au Nom de l'Autre*. Paris. La Decouverte.

FRA (2007) European Agency for Fundamental Rights (FRA) *Combating Ethnic and Racial Discrimination and Promoting Equality in the European Union*. http://fra.europa.eu/fraWebsite/research/publications/publications_per_year/2007/pub_tr_trendscombatingdiscrimination_en.htm

(2009) *Annual Work Programme* [Online] Available at http://fra.europa.eu/fraWebsite/news&events/news&events_en.htm

(2009 01) *EU-MIDIS at a Glance*. [Online] Available at http://fra.europa.eu/fraWebsite/attachments/EU-MIDIS_GLANCE_EN.pdf

(2009 02) *EU MIDIS Data in Focus Report: Muslims* [Online] Available at http://fra.europa.eu/fraWebsite/attachments/EU-MIDIS_MUSLIMS_EN.pdf

(2009 03) *EU MIDIS Main Results Report* [Online] Available at http://fra.europa.eu/fraWebsite/attachments/eumidis_mainreport_conference-edition_en_.pdf

(2010) Experience of Discrimination, Social Marginalisation and Violence. [Online] Available at http://fra.europa.eu/fraWebsite/attachments/Pub-racism-marginalisation_en.pdf

(2010 05) *EU-MIDIS Data in Focus Report: Multiple Discrimination*. [Online] Available at www.fra.europa.eu/fraWebsite/attachments/EU_MIDIS_DiF5-multiple-discrimination_EN.pdf

Freeman, G. and Ögelman, N. (1998) Homeland Citizenship Policies and the Status of Third Country Nationals in the European Union. *Journal of Ethnic and Migration Studies* 24 (4): 769–788.

Gallisot, R. (1989) Nationalité et Citoyenetté, *Après-Demain*, 286: 8–15.

Geddes, A. (2003) *The Politics of Migration and Immigration in Europe*. London: Sage.

Geddes, A. and Wunderlich, D. (2009) Policies and 'Outcomes' for Third Country Nationals in Europe's Labour Markets in J. Niessen and T. Huddleston (eds) *Legal Frameworks for the Integration of Third-Country Nationals*. Leiden: Martinus Nijhoff Publishers, pp. 195–215.

Geiser, V. (2004) Islamophobia in Europe in I. Ramberg (ed.) *Islamophobia and its Consequences on Young People.* Council of Europe, pp. 36–46.

Genderace, see European Union Seventh Framework Programme.

Geschiere, P. (2009) *The Perils of Belonging: Autochthony, Citizenship, and Exclusion in Africa and Europe*, University of Chicago.

Giry, S. (2006) France and its Muslims. *Foreign Affairs* 85 (5): 87–104.

Gjoksi, N. (2010) (December) *National Approaches to Measure Wealth and Well-being in the Context of Sustainable Development.* ESDN Case Study No. 4. [Online] Available at www.sd-network.eu/pdf/case%20 studies/04_ESDN%20Case%20Study%204_FINAL.pdf

Goldberg, A. (2002) Islam in Germany in S. T. Hunter (ed.) *Islam, Europe's Second Religion: The New Social, Cultural and Political Landscape.* Westport, CT: Praeger.

Goodman, S. W. (2010) Integration Requirements for Integration's Sake? Identifying, Categorizing and Comparing Civic Integration Policies. *Journal of Ethnic and Migration Studies* 36 (5) (May): 763–772.

Goody, J. (2004). *Islam in Europe.* Malden, MA: Polity Press.

Graziano, P. and Vink, M. (eds.) (2006). *Europeanization: New Research Agendas.* Basingstoke: Palgrave Macmillan.

Grillo, R. (2010) British and Others: From Race to Faith in S. Vertovec and S. Wessendorf *The Multicultural Backlash.* London: Routledge, pp. 50–71.

Guenif, N. (2006) La Française voilée, la buerette, le garçon arabe et le musulman laïc: Les figures assignees du racism vertueux in N. Guenif (ed.) *La Republique mise a nu par son immigration.* La Fabrique: Paris, pp. 109–132.

Guiraudon, V. (2000) European Integration and Migration Policy: Vertical Policy-making as Venue Shopping. *Journal of Common Market Studies* 38 (2): 251–271.

(2006) Different Nation, Same Nationhood in P. D. Culpepper, P. A. Hall and B. Palier (eds) *Changing France.* Basingstoke: Palgrave Macmillan, pp. 129–149.

(2008) Integration Contracts for Immigrants: Common Trends and Differences in the European Experience. Real Instituto Elcano: Demography, Population and International Migrations. [Online] Available at

http://129.35.96.152/wps/portal/rielcano_eng/Content?WCM_ GLOBAL_CONTEXT=/elcano/elcano_in/zonas_in/ari43-2008

Guiraudon, V, Phalet, K. and ter Wal, J. (2005) Monitoring Ethnic Minorities in the Netherlands. ISSJ 183 UNESCO. Oxford: Blackwell Publishing Ltd, pp. 75–87. [Online] Available at: http://ics.uda. ub.rug.nl/FILES/root/Articles/2005/PhaletK-Measuring/PhaletK-Measuring-2005.pdf

Haller, G. (2002) *Die Grenzen der Solidarität. Europa und die USA im Umgang mit Staat, Nation und Religion (The Boundaries of Solidarity in Europe and the USA: State, Nation and Religion).* Berlin: Aufbau.

Hammar, T. (1994) *Democracy and the Nation State: Aliens, Denizens and Citizens in the World of International Migration.* Aldershot, UK: Avebury.

Hargreaves, A. (1995). *Immigration, 'Race' and Ethnicity in Contemporary France.* London: Routledge.

Haug, S. S. Musig and A. Stichs (2009). See BAMF (2009).

Heitmeyer, W., Müller, J. and Schröder, H. (1998) *Verlockender Fundamentalismus. Türkische Jugendliche in Deutschland. (Seductive Fundamentalism. Turkish Youngsters in Germany.)* Frankfurt am Main: Suhrkamp.

Hobsbawm, E. and Ranger, T. (eds) (1992) *The Invention of Tradition.* Cambridge: Cambridge University Press.

Hollo, L. (2009) *The European Commission against Racism and Intolerance (ECRI).* Strasbourg: Council of Europe.

Home Office (2008a) *The Path to Citizenship.* London: HMSO.

(2008b) *Persons Granted British Citizenship: United Kingdom, 2007.* London: HMSO.

Hunger, U. (2001) Party Competition and Inclusion of Immigrants in Germany, *German Policy Studies* 1 (3): 302–330.

Huntington, S. (1996) *The Clash of Civilizations: Remaking of World Order.* New York: Touchstone.

Hurwitz, J. and Peffley, M. (2005) Explaining the Great Racial Divide: Perceptions of Fairness in the U.S. Criminal Justice System. *The Journal of Politics* 67 (3) August: pp 762-85.

Hussain, D. (2004) Muslim Political Participation in Britain and the 'Europeanisation' of FIQH. *Welt des Islams*, 44 (3): 376–401.

Huysmans, J. (2006) *The Politics of Insecurity: Fear, Migration and Asylum in the EU.* London: Routledge.

Inglehart, R. and Norris, P. (2003) The True Clash of Civilizations, *Foreign Policy*, 135: 63–70.

Ipgrave, J. (2010) Including the Religious Viewpoints and Experiences of Muslim Students in an Environment that is both Plural and Secular, *International Migration and Integration*, 11: 5–22.

Ipgrave, J., Miller, J. and Hopkins, P. (2010) Responses of Three Muslim Majority Primary Schools in England to the Islamic Faith of Their Pupils. *International Migration and Integration*, 11: 73–89.

Ireland, P. (1994) *The Policy Challenge of Ethnic Diversity*. Cambridge: Harvard University Press.

Jackson, P. I. (1995) Minority Group Threat, Crime, and the Mobilization of Law in France in D. F. Hawkins (ed.) *Ethnicity, Race, and Crime*, Albany, NY: State University of New York Press.

(1997) Minorities, Crime, Criminal Justice in France in I. H. Marshall (ed.), *Minorities, Migrants and Crime*. California: Sage, pp. 130–150.

(2009) Measuring Muslim Integration in Europe, *Democracy and Security*, 5: 223–248.

(2010) Race, Crime and Criminal Justice in France in A. Kalunta-Crumpton (ed.) *Race, Crime and Criminal Justice*. Hampshire, UK: Palgrave MacMillan, pp. 51–71.

Jackson, P. I. and Parkes, R. (2007) Parallel Societies, Cultural Tolerance and Securitization." *Journal of Social and Ecological Boundaries* 3 (1): 7–42.

Jackson, P. I. and Warner, J. (2007) Muslim Integration in Postindustrial Democracies. *Journal of Social and Ecological Boundaries*, Fall/Winter, 2007–2008, 3 (1) Special Issue.

Jackson, P. I., Zervakis, P. and Parkes, R. (2005) A Contextual Analysis of the Integration of Muslims, *Discourse of Sociological Practice* 7: 205–216.

Jacobs, D. and Herman, B. (2009) in J. Niessen and T. Huddleston (eds.) *Legal Frameworks for the Integration of Third-Country Nationals*. Leiden: Martinus Nijhoff Publishers, pp 113–39.

Jansson, K., Budd, S. Lovbakke, J., Moley, S. and Thorpe, K. (2007) *Attitudes, Perceptions and Risks of Crime: Supplementary Volume 1 to Crime in England and Wales 2006/7*, second edition. Home Office. [Online] Available at http://rds.homeoffice.gov.uk/rds/pdfs07/hosb1907.pdf

Jenkins, P. (2006) Demographics, Religion, and the Future of Europe. *Orbis: A Journal of World Affairs* 50 (3): 519–539.

John, B. (1997) *Berliner Jugendliche turkischer Herkunft*. Berlin: Seantsverwaltung fur Gesundheit und Soziales.

Joppke, C. (2007) Beyond National Models: Civic Integration Policies for Immigrants in Western Europe. *West European Politics* 30 (1): 1–22.

Kaina, V. (2008) Declining Trust in Elites and Why We Should Worry About It – With Empirical Evidence From Germany. *Government and Opposition* 43 (3): 405–423.

Kasse, M. (1999) Interpersonal Trust, Political Trust and Non-institutionalized Political Participation in Western Europe. *West European Politics* 22 (3): 1–21.

Keele, L. (2007) Social Capital and the Dynamics of Trust in Government, *American Journal of Political Science* 51 (2): 241–254.

Klingemann, H-D. (1999) Mapping Political Support in the 1990s: A Global Analysis in P. Norris (ed.) *Critical Citizens: Global Support for Democratic Governance*. Oxford: Oxford University Press, pp. 31–56.

Klingemann, H-D. and Fuchs, D. (1995) *Citizens and the State*. Oxford: Oxford University Press.

Klausen, J. (2008) Public Policy for European Muslims: Facts and Perceptions. Institute for Strategic Dialogue. [Online] Available at www.strategicdialogue.org/PublicPolicyMuslimsWEB.pdf

Koenig, M. (2005) Incorporating Muslim Migrants in Western Nation States, *Journal of International Migration and Integration* 6 (2): 219–234.

(2007a) *Religionspolitik in Europa*. Frankfurt am Main: Campus.

(2007b) Europeanising the Governance of Religious Diversity. *Journal of Ethnic and Migration Studies* 33 (6): 911–932.

König, T. and Mäder, L. (2009) The Myth of 80% and the Impact of Europeanisation on German Legislation. Working Paper. Mannheim Centre for European Social Research. [Online] Available at www. mzes.uni-mannheim.de/publications/wp/wp-118.pdf

Koopmans, R. and Statham, P. (1999) Challenging the Liberal Nation-State? Postnationalism, Multiculturalism, and the Collective Claims Making of Migrants and Ethnic Minorities in Britain and Germany., *American Journal of Sociology* 105 (3): 652–696.

(2000) Challenging the Liberal Nation-State? Postnationalism, Multiculturalism, and the Collective Claims-Making of Migrants and Ethnic Minorities in Britain and Germany in R. Koopmans and P. Statham (eds) *Challenging Immigration and Ethnic Relations Politics: Comparative European Perspectives*. Oxford: Oxford University Press.

Laborde, C. (2001) The Culture(s) of the Republic: Nationalism and Multiculturalism in French Republican Thought, *Political Theory* 29 (5): 715–735.

Ladis Bulletin. National Alcohol and Drugs Information System, pp. 1–5. [Online] Available at: www.ladisonline.nl/files/pdf/bulletin/eng/Bulletin%20ethnic%20 minorities%202005%20eng.pdf

Ladrech, R. (1994) Europeanization of Domestic Politics and Institutions: The Case of France. *Journal of Common Market Studies* 32 (1): 69–88.

Lanz, S. (2010) The German Sonderweb: Multiculturalism as 'Racism with a Distance' in A. Silj, *European Multiculturalism Revisited*. London: ZED Books, pp. 105–146.

Lavenex, S. (2001) Europeanization of Refugee Policies: Normative Challenges and Institutional Legacies. *Journal of Common Market Studies,* 39 (5): 851–874.

Laurence, J. and Vaisse, J. (2006) *Integrating Islam.* Washington, DC: Brookings Institution Press.

Law Library of Congress (2011) "Netherlands: Local Ruling Upholding Headscarf Ban in Catholic School." April 11. Available at: www.loc.gov/lawweb/servlet/lloc_news?disp3_l205402618_text (accessed April 5, 2012).

Leweling, T. (2005) Exploring Muslim Diaspora Communities in Europe through a Social Movement Lens: Some Initial Thoughts. *Strategic Insights* IV (5). [Online] Available at www.nps.edu/Academics/centers/ccc/publications/OnlineJournal/2005/May/lewelingMay05.pdf

Lewis, P. (2007) *Young, British and Muslim.* London: Continuum.

Lind, E. and Tyler, T.R. (2008) *The Social Psychology of Procedural Justice.* New York: Plenum Press.

Liska, A. E., Lawrence, J. J. and Sanchirico, A. (1982) Fear of Crime as a Social Fact. *Social Forces* 70 (3): 760–770.

Lochak, D. (1989) Les minorités et le droit publique français: Du refus des différences a la gestion des différences in A. Fenet and G. Soulier (eds), *Les Minorities et leurs Droits Depuis 1789.* Paris: L'Harmattan, pp. 111–184.

Lorcerie, F. (2010) A French Approach to Minority Islam? A Study in Normative Confusion. *Journal of International Migration and Integration,* 11: 59–72.

Mail Online (2009) *Sarkozy includes Happiness and well-being in France's measure of economic progress.* September 15. Available at: www.dailymail.co.uk/news/article-1213361/Sarkozy-includes-happiness-Frances-measure-economic-progress.html

Malik, M. (2010) Progressive Multiculturalism: The British Experience in A. Silj *European Multiculturalism Revisited.* London: ZED Books, pp. 11–64.

Manchin, R. (2004) *Religion in Europe: Trust not Filling the Pews.* Gallup Survey Analysis, [Online] Available at www.gallup.com/poll/13117/Religion-Europe-Trust-Filling-Pews.aspx?utm_source=email%2Ba%2Bfriend&utm_medium=email&utm_campaign=sharing&utm_term=Religion-Europe-Trust-Filling-Pews&utm_content=morelink

Maussen, M. (2006) The Governance of Islam in Western Europe, IMISCOE Paper 16. Available at: http://imiscoe.socsci.uva.nl/publications/workingpapers/documents/GovernanceofIslam-stateoftheart_000.pdf

Maxwell, R. (2010a) Evaluating Migrant Integration: Political Attitudes Across Generations in Europe. *International Migration Review* 44 (1): 25–52.

(2010b) Trust in Government Among British Muslims: The Importance of Migration Status, *Political Behavior* 32: 89–109.

Messina, A. (2006) The Political Incorporation of Immigrants in Europe: Trends and Implications. in A. Messina and G. Lahav (eds). *The Migration Reader: Key Contributions to Policy and Politics.* Colorado: Lynne Rienner Publishers, pp 470-93.

(2007) *The Logics and Politics of Post-World War II Migration to Western Europe.* Cambridge: Cambridge University Press.

Messina, A. and Lahav, G. (eds) (2006) *The Migration Reader: Key Contributions to Policy and Politics.* Colorado: Lynne Rienner Publishers

Miller, M. (1981) *Foreign Workers in Western Europe: An Emerging Political Force?* New York: Praeger.

Modood, T. and Meer, N. (2010) Contemporary Developments in Cases of Muslim-State Engagement in A. Triandafyllidou (ed.) *Muslims in 21st Century Europe.* London: Routledge, pp. 78–102.

Modood, T., Triandafyllidou, A. and Zapata-Barrero, R. (2006) *Multiculturalism, Muslims and Citizenship.* New York: Routledge

Mogahed, D. and Nyiri, Z. (2007) Reinventing Integration: Muslims in the West, *Harvard International Review* (Summer): 14–18. [Online] Available at www.thefreelibrary.com/Reinventing+integration%3a+Muslims+in+the+West.-a0167969652.

Mucchielli, L. (2009) Autumn 2005: A Review of the Most Important Riot in the History of French Contemporary Society, *Journal of Ethnic and Migration Studies* 35 (5): 731–751.

Mulholland, H. and Watt, N. (2010) David Cameron defends plans for wellbeing index, *Guardian*.co.uk [Online] Available at http://www.guardian.co.uk/politics/2010/nov/25/david-cameron-defends-wellbeing-index/print.

Munson, H. (2004) Lifting the Veil: Understanding the Roots of Islamic Militancy. *Harvard International Review* 25 (4): 20–23.

Negrin, K. (2003) Collecting Ethnic Data: An Old Dilemma, The New Challenges, *EUMAP: EU Monitoring and Advocacy Program Online Journal.* Reprinted in 2009 at the link below: www.soros.org/resources/articles_publications/articles/ethnic-data-20030403/ethnic-data-20030403.pdf

New York Times (2007) *Muslims' Veils Test Limits of Britain's Tolerance.* [Online] Available at www.nytimes.com/2007/06/22/world/europe/22veil.html?pagewanted=print

Niessen, J. (2009) Construction of the Migrant Integration Policy Index in J. Niessen and T. Huddleston (eds) *Legal Frameworks for the Integration of Third-Country Nationals.* Leiden: Martinus Nijhoff Publishers, pp. 1–14.

Niessen, J. and Huddleston, T. (eds) (2009) *Legal Frameworks for the Integration of Third-Country Nationals.* Leiden: Martinus Nijhoff Publishers.

Nyiri, Z. (2007) *European Muslims Show No Conflict Between Religious and National Identities.* Gallup Survey Analysis, April 27 [Online] Available at www.gallup.com/poll/27325/European-Muslims-Show-Conflict-Between-Religious-National-Identities.aspx?utm_source=email%2Ba%2Bfriend&utm_medium=email&utm_campaign=sharing&utm_term=European-Muslims-Show-Conflict-Between-Religious-National-Identities&utm_content=morelink

OECD (2000) (2004) (2006) Analyses of PISA results (Programme for International Student Assessment). [Online] Available at www.pisa.oecd.org

(2007) Social, Employment and Migration Working Papers No. 47. *Labour Market Integration of Immigrants in Germany.* Thomas Liebig: OECD.

Office for National Statistics (2004) Focus on Religion. [Online] The report is now available at www.statistics.gov.uk (where all the national Statistics Reports can be found by typing the title into the search box at the top).

(2006) *Focus on Ethnicity and Religion.* Basingstoke: Palgrave Macmillan.

Őgelman, N. (2003) Documenting and Explaining the Persistence of Homeland Politics among Germany's Turks. *International Migration Review* 37 (1): 163–193.

Open Society Institute (2005) *Muslims in the UK: Policies for Engaged Citizens.* OSE/EU Monitoring and Advocacy Program.

(2007) *Muslims in the EU: Cities Report, Germany.* EU Monitoring and Advocacy Program. [Online] Available at www.soros.org/initiatives/home/articles_publications/publications/museucities_20080101/museucitiesger_20080101.pdf

(2009) *Ethnic Profiling in the European Union: Pervasive, Ineffective and Discriminatory.* [Online] Available at www.soros.org/initiatives/justice/focus/equality_citizenship/articles_publications/publications/profiling_20090526

(2010) *Muslims in Europe: A Report on 11 EU Cities.* At Home in Europe Project. [Online] Available at www.soros.org/initiatives/ home/articles_publications/publications/muslims-europe-20091215

Ozyurek, E. (2009) Convert Alert: German Muslims and Turkish Christians as Threats to Security in the New Europe. *Comparative Studies in Society and History* 51 (1): 91–116.

Penninx, R. (2006) Dutch Immigrant Policies Before and After the Van Gogh Murder. *Journal of Migration and Integration* 7 (2): 242–254.

Pfaff, S. and Gill, A. J. (2006) Will a Million Muslims March? *Comparative Political Studies* 29 (7): 803–828.

Prime Minister's *Portal Du Government,* France (2008) [Online] Available at www.premierministre.gouv.fr/en/information/latest_news_97/ controlling_immigration_56561.html (accessed 21 November 2008).

Prins, B. and Saharso, S. (2010) From Toleration to Repression: The Dutch Backlash Against Multiculturalism in S. Vertovec and S. Wessendorf (eds.) *The Multicultural Backlash.* London: Routledge, pp. 72–91.

Putnam, R. D., Pharr, S. J. and Dalton, R. J. (2000) Introduction: What's Troubling the Trilateral Democracies in S. J. Pharr and R. D. Putnam (eds) *Disaffected Democracies.* Princeton: Princeton University Press, pp. 3–27.

RAXEN (Racism and Xenophobia Network) reports below are available through the following link sponsored by the Fundamental Rights Agency. Available at: http://fra.europa.eu/fraWebsite/research/ background_cr/background_cr_en.htm

RAXEN (2005) Focal Point for France (ADRI). *National Analytical Studies on Racist Violence and Crime* published by EUMC.

(2005) Focal Point for Germany/European Forum for Migration Studies (EFMS), University of Bamberg. *National Analytical Studies on Racist Violence and Crime* published by EUMC.

(2005) Focal Point for the Netherlands (DUMC) *National Analytical Studies on Racist Violence and Crime* published by EUMC.

(2005) Focal Point for the UK (Commission for Racial Equality), *National Analytical Studies on Racist Violence and Crime* published by EUMC

(2009) Racism, Xenophobia and Ethnic Discrimination in Germany. *National Analytical Studies on Racist Violence and Crime* published by EUMC [Also online] Available at www.efms.uni-bamberg.de/pdf/ Rassismus%20update%202008.pdf

Rheault, M. and Mogahed, D. (2008) *Moral Issues Divide Westerners from Muslims in the West*. Gallup Survey Analysis [Online] Available at www.gallup.com/poll/107512/Moral-Issues-Divide-Westerners-From-Muslims-West.aspx?utm_source=email%2Ba%2Bfriend&utm_medium=email&utm_campaign=sharing&utm_term=Moral-Issues-Divide-Westerners-From-Muslims-West&utm_content=morelink

Roy, O. (2006) Foreword in J. Laurence and J. Vaisse *Integrating Islam*. Washington DC: Brookings Institution Press.

Rosenow, K. (2009) The Europeanisation of Integration Policies. *International Migration* 47 (1): 133–159.

Saggar, S. (2000) *Race and Representation: Electoral Politics and Ethnic Pluralism in Britain*. Manchester: Manchester University Press.

Saggar, S. (2001) *Race and Representation: Electoral Politics and Ethnic Pluralism in Britain*. Manchester, UK: Manchester University Press.

Saharso, S. and Lettinga, D. (2008) Contentious Citizenship: Policies and Debates on the Veil in the Netherlands. *Social Politics: International Studies in Gender, State and Society* 15 (4): 455–480.

Sarrazin, T. (2010) *Germany Does Away With Itself.* Deutsche Verlags-Austalt.

Schain, M. (2008) *The Politics of Immigration in France, Britain, and the United States.* New York: Palgrave.

Scheffer, P. (2000) Het Multiculturele Drama, *NRC Handelsblad,* 29 January.

Schiffauer, W. (2006) Enemies within the Gates in T. Modood, A. Triandafyllidou and R. Zapata-Barrero, *Multiculturalism, Muslims and Citizenship.* New York: Routledge, pp. 94–116.

Schmeets, H. and te Riele, S. (2010) *A Decline of Social Cohesion in the Netherlands? Participation and Trust, 1997–2010.* Paper presented at the OECD International Conference on Social Cohesion and Development, Paris, 20 January. [Online] Available at www.oecd.org/dataoecd/13/31/46804565.pdf

Schneider, P. (2005) The New Berlin Wall, *New York Times,* 4 December [Online] Available at http://www.nytimes.com/2005/12/04/magazine/04berlin.html?pagewanted=print

Schönwälder, K. (2010) Germany: Integration Policy and Pluralism in a Self-Conscious Country of Immigration in S. Vertovec and S. Wessendorf (eds) *The Multicultural Backlash.* London: Routledge, pp. 152–169.

Schuerkens, U. (2007) France in A. Triandafyllidou and R. Gropas *European Immigration: A Sourcebook.* Great Britain: Ashgate, pp. 113–126.

Shore, Z. (2006) *Breeding Bin Ladens: America, Islam and the Future of Europe.* Baltimore: Johns Hopkins Press.

Silj, A. (ed.) (2010) *European Multiculturalism Revisited*. London: ZED Books.

Simon, P. and Sala Pala, V. (2010) 'We're not all multiculturalists yet': France Swings Between Hard Integration and Soft Anti-Discrimination in S. Vertovec and S. Wessendorf (eds) *The Multicultural Backlash*. London: Routledge, pp. 92–110.

Singh, G. (2005) British Multiculturalism and Sikhs, *Sikhs Formations*, 1 (2): 157–173.

Smith, D. J., McVie, S., Woodward, R., Shute, J., Flint, J. and McAra, L. (2001) *The Edinburgh Study of Youth Transitions and Crime: Key Findings at Ages 12 and 13*. ESRC Report. [Online] Available at www.law.ed.ac.uk/cls/esytc

Soysal, Y. (1997) Changing Parameters of Citizenship and Claims-making: Organized Islam in European Public Spheres. *Theory and Society* 26 (4): 509–527.

Spiegel Online (2009) *How Blunt Can One Be About Integration?* [Online] Available at

www.spiegel.de/international/germany/0,1518,druck-654921,00.html

Statistics Netherlands (2004) *The Dutch Virtual Census of 2001: Analysis and Methodology*. Statistics Netherlands: Voorburg. [Online] Available at www.cbs.nl/NR/rdonlyres/D1716A60-0D13-4281-BED6-3607514888AD/0/b572001.pdf

Stiglitz, J, Sen, A. and Fitoussi, J-P (2009) Report by the Commission on the Measurement of Economic Performance and Social Progress. [Online] Available at www.stiglitz-sen-fitoussi.fr/documents/rapport_anglais.pdf

Sunier, T. (2010a) Islam in the Netherlands, Dutch Islam in A. Triandafyllidou, *Muslims in 21st Century Europe*. London: Routledge, pp. 121–134.

(2010b) Assimilation by Conviction or by Coercion? Integration Policies in the Netherlands in A. Silj *European Multiculturalism Revisited*. London: ZED Books, pp. 214–234.

Swann, M. (1985) *Education for All: The Report of the Inquiry into the Education of Pupils from Ethnic Minority Groups*. London: HMSO.

Tausch, A., with Bischof, C., Kastrun, T. and Mueller, K. (2006) *Why Europe has to offer a   better deal towards its Muslim Communities: A Quantitative Analysis of Open International Data*. Centro Argentino de Estudios Internacionales (CAEI) [Online] Available at www.caei.com.ar/ebooks/ebook16.pdf

Tellegen, A. (1982) *Brief Manual for the Multidimensional Personality Questionnaire*. Minneapolis: University of Minnesota.

Theiss-Morse, E. and Hibbing, J. R. (2005) Citizenship and Engagement. *Annual Review of Political Science* 8 (1): 227–249.

Tillie, J. (1998) Explaining Migrant Voting Behavior in the Netherlands: Combining the Electoral Research and Ethnic Studies Perspectives. *Revue Européene des Migrations Internationales* 13(2) pp 71-94.

Togeby, L. (1999) Migrants at the Polls: An Analysis of Immigrant and Refugee Participation in Danish Local Elections. *Journal of Ethnic and Migration Studies* 25 (4): 665–684.

Toth, J. (2009) Acquiring Nationality: Is it a Goal, a Tool, or an Assessment of Integration? in J. Niessen and T. Huddleston (eds), *Legal Frameworks for the Integration of Third-Country Nationals.* Leiden: Martinus Nijhoff Publishers, pp 159-94.

Triandafyllidou, A. (ed.) (2010) *Muslims in 21st Century Europe.* London: Routledge.

Tyler, T.R. (1990) *Why People Obey the Law.* New Haven: Yale University Press.

Tyler, T. R. (1998) Trust and Democratic Governance in V. Braithwaite and M. Levi (eds) *Trust and Governance,* New York: Russell Sage Foundation.

Tyler, T.R. and Folger, R. (1980) Distributional and Procedural Aspects of Satisfaction with Citizen-Police Encounter. *Basic and Applied Social Psychology* 1: pp 281-92.

U.S. Department of State (2010) *International Religious Freedom Report: Netherlands.* [Online] Available at www.state.gov/g/drl/rls/irf/2010/148969.htm

Vaïsse, J. (2007) La France et ses Musulmans: une politique étrangère sous influence? *Foreign Policy: Edition Française* 66.

Van der Noll, J. (2010) Public Support for a Ban on Headscarves: A Cross National Perspective. *International Journal of Conflict and Violence* 4 (2): 191–204.

van Heelsum, A. (2000) *Political Participation of Migrants in the Netherlands.* Paper presented to the Metropolis Conference, Rotterdam, November 13-20.

Vertovec, S. and Wessendorf, S. (eds) (2010) *The Multicultural Backlash.* London: Routledge.

Warner, C. and Wenner, M. (2006) Religion and the Political Organization of Muslims in Europe. *Perspectives on Politics* 4 (3): 457–479.

Washington Post (2005) France Beefs Up Response to Riots, 8 November [Online] Available at

www.washingtonpost.com/wp-dyn/content/article/2005/11/07/AR2005110700295_pf.html

(2007) EU Proposes Monitoring Radical Mosques 12 May [Online] Available at www.washingtonpost.com/wp-dyn/content/article/2007/05/12/AR2007051200749_pf.html

Weil, P. and Crowley, J. (1994) Integration in Theory and Practice: A Comparison of France and Britain, *West European Politics* 17 (2): 110–126.

Wüst, A. (2000) New Citizens – New Voters? Political Preferences and Voting Intentions of Naturalized Germans: A Case Study in Progress, *International Migration Review* 34 (2): 560–567.

(2002) *Wie wählen Neuburger? Politische Einstellungen und Wahlverhalten eingebürgerter Personen in Deutschland.* Opladen: Leske + Budrich.

(2004) Naturalised Citizens as Voters: Behaviour and Impact, *German Politics* 13 (2): 341–359.

Zentralinstitut Islam-Archiv-Deutschland e.V. (2000) *Muslime vor den Landtagswahlen in Nordrhein-Westfalen*, Soest.

Index